To Edwin Jahiel,
about whom Bulgarian directors
have never ceased to sing
your praises at Urbana.

Sincerely,
Ron Holloway
Karlovy Vary, 1988

THE BULGARIAN CINEMA

Lyudmil Staikov's *Khan Asparukh* **(1981).**

THE BULGARIAN CINEMA

RONALD HOLLOWAY

RUTHERFORD • MADISON • TEANECK
FAIRLEIGH DICKINSON UNIVERSITY PRESS
LONDON AND TORONTO: ASSOCIATED UNIVERSITY PRESSES

© 1986 by Associated University Presses, Inc.

Associated University Presses
440 Forsgate Drive
Cranbury, NJ 08512

Associated University Presses
25 Sicilian Avenue
London WC1A 2QH, England

Associated University Presses
2133 Royal Windsor Drive
Unit 1
Mississauga, Ontario
Canada L5J 1K5

Library of Congress Cataloging in Publication Data

Holloway, Ronald.
  The Bulgarian cinema.

  Includes index.
  1. Moving-pictures—Bulgaria—History. 2. Moving-
pictures—Bulgaria—Plots, themes, etc. 3. Moving-
pictures—Bulgaria—Catalogs. 4. Moving-picture
producers and directors—Bulgaria—Biography. 5. Moving-
picture actors and actresses—Bulgaria—Biography.
I. Title.
PN1993.5.B8H65   1985   791.43′09497′7   82-49318
ISBN 0-8386-3183-5 (alk. paper)

Printed in the United States of America

Dedicated to Bulgarian Friends and Filmmakers

CONTENTS

FOREWORD

Perhaps the most important thing to say about the Bulgarian cinema is that it is not as well known as it deserves to be. People do not, as yet, talk about Bulgarian films in the way, for example, that they discuss the cinemas of such other Eastern European countries as Poland and Hungary. The principle reason for this is simple: no Bulgarian film director has yet acquired the kind of international reputation (like Wajda in Poland or Jancso in Hungary) that automatically directs attention to the rest of the films made in his country. And yet there are many fine directors working in Bulgaria, and they have made films that have aroused international admiration and garnered festival prizes. Bulgaria's time of cinematic glory will, however, certainly come, for the standard of filmmaking in what is, after all, a rather small country is surprisingly high. Already there are a few titles that arouse instant recognition from connoisseurs of cinema around the world, most notably Radev's *The Peach Thief,* Andonov's *The Goat Horn,* and Vulchanov's *The Unknown Soldier's Patent Leather Shoes,* and there are other equally splendid films which have not aroused the attention they merit,

like Nichev's *Stars in the Hair, Tears in the Eyes* and Zahariev's *Villa Zone.* It is hoped that Ron Holloway's carefully researched new book on this undervalued cinema will help to widen and deepen international understanding of Bulgarian cinematography. Already Bulgarian animated films are highly represented by experts in the international animation world, and Bulgarian children's films are winning their own way; it is only a matter of time until the feature films make their deserved breakthrough. It should be stressed, as well, that the Bulgarian cinema has quite a lot to offer the international film community—for example, its brilliant and inventive use of folk traditions, colorfully and meaningfully displaying the roots of Bulgarian culture. Cinema is, in the truest sense, today's international language speaking across borders and politics in a way that no other form of communication can. The best of Bulgarian cinema opens a window for the rest of the world to gaze upon a rich, varied, and fascinating culture.

KEN WLASCHIN
Artistic Director, Los Angeles Film Exposition

PREFACE

This modest historical account of the Bulgarian cinema was inspired by Jay Leyda's similar, but far more complete, histories of the Soviet and Chinese cinematographies. It grew out of frequent visits and contacts with knowledgeable colleagues in Sofia and at various international film festivals. Since I have reviewed several contemporary feature films made in Bulgaria in *Variety,* usually on the spot and often after conversations with the directors, I felt a certain competency in the course of time to write this portrait of a socialist cinema.

My approach to the material is journalistic, rather than academic. By this, I mean that I have not had recourse to lengthy analyses of important films to the utter neglect of minor but relevant ones. I am of the opinion that a national cinema develops at its own pace: thus, the long view offers more insights into the making of a "milestone film" than a shortsighted weighing of style and aesthetics in that same "masterpiece."

Chapter One offers a cultural background embracing the arts related to filmmaking; Chapter Two highlights the principal directors in the postwar period; and Chapter Three covers trends, and comments on the key films that fostered the development of Bulgarian cinema, both domestically and internationally. Part Two consists of a complete annotated filmography on every feature film made in Bulgaria, beginning in the silent era and carrying on through the war years until the birth of a Socialist cinema in 1950. Each section can be read for itself, and it is not unusual to find certain films rising to the surface on each occasion but for different reasons.

Three books have been consulted in writing this history: Sergio Micheli's *Il Cinema Bulgaro* (Padua: Marsilio Editori, 1971), Albert Cervoni's *Les écrans de Sofia* (Paris: Filméditions Pierre L'Herminier Editeur, 1976), and Maria Ratschewa and Klaus Eder's *Der bulgarische Film* (Frankfurt: Kommunales Kino, 1977). In addition, Sergio Micheli's *Cinema di animazione in Bulgaria* (Bologna: Cappelli Editore, 1975) was consulted in regard to the country's major contribution to the animated film. Also, the journal *Bulgarian Films* proved to be a helpful source for interview information. Lastly, David Marshall Lang's *The Bulgarians: From Pagan Times to the Ottoman Conquest* (London: Thames and Hudson, 1976) offered the historical balance needed in viewing and evaluating many historical epics in current feature-film production.

A word of caution for some readers may be necessary in regard to the term "Socialist Realism." Western critics are prone to use capital letters in referring to that brand of Socialist Realism practised in the 1950s under the Personality Cult. Eastern critics prefer to view the phenomenon as an evolving film style still effectively in use at the present time—this brand of socialist realism, however, is usually spelled with small letters by perceptive Western critics. Also, the term "Eastern" used in this book refers to the action-packed partisan or war film: it has nothing to do with the "Kung Fu Eastern."

So far as the American spelling of Cyrillic-written names is concerned, a difference is to be noted from British and French usage. The French prefer Tchaikovsky, the British Chaikovsky, and the Americans Tchaikovsky. Thus, when it came time to write Hristo, instead of Christo or Kristo, I did so in despairing hope that others in the future would follow suit. By the same token, Angel Wagenstein is preferred over Anzhel Vagenshtine, and Georgi Djulgerov over Georgy Dyulgerov. Nevertheless, it should be admitted that the variations in French, German, British, and American spellings of transliterations of Cyrillic-written names is a matter of endless dispute.

I wish to thank the *New Orleans Review* for permission to reprint material which appeared in that journal in shortened form in Summer 1981 (Volume 8, number 2). And I want to take this opportunity to thank several individuals at the Bulgarian Cinematography State Corporation, particularly Ivan Stoyanovich and his staff at *Bulgarian Films,* for advice in preparing the book. An acknowledgment goes to the same organization for the permission to reproduce over two hundred stills and photographs, many selected with the intention of illustrating passages in the text. Another vote of thanks and appreciation is extended to Mr. Donald C. Yelton, Ms. Katharine Turok, Ms. Beth Gianfagna, and Mr. Edward Dimendberg for assistance in editing the manuscript, particularly in regard to transliterations from the Cyrillic.

Originally, the book was planned for the 1,300th anniversary of the founding of Bulgaria, in 1981, but publication was delayed in view of a decision to include an estimate of the major epic productions begun before, during, and after that year to commemorate the occasion. The decision was justified upon taking note of the high quality of Georgi Djulgerov's *Measure for Measure* and Lyudmil Staikov's *Khan Asparukh* in 1981, followed by Georgi Stoyanov's *Constantine the Philosopher* in 1983. Borislav Sharaliev's epic *Boris the First* was subsequently completed at the end of 1984. In the meanwhile, a shortened version of *Khan Asparukh* has been released for export: it bears the English title *681 —The Glory of Khan.* At this writing a retrospective of Bulgarian feature films is being prepared for programming in Great Britain, Australia, Canada, and the United States. There is little doubt that this retrospective will offer conclusive evidence of the high esthetic standards practiced today in Bulgarian cinematography.

THE BULGARIAN CINEMA

PART I

1
ART AND HISTORY

A Game Played by Ethnic Rules

Why not view Bulgarian cinema as the tip of an iceberg?

For below its visible surface does lie a vast area of art and history to be appreciated along with the pleasure of seeing a movie. Indeed, most of Bulgarian cinema only makes sense in juxtaposition with its vast cultural and national heritage.

"All art is a game played by ethnic rules," concluded the critic Vernon Young. He was right. Just as Scandinavian films differ fundamentally from Italian, so also has Bulgarian cinema little in common with Hungarian or Polish movies, however binding the ties in what is known as "East Europe."

Appreciation is often a question of style. Once the narrative style of a Bulgarian filmmaker is comprehended, it's easier to determine the scope of his vision and the depth of his talent. Once the Bulgarian Literary Revival of the past century is perceived as belated renaissance, it helps to explain why, in general, the theatrical narrative dominates over visual expression for the Bulgarian film artist. His images have their inspiration in the icon, rather than in Western painting tempered by the Renaissance. And historical epics might require a passing knowledge of the Thracians, the Proto-Bulgars, and the ongoing conflicts with the Byzantines and the Turks.

The more one studies Bulgarian art, culture, and history, the more he is conscious of how massive the iceberg is below that tip of cinematic expression. The Thracian art exhibit stunned visitors to the world's museums by the quantity of the archaeological discoveries in the Balkans since the Second World War. Bulgaria celebrated its 1,300th anniversary as a nation in 1981, an event that highlighted its place as the "Cradle of Slavonic Orthodoxy." The richness of the Bulgarian icon and old Slavonic manuscripts is just beginning to dawn on historians, who, in the past, have interpreted Western civilization through Latin Christianity.

It is ironic that theater schedules in Sofia offer a third of the repertoire to foreign dramatists, in order to acquaint home audiences with O'Neill and Albee—yet American and British audiences are quite ignorant of the dramas penned by Nikolai Haitov, Valeri Petrov, and Yordan Radichkov, for the simple reason that no one has even bothered to translate them into English.

Bulgarian films have often been accused by critics as being too "heavy" or "literary," as though this were an aesthetic flaw. To be sure, Bulgarian cinema did suffer from stiff scenarios in the beginning, but the tables were balanced

Todor Dinov and Hristo Hristov's *Iconostasis* (1969).

Rangel Vulchanov's *On a Small Island* (1958).

when a director, scriptwriter, and cameraman collaborated on a breakthrough film, *On a Small Island* (1958). Thereafter, Bulgarian cinema struggled to match these successes, and in the 1970s it compared well with the best that emerged from Eastern Europe. Today, a national film school assures that potential filmmakers do not have to travel to Moscow or Prague for proper training. Result: the emergence of a national film style, one that is today more visual than literary, more daring and complex in handling contemporary themes.

The film buff and festivalgoer is well advised to visit the Varna Film Festival, a biannual affair on the Black Sea coast in September. This national showcase offers a great deal more than a preselection of the best Bulgarian feature films over the past two years; it is a haven for the student of history and archaeology as well. Within walking distance from the festival is the Aladja Monastery carved into the rocks (the dawn of Christianity), while a couple of hours away by car are the "Horse of Madara" rock sculpture

(Proto-Bulgarian period), the ruins of Aboba Pliska (Bulgaria's first capital), Varna's archaeological diggings (the Proto-Thracians), and the peninsular city of Nesebŭr (early Christian architecture).

Another trip to Bulgaria might include Plovdiv, site of the principal findings of the Thracian art treasures, a city known as Philippopolis in ancient times. South of Plovdiv is Bachkovo Monastery, whose paintings supplied the motif in *Iconostasis* (1969), the film that signaled the second awakening of New Bulgarian Cinema. The Thracian Plain in this area gives way to the lovely Rhodope Mountains, separating Bulgaria from Greece, the setting for Nikolai Haitov's stories that both inspired and nourished Bulgarian cinema.

For pure tourists the country's chief attraction is Kazanlik, the Valley of Roses, which produces the country's famous rose oil. Rose attar and goat rugs were peddled across Europe by the best known and most controversial figure in Bulgarian literature, Bay Ganyu, the creation of

Todor Dinov and Hristo Hristov's *Iconostasis* (1969).

19

Vulo Radev's *The Peach Thief* **(1964).**

Zahari Zhandov's *Master of Boyana* **(1981).**

satirist Aleko Konstantinov in 1895 at the dawn of the motion picture age. North of the Valley of the Roses is Turnovo, capital of the Second Bulgarian Kingdom in the Middle Ages, which forms the backdrop of *The Peach Thief* (1964), a popular film at home and abroad. Again, the nearby Preobrazhenski Monastery should not be bypassed for its church relics.

Sofia—Serdica, in Roman times—is said to be Europe's second oldest living city, following Athens. Its baths and springs were prized by Roman legionaries after encounters with the barbarians on the border. Sofia takes its name from the first Christian church, Saint Sofia, erected in the sixty century in tribute to Hagia Sophia in Constantinople. One of the ancient baths was turned into a chapel, Saint George's, whose frescoes are a link with early Christianity. So are the frescoes in the Boyana Church near Sofia; the chapel lent its name to the Boyana Film Studios, situated on a hill overlooking the city.

Another national shrine is the Rila Monastery south of Sofia. It was here that a rich heritage was preserved in art and literature during harsh suppression under Byzantium and the Ottoman Empire. In times of danger, the Old Slavonic manuscripts were packed on donkeys for safekeeping abroad—once, in the fourteenth century, to Kiev and Moscow, where the Russian Orthodox Church cared for them.

The close friendship between the Russians and the Bulgarians dates from this time. During the five-hundred years under the yoke of the Turks, the Bulgarians kept their national identity by protecting the Old Church Slavonic at all costs. When a Russian army liberated Sofia in 1878, plans were drawn for the construction of Saint Alexander Nevski Cathedral in the center of the city. A Russian painter lay on his back for a year to complete the majestic God the Father in the dome; the cathedral was finished in 1912, just as the Balkan Wars broke out.

Bulgaria both influenced and missed the Italian Renaissance. As a result, the tradition of arts and letters in this corner of the Balkans differs from the heritage of the Czechs, the Slovaks, the Poles, the Russians, the Slovenes, and the Croatians—other members of the Slav family who escaped the Turkish yoke. Still, Bulgaria, as the "Cradle of Old Church Slavonic," serves as a far more important link with early Christianity and the dawn of Western civilization.

One feels this tie with the past at national festivals. The Bulgarian Theater Festival, for instance, faithfully and regularly stages a drama about the monks Cyril and Methodius in Rome.

It takes place in the crypt of Saint Alexander Nevski Cathedral, and singers from the opera intone Old Slavonic hymns as a choral background.

The story has yet to be written about the impact the Slavonic Orthodox Church had upon Western Christianity.

The Thracians

The Thracian Art Exhibit is continually booked up for a decade in advance. As a cultural calling card, its renown is equaled only by the country's operatic basses. The collection of a thousand artifacts dates back to the beginning of the Iron Age. Homer testified that the Thracians, with "the biggest and handsomest horses I ever saw," fought on the side of the Trojans against the Greeks.

Magnificent horses weren't the only things they loved. Gold and silver decorated their armor; the area they inhabited north of Greece (today's Bulgaria) was noted for its gold mines. They were such hardy fighters that the Greeks found it difficult to settle colonies along the Black Sea coast. They were referred to as "barbarians" because no one could understand what they were saying.

The tomb of a Thracian chief who lived around 1500 B.C. was unearthed in 1924 by a farmer ploughing his field in the Pleven district of northern Bulgaria; the gold taken from his tomb matched the findings in those of Agamemnon and Clytemnestra, discovered by Heinrich Schliemann in Mycenaean Greece the century before. The Thracians were definitely on the scene by 3000 B.C., according to archaeologists and historians attending the First Plovdiv Symposium on the Proto-Thracians, held in 1974.

Descriptions of the Thracians have come down to us from Herodotus, Pindar, and Xenophon. Aeschylus wrote a trilogy of plays (unfortunately lost) about Dionysus in Thrace; the god of fertility and wine had his origin there. Another favorite was Bendis, the goddess of the hunt who corresponded to Artemis of the Greeks and Diana of the Romans. The legend of Orpheus, the master of song and music who descended into Hades, is Thracian; according to mythology, he was the son of a Thracian king and the Muse Calliope. Mystic cults, like the Dionysian cult, flourished first in Thrace, then were absorbed into Greek and Roman rituals.

Aristophanes made fun of a swaggering Thracian soldier in *Lysistrata*. The race provided

The mural paintings in the
Kazanlik Tomb: Thracian horses.

Binka Zhelyazkova's *The Big Night Bathe* (1980).

prized mercenaries in Greek times and gladiators (Spartacus) in Roman times. No Roman emperor was able to completely subdue them until Trajan erected Roman fortresses in their territory to protect the border along the Danube. Thereafter, Greek was spoken in the cities, but the Thracian native tongue was maintained in the mountains until the coming of Christianity and the conversion of the Bulgars and Slavs (who had absorbed the Thracians).

Not even the advent of Christianity, however, could completely subdue the ancient ways of the Thracians. The rites of Dionysus and the legend of Orpheus were handed down in varying stories and festival celebrations. The proud Thracian horseman with a spear became Saint George on horseback killing the dragon in the religious icon. The pagan's rejoicing in life and merry-making is echoed in paintings on church walls depicting devils in hell impishly plying their trade—they catch the visitor's eye before entering the church. The springtime "kukeri" dancers, with their fantastic costumes, are Thracian in origin.

So far as Bulgarian literature is concerned, the Thracian spirit is best reflected in the stories of Nikolai Haitov, whose tales are drawn from the people of the Rhodope Mountains. This was the last refuge of a fading culture before the entrenchment of Christianity, the rugged area between the fruitful Thracian Plain and the Aegean Sea where several priceless treasures were discovered.

The tale of revenge in Metodi Andonov's *The Goat Horn* (1972), the story of a boy's advancement to manhood in Georgi Dyulgerov's *The Test* (1971), and the reworking of a legend ("It happened long ago . . .") in Eduard Zahariev's *Manly Times* (1977)—screenplays based on Haitov's stories—match in flavor the reports handed down by the Greeks who once paid these hills a visit. There is the same aura of romantic legend enveloping Thracian opulence as a whole.

"Thracian gold" in the exhibit dates mostly from the third and fourth centuries B.C., the most breathtaking findings being the Panagyurishte Treasure: seven gold goblets with carved centaurs as handles, a gold amphora with centaur handles, gold amphora-rhytons, and a magnificiently carved gold serving tray—once possibly decorating the table of a Thracian king. Like the chieftain Seuthes, mentioned in Xenophon's *Anabasis.* Xenophon describes a lusty banquet thrown for the returning Ten

Eduard Zahariev's *The Hare Census* (1973).

Johan Rozev's documentary *Monuments of the Great Rila Wilderness:* **an icon depicting St. George.**

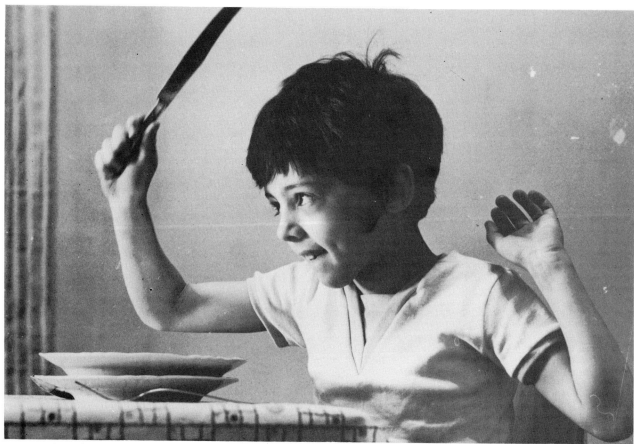

Borislav Sharaliev's *Knight without Armor* **(1966).**

Metodi Andonov's *The Goat Horn* **(1972).**

Eduard Zahariev's *Manly Times* **(1977).**

The Panagyurishte Treasure of gold objects.

The Panagyurishte Treasure of gold objects.

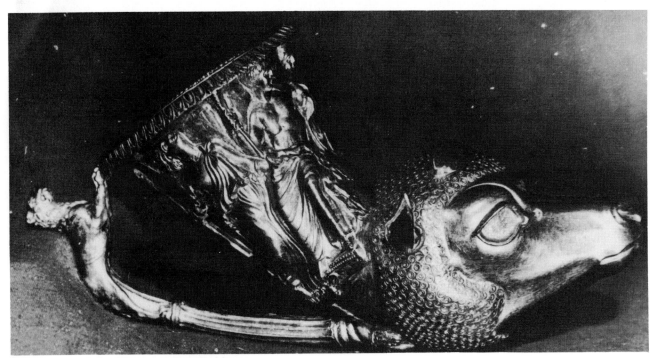

The Panagyurishte Treasure of gold objects.

Thousand, followed by drinking bouts and wild dancing—Haitov's "manly times" as they were long, long ago.

In October 1981, the month Bulgaria officially celebrated its 1,300th anniversary, I had the good fortune to attend the Second Varna World Animation Festival. Its awards are replicas of "kukeri" masks, still worn in colorful pageants celebrating spring fertility rites. The harvest was in—from orchards of apples and peaches, from the vineyards.

> . . . in this land I dwell,
> Thracian Land, full of grape-vines
> and so rich in fruit.
>> Pindar, *Fragment 34*

On the way to Sofia by car, we stopped at the Thracian tomb at Kazanlik in the Valley of the Roses. it was here in 1944 that a group of soldiers, digging an air-raid shelter out of a convenient hillock, stumbled upon what can now be described as the country's national monument: a Thracian tomb, seven meters high and forty meters in diameter. Judging from the gigantic mural paintings in four colors, it had belonged to a princely individual of the late fourth or early third centuries and leaves a powerful impression of pomp and serenity upon the viewer.

The Thracian people, after the Indians, are the largest on earth. Were they united and had they a leader, they would have been invincible and, in my opinion, the most powerful people by far.

> Herodotus 5.3

And in Sofia, where the Thracian treasures have returned home for a few months of rest before touring the world's museums again over the next decade, I stood before glittering gold and silver armor and remembered the lusty praise of Aristophanes:

> Nearby a soldier, a Thracian, was wildly
> shaking his spear, like Tereus at play,
> To frighten a fig-girl, so that, unseen,
> he could filch her ripest fruit away.
>> Aristophanes, *Lysistrata*

The greatest literary tribute paid to the Thracians was by Euripides. His play *Rhesus* was written between 455 and 440 B.C.,—if the contested drama was written at all by him—and states flatly, drawing on the tenth book of Homer's *Iliad,* that if the King of Thrace, Rhesus, were to live to fight on the side of Hector and the Trojans, the Greeks would lose the war. The feared king is then murdered in his sleep, and his magnificent white horses stolen—whereupon, the Muse of the Mountains, mother of King Rhesus, appears to lament the death of her son.

The mural paintings in the Kazanlik Tomb: funeral rites.

A summer rain in the Rhodopes, says a Bulgarian shepherd, is the Muse of the Mountains still lamenting for her son. The blessing of a summer rain is a common symbol in Bulgarian cinematography, indeed in all of East Europe. A weeping mother lamenting the loss of her children during one or another of the many national tragedies is also the Bulgarian version of the *Pietà*.

28

Hristo Kovachev's documentary *Hello, Dear Children!*

Old Church Slavonic

Recently, UNESCO set aside for preservation a selected number of monuments of worldwide importance. So far as Bulgaria was concerned, four were chosen for special consideration: (1) the aforementioned Thracian Tomb at Kazanik, with its frescoes of racing chariots and the solemn funeral feast; (2) the Horseman of Madara, an eighth-century rock-face sculpture depicting a triumphant Bulgarian monarch; (3) the Boyana Church near Sofia, whose frescoes, painted in 1259, are treasured examples of realism in Bulgarian art before the Italian Renaissance; and (4) the rock-cut cave churches at Ivanovo in the gorge of the Rusenski Lom River, whose fourteenth-century frescoes are representative of the late flowering of Bulgarian Christian art in stylized human proportions, as practised by the Turnovo school.

Besides these four monuments, the Bulgarian government is seeking to have UNESCO place the site of Nesebŭr under protection as a historical architectural preserve. In addition, there are the famous cloisters at Rila, Bachkovo, Troyan, Turnovo (Preobrazhenski monastery), Rozhen, and Dryannovo—among more than forty such monasteries, six hundred exceptional churches, and fourteen extraordinary architectural preserves.

When, in 1981, Bulgaria celebrated its 1,300th anniversary as a state, the entire country was turned into a monumental cultural exhibition. And in the process, four superspectacles were produced by the authorities at the Boyana Studios to record on film the history of a people with rich cultural traditions. They are: Lyudmil Staikov's *Khan Asparukh*, celebrating the ruler who founded a new state of Bulgars and Slavs in 681; Georgi Stoyanov's *Constantine the Philosopher*, about the future Cyril who, together with his brother Methodius, prepared around 850 a Slavonic alphabet for the conversion of the Slav nations; Borislav Sharaliev's *Boris the First*, about

29

The Horseman of Madara: rock relief near Varna.

Fresco in the Boyana Church near Sofia.

the Bulgarian king who accepted Byzantine Orthodox Christianity on his own terms in 864; and Zahari Zhandov's *Master of Boyana*, the protagonist of which was the unknown but immortal painter of the frescoes in the Boyana chapel in 1259.

It cost the Bulgarian government a small fortune to make these superproductions. The question is why. And the answer lies in history, in the story of Old Church Slavonic.

In the sixth century, just as the Emperor Justinian was bringing the Byzantine Empire to the height of its glory, a tribe of Slav barbarians (as they were called) migrated to the Balkan Peninsula from the north, maintaining a loose contact with other Slav tribes through a common tongue. About a century later, as the Byzantines were occupied elsewhere, they were joined by the Proto-Bulgarians, a Turkic tribe from the East. In 681, to counteract Byzantine subjugation, the tribes fused into the Slav Bulgarians, who then defeated the Emperor Constantine IV Pogonatus under their pagan chieftain, Khan Asparukh, a remarkable general and leader. By this time, having been gradually fused into one people, the Bulgars had fully adapted to Slav ways and language.

Asparukh established his capital at Pliska. His successors codified laws, built royal palaces, and invited Greek artisans from Constantinople to decorate them. But unable to capture the fortress city of the Byzantine Empire, they feared the political influence of Constantinople and thus resisted conversion to Christianity.

"Desislava" fresco in the Boyana Church.

"Desislava" in Zahari Zhandov's *Master of Boyana* (1981).

Another Slav nation to the north, the Moravians, equally feared the political influence of powerful neighbors, the Germans, who were converted to Christianity in the ninth century. To prevent the influence of the Latinized Germans, the Moravian king in 862 appealed to the Greek Christian Church in Constantinople to send missionaries to preach in their native Slav tongue. Two monks at Thessalonica (Salonica), the brothers Cyril and Methodius, had studied at a Slav institute in Constantinople and devised a Slav alphabet (first Glagolitic and then Cyrillic, under their disciples).

Old Church Slavonic, also known as Old Bulgarian and Church Slavonic, was the institution of these two "Apostles to the Slavs." By definition, it is a literary language based on the Macedonian dialect of Bulgarian, but influenced significantly by Greek.

While on their mission to the Moravians, Cyril and Methodius encountered the "three-tongue heresy," whereby their Slavonic language and liturgy were denied acceptance in Rome on the grounds that God should be worshiped only in Latin, Greek, and Hebrew. Shortly thereafter, when the German neighbors subdued the Moravians, the brothers were first imprisoned, and then were expelled from the country. Old Church Slavonic, however, had already become the literary lingua franca for the conversion of the Slav nations to Christianity.

So it was that the Slav Bulgarians, who were later willing to accept Christianity from Rome in exchange for a Franco-Bulgar alliance to counter Byzantine and Greek Church influences, decided in the end against receiving Christian missionaries from Germany when it was clear that they would thereby be denied a liturgy in their own language.

Many speculative historians feel that the decision of King Boris I of Bulgaria to accept a Slavonic-speaking Christianity from the Greek Patriarch in Constantinople altered the course of Western civilization, for thus Europe was effectively divided into separate halves long before the Greek Schism of 1054. Shortly after Boris adopted Christianity from Constantinople in 865, Pope Stephen VI condemned the use of Slavonic in the liturgy (885) and the German Franks put an end to an independent Moravia (906). Thereafter, Roman Christianity was imposed on the Moravians, Czechs, Slovaks, Slovenes, Croatians, and Poles. (Poland, in fact, was the only Slav nation untouched by the Slavonic-language missionaries; its form of Latin Christianity came in the tenth century from the Germans.)

The disciples of Cyril and Methodius, upon being expelled from Moravia, took up residence in Bulgaria in 885 (the year Pope Stephen VI condemned the Slavonic liturgy) at the invitation of King Boris I. They brought with them the Slavonic translations of the Bible made by their teachers, Cyril (also known as Constantine) and Methodius. Two schools were established in the kingdom: one at Preslav, the new capital, and the other at Ohrid in Macedonia (today a republic in Yugoslavia).

Zahari Zhandov's *Master of Boyana* **(1981).**

Old Bulgarian literature, or Old Church Slavonic, dates from the activities of these two schools from the end of the ninth century onwards, but particularly Ohrid under Clement, one of the original disciples of Cyril and Methodius. Saint Clement of Ohrid (d. 916) founded a school in Macedonia so famous for translations, letters, hymns, and prayers in the Slavonic that it has been referred to as "Europe's first university."

Bulgaria's literary heritage, however, stems from the Royal School at Preslav under Constantine, a pupil of Methodius consecrated a bishop in 906. This school was to reach its height during the reign of King Simeon (893–927), the son of Boris I, who was educated at Constantinople and dubbed "the Half-Greek" by his Bulgarian contemporaries. At Preslav, ecclesiastical autonomy—a lesson the enlightened king learned at Constantinople—became a way of life to unite the spreading Bulgarian kingdom.

Palace ruins at Preslav during the period of the First Bulgarian Kingdom (681–1018) attest to a Golden Age of Slavonic art and literature. King Simeon himself wrote and translated several books; he may have been the first Bulgarian writer using the vernacular for storytelling.

Greek apocryphal literature and works from Latin Christianity found their way into Slavonic translations at Preslav. Records of heretical movements, such as the Bogomil sect, and resistance of pagans to Christianity are extant. Old Bulgarian Literature became a mixture of the religious and the secular.

The First Bulgarian Kingdom reached its political crest during the reign of Simeon. Its eastern boundary was the Dnieper River, and its western the Adriatic Sea–Bulgaria, in fact, controlled the trade routes between East and West. The southern Slav tribes were united into a single power. Simeon, on a military expedition against Byzantium, nearly conquered Constantinople and enjoyed at least the pleasure of walking in the suburbs of the city that had nourished him intellectually as a boy.

Within a century after Simeon's death, Bulgaria was at the mercy of the Byzantines once again. The fall of the First Bulgarian Kingdom in 1018 resulted in some destruction of indigenous church icons and Slavonic manuscripts, while "Hellenization" in art, liturgy, and alphabet was hurried by the Greek Schism of 1054. Preslav declined, while the Black Sea cities of Nesebŭr and Sozopol prospered by affiliating

Zahari Zhandov's *Master of Boyana* **(1981).**

Hristo Hristov's *The Last Summer* (1974).

their liturgies to the Greek Orthodox Church in Constantinople.

It was in a period of rather suppressive Hellenization that the Old Slavonic books, now made sacred by more than a century of liturgical use, were guarded by pious monks or packed overland to Kiev. (A Kievan Grand Duke, Vladimir, had accepted the Christian Orthodox faith from the Byzantines in 988, and eventually imposed it as a state religion on all the Russian principalities. The conversion, however, was only a nod to Constantinople, for the official liturgy of the Russian Orthodox Church became the Old Slavonic inherited from the Bulgarians under Byzantine suppression.)

When the marauding Crusaders sacked Constantinople in 1204, Byzantium was already weakened by the revolt of the brothers Peter and John (Ivan) Assen in 1186, which paved the way for the Second Bulgarian Kingdom (1186–1395). The height of this kingdom was reached under the reign of John Assen II (1218–41), who controlled the present territory of Bulgaria,

the northern part of Greece, a portion of Albania, and the whole of Serbia and Macedonia. Turnovo, a natural mountain fortress, became the capital, and was sometimes referred to as the "Third Rome."

A strong revival in Church Slavonic and Bulgarian art and literature took place during the Second Bulgarian Kingdom. Just as the capital was an impregnable fortress, so also were the monasteries founded in the mountains, like the Rila Monastery opened by the hermit Saint John of Rila in the tenth century. Here, the holy monk translated the Bible into Old Slavonic, the Codex Suprasliensis, thus assuring the enduring fame of the Rila Monastery as a guardian of Bulgaria's past traditions.

Among all the monasteries in Bulgaria—Ohrid, Bachkovo, and Poganovo were others—Rila, near Sofia, became the main center of national pride during the oppressive periods of Hellenization and Ottoman rule. After 1395, when the Turks put an end to Bulgarian independence for the next five hundred years, the

Rangel Vulchanov's *The Unknown Soldier's Patent Leather Shoes* **(1979).**

Rila Monastery, in fact, became the protectorate of a past tradition and culture, vital to the spirit of a suffering people.

It is highly significant that, on one side, Old Bulgarian literature developed into an ecclesiastical institution of the Byzantine Empire for the Christianizing of the Slav nations, while, on the other, it produced such readable and enduring manuscripts as a popular life of Saint John of Rila, Bogomil patriotic stories, and the Salonica legend of how Saint Cyril converted the Bulgarians. That same Salonica legend in a more dramatized version is presented regularly in the crypt of Saint Alexander Nevski Cathedral in Sofia during the Bulgarian Drama and Theater Festival.

Once a vital crossroads in the transfer of European art, history, and civilization, Bulgaria today is still the custodian of more than thirteen hundred years of a rich national heritage.

Iconostasis

If there is such a phenomenon as a nation's heart, it beats in the crypt of the Cathedral of Saint Alexander Nevski—where a magnificent collection of medieval Bulgarian art treasures is housed. The glory of that collection is the icon, the supreme expression of the aesthetic spirit in the Orthodox religion.

The Soviet film by Andrei Tarkovsky, *Andrei Rublev* (1966, released 1968), recounts the passion of Russia's (and the world's) incomparable icon painter in the early fourteenth century. The Bulgarian film, Todor Dinov and Hristo Hristov's *Iconostasis* (1969), was set at the height of the Bulgarian Renaissance, the late nineteenth century during the Turkish occupation; it, too, is the story of an icon painter, an artist who follows his conscience and defies the established order. The subject of both films was a culture, rather

A Bulgarian icon preserved in the crypt of the Cathedral of Saint Alexander Nevski in Sofia.

than an individual artist or religious art in itself.

The icon is profoundly wedded to Eastern Orthodoxy, just as the cross is inseparable from Latin Christianity. The iconostasis in the East serves the same function as the altar triptych in the West; both owe their existence to a religion that prompted sublime examples of European art.

For the believer, the spiritual truths contained in an icon are usually conveyed in the subtlest and most intelligent manner possible. For the artist and his admirers, the same spiritual dimension is proportionate to the subtlety of the line, the richness of the color, and the peculiar idealized representation of the divine in the image. No attempt is made to transmit human emotions—instead, a mystical feeling of a heavenly world in communion with mankind (that is, the believer) is conveyed. A Neoplatonist philosopher could appreciate an icon in much the same manner as a Byzantine dogmatist could venerate its image.

Veselina Gerinska's *Pray for Me, Brothers!:* a wood-carved iconostasis.

The icon yields its mysteries through symbols and an image of Christ or one of the saints. The application of gold leaf and plating, together with other ornamentation (such as precious stones), endows the icon with a sophisticated magnificence, all the more striking if the painting itself is masterfully executed. Add to this the mystic elements in the Old Slavonic liturgy, plus the high solemnity of an Orthodox feast day, and both the icon and the iconostasis become indispensable components of a national culture.

Byzantine art reached its Golden Age in the sixth century, and icon painting along with it. It was a time when Oriental forms and theology finally subdued a resisting Hellenism enriched by its own heritage of art and philosophy, now on the wane. The fusion resulted in the Hagia Sophia, a shrine to Holy Wisdom erected by the Emperor Justinian in Constantinople, and a tradition of icon painting that spread as far west as Siena and as far north as Novgorod. In particular, the icon impregnated the liturgies of the Old Slavonic.

The oldest surviving Bulgarian icon, a ceramic-tile image of Saint Theodore, dates from the ninth or tenth century and was unearthed near Preslav. Although the pattern of expression is definitely Eastern, the image is more human than mystic and resembles a Slav monk rather than a saint. This gives rise to the theory that Slavonic art deviated from Byzantine standards and drew its inspiration equally from early Christian schools.

Old Bulgarian literature texts, however, confirm that Slavonic icons matched the best of the Byzantine schools in the tenth century, when Preslav and Ohrid were competing for artistic and literary honors under King Simeon. The vast majority of these icons, however, were destroyed in 1018 or thereafter, when Hellenization was imposed by Byzantium on the Slavonic churches and the Crusaders came to pillage. The artistic expression of the First Bulgarian Kingdom can therefore never be fully estimated.

The icons of the Second Bulgarian Kingdom in the thirteenth and fourteenth centuries

The oldest surviving Bulgarian icon: Saint Theodore painted on ceramic tile, dating from the ninth or tenth century.

benefited, in turn, from the presence of Greek painters who left Constantinople after it was sacked by the Crusaders (1204). The same Greek, and Slavonic, icon painters brought the traditions of Byzantine art to the Italian Renaissance painters, just as Theophanes the Greek transmitted the past glories of Constantinople to distant Russia through his prized pupil Andrei Rublev.

Humanistic influences in the Slavonic icon are discernible. During the period of the Latin Empire of the Balkans (1204–61), the frescoes in the Boyana Chapel near Sofia were painted (1259); they anticipated the humanism of Cimabue and Giotto a generation or so later in Italy. Were these Byzantine, Western, or Slavonic in character? The human elements of affection and tenderness, particularly in paintings of the Virgin, were common in the icons of the Second Bulgarian Kingdom.

After the fall of Turnovo (1393) and Constantinople (1453), the Ottoman Turks suppressed Slavonic and Greek art in all the major cities. The Bulgarian icon then went underground for five hundred years as a folk art, protected and nourished by the monasteries that supplied the inspirational force. Once again, during this interim period, Russia became the center of East-

Hristo Hristov's *The Truck* (1980): the intellectual figure.

ern Orthodoxy and Moscow was now referred to as the "Third Rome," after the fall of Constantinople.

The Bulgarian icon in homes became a symbol of national fervor. Only on certain occasions could artists paint for the few churches that remained intact. The severity of Ottoman rule (1396–1878) reduced icon painting to a folk art. Favorite themes of these naïve painters were scenes from daily life and legends of the popular Bulgarian saints, particularly Cyril and Methodius, John of Rila, Saint George Slaying the Dragon, and martyrs of the Slavonic Church. When a Suffering Christ, the Nativity, the Birth of the Virgin, or a fiery Archangel Michael were depicted, the icon served as an effective household symbol for hope and perseverance.

The icon became an open symbol for courage and resistance when the ban on building churches was lifted in the seventeenth century. The transition in image from martyr to warrior is noticeable. National fervor mounted—until

the revival in art and literature, the Bulgarian Renaissance, took place like a brush fire sweeping the countryside. The revival began during the second half of the eighteenth century, continued on sporadically from posts of exile, and then exploded in all the arts about the middle of the nineteenth century. Bulgarian poets and artists gave their lives in uprisings. When the Russian army finally came to the aid of Bulgaria in revolt, expelling the Turks in 1878, the stage was set for a rediscovery of a past heritage.

One has to appreciate the beauty of an iconostasis, the screen dividing the sanctuary from the laity in an Orthodox Church, and one can perhaps only appreciate it fully during a solemn ceremony on a high liturgical feast day. To comprehend the importance of Dinov and Hristov's *Iconostasis* (1969), their national breakthrough film, one has to understand too the significance of the Bulgarian Renaissance, with which it deals. It is the story of an iconostasis artist, a woodcarver, who is inspired by the range and

Georgi Djulgerov's *Measure for Measure* (1981): the shepherd debating with Saint George, against the background of the Ilinden Day Uprising in 1903.

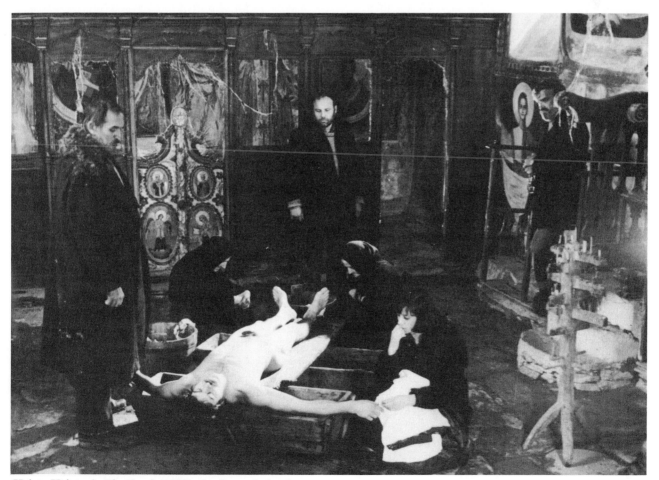

Hristo Hristov's *The Truck* (1980): the funeral ritual.

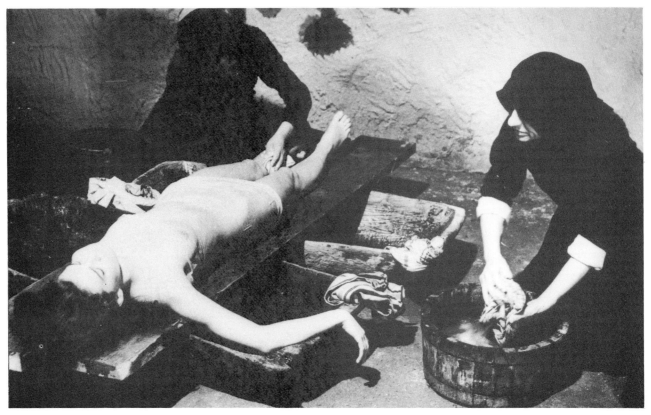

Todor Dinov and Hristo Hristov's *Iconostasis* (1969): the funeral ritual.

depth of folk art as a medium of self-expression and the national spirit.

Iconostasis is much more than just a movie. It is as close to a national epic as any film has come in the short history of Bulgarian cinema.

The Bulgarian National Revival

After five hundred years a phoenix rose from the ashes.

Of all the Balkan countries, Bulgaria had suffered the most under the Ottoman Turks. Severe restrictions were placed on the country because of its close proximity to Constantinople and its strategic location in the Balkans. In 1767, ecclesiastical jurisdiction at Ohrid was abolished in favor of Greek Orthodoxy, and Greeks were put in charge of Bulgarian education. That a Bulgarian literary awakening could take place at all under these circumstances is astonishing.

The way was paved by a new middle class of Bulgarian merchants and teachers, who made inroads toward self-rule among Turkish officials. Then it became widely known that a monk at Mount Athos, Paisy of Hilendar, had completed his *Slav-Bulgarian History* (1762), a nationalistic opus urging a break from Greek ecclesiastical control. Thus the foundation for a literary revival was laid. The stage was then set for the renaissance when the first book in Bulgarian was published in 1806, followed by the first classes in the Bulgarian language in 1835.

Upon reading Paisy's history, Petko Slaveykov, a gifted teacher, left his monastery and, in 1852, began publishing articles urging Bulgarian church autonomy (granted in 1870); he was the first poet of the National Revival. Owing to his activities as a journalist and opponent of the Greek Exarchate, Slaveykov was forced into exile; he joined the Bulgarian colony in Constantinople in 1864, where he translated the New Testament into modern Bulgarian. He supported the April Uprising of 1876 and reported on the "Bulgarian horrors" that followed, when the Turks cruelly suppressed the revolutionaries and roused the ire of the British and Russian governments. His collection of songs, proverbs, and folklore, plus an all-embracing autobiography, earned him a place in the nation's heart

Todor Dinov and Hristo Hristov's *Iconostasis* (1969),
based on Dimiter Talev's classic novel *The Iron Candlestick*, published in the late nineteenth century during the
Bulgarian National Revival.

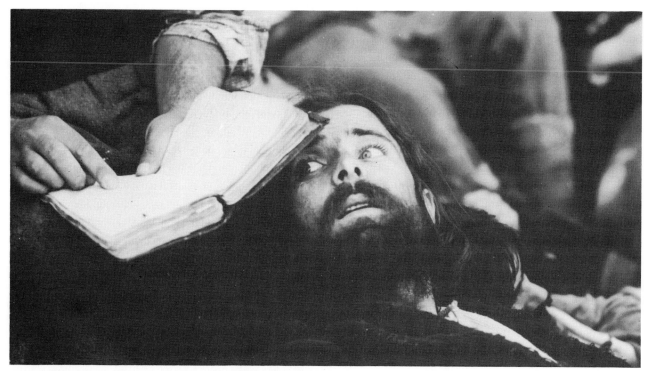

Georgi Djulgerov's *Measure for Measure* (1981): the awakening of the common people in the wake of the Bulgarian
National Revival at the turn-of-the-century.

and the nickname "Grandpa Slaveykov."

Hercegovina was the first Balkan land to succeed in its revolt against the Turks, in 1875, followed by Serbia, Montenegro, and Bulgaria in 1876. A group of exiled Bulgarian patriots living in Bucharest known as the "Apostles" led the April Rising. Their leader was Hristo Botev, a poet and publicist, while another poet, Ivan Vazov, wrote the verses for the battle hymn. The 200-man expedition ended in failure on Mount Vola, but the heroic deaths of Botev and the "Apostles" united the people as never before, and won needed support abroad. Vazov's verses on the tragic suppression of his people were on everyone's lips as Russia came to Bulgaria's aid in 1877, and ended the Turkish occupation.

Ivan Vazov, the poet laureate of Bulgarian literature, crowned the National Revival with verses, drama, and prose during the crucial years of newly won independence. His novel on

Alexander Vazov's *Nastradin Hoggia and Sly Peter* (1939) based on a popular book by National Poet Ivan Vazov.

the circumstances surrounding the April Rising, *Under the Yoke* (1894), won him recognition abroad and became known at home as the "Bulgarian national novel." Written after the long delayed unification of the country—a favorable unification provision in the Treaty of San Stefano in 1878 was nullified in the same year by the Treaty of Berlin, thus making unity possible only by the intervening Serbo-Bulgarian War of 1885—it had to be completed in exile: Vazov had to leave Bulgaria again in 1886 for a brief sojourn in Odessa, due to the constant shift in the country's political climate. Political necessity thus continued to fan the flames of the National Revival.

While Bulgaria fumbled with her fate on the world stage, George Bernard Shaw spoofed the Serbo-Bulgarian war and Balkan political intrigues in *Arms and the Man* (1894); it appeared in the same year as Vazov's *Under the Yoke*. *Arms and the Man* was later adapted by Oskar Straus in a popular operetta, *The Chocolate Soldier* (1908), while another comic operetta on Balkan romance-and-politics was Franz Lehar's *The Merry Widow* (1905).

Vazov, hailed as his country's "national poet," was the founder of modern Bulgarian theater in association with other poets and writers. The roots of a distinct national drama, however, are to be found in the Bulgarian Renaissance days during Ottoman subjugation. Dobry Voinikov, the son of a clergyman educated at a French school in Constantinople, was the real pioneer in drama; he wrote plays on his country's conversion to Christianity, to be performed in churches. Conservative Greek church officials drove him from Bulgaria into exile in Belgrade, and then Braila, a port city on the Danube in Romania, where a colony of Bulgarian revolutionaries had gathered. There Voinikov continued to write patriotic historical plays until the liberation came; he died of typhus in 1878.

The period between 1878 and 1885 was crucial to Bulgaria's national identity, while the time between 1885 and 1912 set the stage for the First World War via the Balkan Wars. The issue in the

Ivan Nichev's *Stars in Her Hair, Tears in Her Eyes* (1977): screenplay writer Angel Wagenstein's description of a typical performance by the "Renewal" theatrical troupe touring the provinces at the turn-of-the-century.

First Balkan War (1912) was the liberation of Macedonia from the Turks; the issue of the Second Balkan War (1913) was Macedonia itself and involved all of Bulgaria's Balkan neighbors.

The Bulgarian National Revival thus splintered into several complementary factions that both nourished and contradicted each other. One of the central questions, of course, was how to depart from time-hallowed ecclesiastical and national commitments to enter the mainstreams of modern European thought. The departure was all the more difficult in view of the martyrdom of the poet Hristo Botev and the years in exile spent by writers Ivan Vasov, Petko Slaveykov, and Lyuben Karavelov. Karavelov (1835–79), publicist and storyteller, had a heavy impact on Bulgarian literature, although living mostly abroad in Moscow (where he studied), Serbia, and Bucharest (where he joined Botev and the revolutionary émigrés).

Karavelov's contribution to the Bulgarian Renaissance was a series of stories about his homeland and the common people, greatly influenced by Russian *narodnik* (populist) writers of the mid-nineteenth century (Gogol, Turgenev, Grigorovich) and the same country's radical thinkers (in support of whom he was forced to leave Russia in 1867). He created Gogol-like patriarchal characters, which were to become prototypes in Bulgarian literature, drama, and cinema, and his knack of bringing literature "closer to the people" was widely imitated throughout the country after independence was won.

A Bulgarian *narodnik* movement swept the country in the 1880s and 1890s with the double aim of rediscovering peasant roots and fostering social and agrarian reform. The stories of Todor Vlaykov are a veritable anthology of Bulgarian village life in the late nineteenth century; as a publicist educated at Moscow in Russian *narodnik* ideals, Vlaykov was instrumental in spreading them among village teachers. Ivan Vazov wrote poems and stories of provincial life, edited a folk newspaper in Plovdiv that campaigned for the union of East Rumelia (South Bulgaria) to Bulgaria, and compiled with Konstantin Velichkov the first Bulgarian anthology of literature. The "Vazov circle," moreover, defended the conservative tradition in Bulgarian literature against new "individualists" led by Pencho Slaveykov, son of Petko "Grandpa" Slaveykov (known for his collection of folklorica).

Pencho Slaveykov, although an ardent student of his country's folk history, formed a "literary circle" to counteract Vasov's influence and res-cue Bulgarian literature from populist social pathos. From his post at the State Library and temporary position as head of the National Theater, he used his talents as a poet, critic, publicist, translator, and philosopher to foster new standards of literary excellence closer to classical and modern European thought (instead of being suffocated by an ecclesiastical national heritage). An extensive knowledge of European literature and an education at Leipzig imbued him with a humanist idealism tempered by a love for aesthetics. When Pencho Slaveykov wrote ballad poems, the folk themes were colored with a new significance. And when he encouraged new writers—Kiril Hristov, Peyo Yavorov, and Petko Todorov—in a monthly journal titled *Misal*, they also developed individual styles emphasizing a new spiritual or symbolic dimension in folklore.

Nearly all the writers who confronted the *narodnik* dilemma were educated abroad, some turning back to European universities to teach Bulgarian literature around the turn of the century. Konstantin Velichkov, who studied French literature in Constantinople and painting in Florence, became minister of education in 1894; he sided for a time with Vazov in the Vazov-Slaveykov debate, then retired to southern France to translate French and Italian literature. Poet and playwright Kiril Hristov, educated in Italy and Leipzig, joined Slaveykov's literary circle at first, then deserted too to teach Bulgarian literature in Leipzig and Prague.

It was in drama that Pencho Slaveykov's principles of aesthetics won out in the end. Anton Strashimirov (educated in Bern) imbued his plays on village life with emotional clashes and inner struggles. Petko Todorov, Slaveykov's prized pupil (educated in Bern, Toulouse, Berlin, and Leipzig), vigorously searched for spiritual and symbolic depth in folk themes. Peyo Yavorov, upon visiting France only once and studying under Slaveykov's influence, drifted away from the populist camp to a complete espousal of the symbolist, psychological sensitivity.

The Yavorov tradition in poetry was furthered, in turn, by Nikolai Liliev; a symbolist poet trained in Lausanne and Paris, he specialized in the evocative, musical element of Bulgarian verse. Another symbolist poet with a love for French literature, Dimcho Debelyanov brought a melancholic note into national verse—all the more powerful through a tragic premonition of his death on the battlefield in 1916. His death at a young age linked him with both Hristo Botev and the "Bulgarian Mayakovsky" of the next generation, Nikola Vaptsarov. Vaptsarov,

Dimiter Minkov's *Bulgarians of Ancient Times* **(1945),**
based on a classic novel by Lyuben Karavelov.

Alexander Vazov's *Cairn* **(1936), based on Ivan Vazov's**
popular poem.

executed by a firing squad in 1942, was remembered as a heroic figure in the first films produced in Bulgaria after the Second World War.

In novels and short stories, where the populist *narodnik* tradition got its start, a gradual change in style and content developed from within. In particular, Yordan Yovkov's cycle of village stories, set in his native Dobruja region (near Romania, between the Danube River and the Black Sea), leaned on a Bulgarian mystique for effect and employed an original prose style. Another storyteller, Elin Pelin, used a dialect to color his humorous tales of village life, set in the hamlets near Sofia.

One of the members of the Vazov circle was Stoyan Mihaylovski, a poet with a liking for satire. Restless and pessimistic by nature, the French-educated lawyer and officeholder used his pen on the side to attack evil in the government; he thereby introduced moral and intellectual motifs into Bulgarian verse. Mihaylovski paved the way for the remarkable Aleko Konstantinov.

Konstantinov, like Mihaylovski, turned to satire while practicing law; his idealism and sense of integrity seem to have driven him to journalism, and then globetrotting. On his travels, he covered for newspapers the European continent and eventually got as far as Chicago; these adventures resulted in travel books, encouraged into print by Pencho Slaveykov. Konstantinov became known as the "Father of Bulgarian Tourism."

An irascible type, Aleko Konstantinov was praised for his satirical pen when poking fun at the West and comparing the foibles of industrialized countries with his nascent, rural Bulgaria. His classic, *Bay Ganyu* (1895), featured the "improbable tales" of a contemporary Bulgarian abroad—a brash, outspoken, acerbic peddler of rose-attar and goat-rugs in the capitals of Europe. This merry forerunner of Schweik, Jaroslav Hašek's Czech equivalent, was later the hero of the first successful Bulgarian feature film, *Bay Ganyu* (1922). By that time, Konstantinov himself was no longer around: his acid pen

Peter Stoychev's *Land* (1930), based on Elin Pelin's novel.

was halted by an assassin's bullet in 1897.

Not only *Bay Ganyu*, but nearly the whole of Bulgarian cinema until well into the postwar years was based on national literature. All the beloved classics were adapted either to the screen or the stage, and the shortcut for most film studios was to reach for a dramatized property of the state. This explains the excess of theatricality in Bulgarian cinema up to approximately a decade ago. As the audience matured, the films became more sophisticated. It was only a matter of time.

All the same, a naïve film—like a primitive painting—can be a joy to watch. Spend a day at the Bulgarska Nacionalna Filmoteka, and see for yourself.

Coming of Age

Bulgaria shared in the tragedies of two world wars by being on the losing sides in both of them. In the interim, a military dictatorship and several bloody uprisings allowed little time throughout the 1920s and 1930s for progress in art and literature according to the standards of West Europe. Still, the poetic soul of the Bulgarian writer was moved to greater things—a voice of fervor and commitment could always be heard, particularly in times of the greatest adversity.

As stated in the previous chapter, the modern tradition in Bulgarian literature owes its advent to Pencho Slaveykov, whose monthly journal, *Misal*, encouraged writers with individual styles honed by experiences in the European capitals. In the formative years of the nation, this movement was complemented by the Vasov circle of writers anchored to provincial life and popular folk tales. Gradually, due to this friction, Bulgarian letters came of age.

The trend upward started on the stage. Poet Peyo Yavorov introduced psychological analysis into his plays. Then Anton Strashimirov featured emotional clashes in popular dramas, his *The Mother-in-Law* containing one of Bulgarian literature's most colorful characters. The Sofian cafés buzzed with writers and artists. Between the wars, the first major dramatist to devote himself solely to the theater, Stefan L. Kostov, wrote a number of satirical comedies in a Gogol vein. The best of these, *Golemanov*, featured a miser aspiring to political power. Another playwright influenced by Gogol was Yordan Yovkov, who was also one of the country's most popular prose writers. His female portraits—Albena, Boryana, Nona—proved to be memorable figures on stage and screen.

Lev Arnstam's *History Lesson* (1957): Stefan Savov as Georgi Dimitrov, during the 1933 Leipzig Trial.

49

Vulo Radev's *Tsar and General* **(1966): Naum Shopov as Tsar Boris, on the eve of World War II.**

A third playwright of the 1930s, Racho Stoyanov, enriched the national repertoire with *Masters,* a popular drama on the conflict between art and love. And an avid student of the Stanislavsky method, N. O. Massalitimov, managed the National Theater in Sofia during these crucial years; the Russian-born actor and director had left the Moscow Art Theater to accept the post in Bulgaria.

Prose and poetry made headway under Georgi Karaslavov, Dimiter Dimov, and Ivan Peychev during the difficult period of the Second World War and after, while Dimiter Talev, Pavel Vezhinov, and Orlin Vassilev contributed novels and plays. Karaslavov's popular short stories were adapted for the stage, and later for the screen: his *The Daughter-in-Law,* in fact, was filmed twice. Dimov's *Tobacco* and *Damned Souls,* landmarks in the development of the Bulgarian novel, were both made into prominent motion pictures. Peychev departed from poetry to a synthesis of poetry and drama in *Every Autumn Eve-*

ning, accenting human failings during the antifascist struggle of the 1940s.

During the period of the Personality Cult, an attempt was made in drama and film to link the National Revival with the Socialist Realism precepts of art. At this time, a string of historical plays, antifascist dramas, and sociopolitical screenplays were written by Kamen Zidarov, Orlin Vassilev, and Lozan Strelkov. Vassilev was assigned to write the first screenplay after the nationalization of the Bulgarian film industry: *Kalin the Eagle* (1950), directed by Boris Borozanov. He also adapted his play *Alarm* (1951) to the screen, in collaboration with Angel Wagenstein.

With the passing of the Personality Cult in the mid-1950s, an important play about that very period, Georgi Diagarov's *The Prosecutor,* was produced and widely discussed. Then, when a film version of the same play was attempted in 1967, directed by Lyubomir Sharlandjiev, another controversy broke out in regard to its

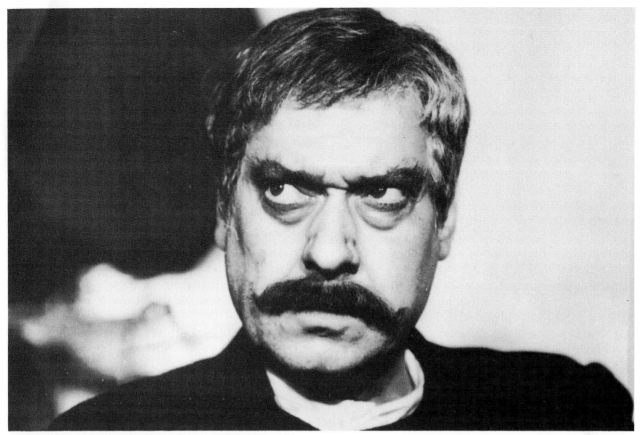

Vassil Mirchev's *The Daughter-in-Law* (1976), based on the
classic by Georgi Karaslavov.

Vulo Radev's *Doomed Souls* (1976), based on Dimiter Dimov's popular novel.

political relevance; the film was never released. (Later, however, during the Bulgarian Theater Festival in 1979, a production of *The Prosecutor* could be seen again on stage in Sofia.)

In addition, dramas about everyday problems appeared on the stage and screen. Dragomir Assenov's plays dealt with all walks of life. Mihail Velichkov specialized in psychological, intimate dramas, winning prizes and recognition abroad. Pancho Panchev, first a critic and then a dramatist, became a prolific writer of comedies with surprising twists and happy endings.

Bulgarian cinema came of age slowly with the passing of the Personality Cult. Its literary foundation prevented a rapid maturing of the art form on its own terms, as was common in Western countries. On the other hand, the gradual influx of writers and dramatists into the medium guaranteed a steady development toward maturity via trial-and-error experiments.

For many years, the screenplay determined the growth of Bulgarian cinema. The novelist Pavel Vezhinov created credible flesh-and-blood contemporary heroes beginning in the mid-1950s; one of his favorite preoccupations was the generation gap. The dramatist Nikola Russev contributed tight dialogue scenes to the cinema. Bogomil Rainov brought his writing talents to the aid of Rangel Vulchanov and Metodi Andonov, talented directors with a penchant for teamwork. Vassil Akyov reduced the partisan theme to antiheroic realism in a pair of screenplays based on personal remembrances as a resistance fighter.

Moreover, important novels were adapted into representative film versions when the time was ripe. Emilian Stanev's *The Peach Thief* (1964), directed by Vulo Radev, became a key film in the acclaimed Bulgarian-style "poetic cinema" of the 1960s. Gencho Stoyev's novel *A Bad Day* was the source for Ivan Terziev's successful *Strong Water* (1975). It can be argued that well over half of Bulgaria's best film productions were based on previous literary material. Some directors, like Hristo Hristov, prefer working from recognized literary sources.

Bulgarian theater matured along parallel lines. Satire, for instance, flourished in the 1970s on stages only after the intervening periods had prepared audiences for the comedies of Ivan Radoev and Stanislav Stratiev. Today, a successful dramatist like Nedyalko Yordanov, who relates his plays to young audiences, has the opportunity to test reactions and make changes while directing his own work. Several playwrights are engaged as artistic advisers, or dramaturges, at theaters in order to assist at rehearsals whenever necessary.

This kind of collective effort bridges all the arts in Bulgaria. It is not surprising to find a dramatist shift to screenplay writing, and then to directing. Nor is it unusual to see a trend in cinema influence the theater at the same time, particularly when a theater director, Metodi Andonov, makes his mark with a Nikolai Haitov story, *The Goat Horn*. The formation of independent film units at the Boyana Studios in 1972 allowed directors and writers to compete against, and complement, each other at the same time.

Teamwork seems to have drawn the best from professional screenplay writers—that and the challenge of writing for cinema, television, and the theater as well as for oneself. Hristo Ganev collaborated with his wife, Binka Zhelyazkova, as writer-director, but he has also directed his own documentaries and taken an interest in animated cartoons for a time. Lyuben Stanev gave up a career in medicine for writing. Svoboda Buchvarova splits her time between scriptwriting and serving as artistic adviser at the Haemus Film Unit. Atanas Tsenev came to screenplays after adapting one of his novels for the screen, and Konstantin Pavlov is still a poet first and then a writer for cinema, stage, and television.

Given this favorable environment for cross-pollination in the arts, why hasn't Bulgaria collected its share of prizes at international film festivals? Until lately, it hasn't for a number of reasons.

The country has been too busy "catching up" with the rest of Europe. The construction of proper movie theaters alone in a predominantly agricultural land with a rural society took time. The foundation of a film industry was simply not there until a decade or two ago. And writers felt an obligation to educate first—before turning to the aesthetics of the art form.

Some, however, accomplished both. They were five: Angel Wagenstein, Valeri Petrov, Yordan Radichkov, Nikolai Haitov, and Georgi Mishev, all worth a moment of consideration.

Angel Wagenstein (born 1922 in Plovdiv)

The author of more than twenty-five screenplays (feature films television plays, documentaries, cartoons), Angel Wagenstein wasted little time making his presence known in Sofia after graduating from the Moscow Film School (VGIK) in 1950, the year the first feature film was made after the nationalization of the Bulga-

Konrad Wolf's East German–Bulgarian coproduction
Stars (1959). Screenplay by Angel Wagenstein.

rian film industry. His collaboration with dramatist Orlin Vassilev on the latter's play *Alarm*
(1951) marked the true beginning of modern
Bulgarian cinema.

The director of *Alarm* was Zahari Zhandov,
who then collaborated with Wagenstein on the
young scriptwriter's diploma work, *Septembrists*
(1954), one of those revolutionary themes common to Bulgarian and East European cinema at
the time. Both *Alarm* and *Septembrists*, however,
were steps forward in the right direction, for the
industry was young and audiences detected the
pulse of life and history in these didactic treatises
on the past.

While studying in Moscow, "Jackie" Wagenstein made the acquaintance of Konrad Wolf.
The East German director collaborated with his
VGIK friend on a coproduction by Bulgaria and
the German Democratic Republic, *Stars* (1959);
it was an instant international success. In view of
the recent past, and a monstrous war that Bulgaria supported for a time as Germany's ally, this

reckoning with the conscience of a nation came
at an opportune time, but there was much more
in the film—the love story dealt realistically with
the fate of a Jewish girl about to be transported
to Auschwitz and a young German officer's disillusionment with his role in an unjust cause. No
positive solution was offered to the dilemma; the
emphasis was placed, instead, on mankind's
common tragedy.

Stars was Wagenstein's first major screenplay.
The vulnerable, warmly human characters presented here are to be found in all his films; a
recent example was Ivan Nichev's *Stars in her
Hair, Tears in her Eyes* (1977), the story of a wandering actors' troupe at the turn of the century.
The writer's sense of the historical moment also
singled him out from others dealing with revolutionary and antifascist themes. His *Amendment to
the Defense-of-State Act* (1976), directed by Lyudmil Staikov, left room for flesh-and-blood portraits of well-known political personalities in the
troublesome 1920s. And his script for Rangel

Vulchanov's coproduction with Czechoslovakia, *Aesop* (1970), has held its own over the years as a political allegory. His latest historical film is *Boris the First* (1984), directed by Borislav Sharaliev.

Besides these, Wagenstein wrote a screenplay on the life of Goya (*Goya*, 1971), an East German production directed by Konrad Wolf; the 70mm film was presented at the Cannes Film Festival. He also worked with Wolf on an interpretation of Saint-Exupéry's fairy tale *The Little Prince* (1966), for East German television. Occasionally, he turns his attention to theater and the documentary film, as in the TV production *Attempt to Fly* (1981), for the anniversary year.

Valeri Petrov (born 1920 in Sofia)

A national poet with a degree in medicine, Valeri Petrov took up freelance writing in 1956 and became famous a few years later through his collaboration with director Rangel Vulchanov on the breakthrough film in Bulgarian film history, *On a Small Island* (1958). After two more films with Vulchanov, *First Lesson* (1960) and *Sun and Shadow* (1962), this trilogy marked the initial poetic phase of a budding national cinema.

As these films collected prizes and critical recognition at international film festivals, Petrov turned his attention elsewhere. One project was the translation of Shakespeare into Bulgarian, a task that alone guaranteed him fame at home and abroad. His dramatic poem *When the Roses Dance* and his comedy *The Word of Honor of a Musketeer* are regular items in Bulgarian theater repertory; he has written, in fact, several poems and plays, in addition to essays and prose.

In the mid-1960s, Petrov lifted the children's film to a respectable genre of its own with the screenplay for Borislav Sharaliev's *Knight without Armor* (1966). The film's view of the world of compromising adults through the eyes of an inquiring, half-grown Don Quixote transfers in midstream to the realm of the poetic, serious-minded "fairy tale." Petrov enjoys questioning the state of the world through the medium of

Rangel Vulchanov's *Sun and Shadow* (1962). **Screenplay by Valeri Petrov.**

the children's film: another was Zako Heskia's *Yo-ho-ho* (1981).

More than a decade after first working with Vulchanov, Petrov collaborated with him on *With Love and Tenderness* (1978). An aging sculptor and a young girl match their visions with bureaucrats, hangers-on, and a cross section of ordinary citizens enjoying the Black Sea Riviera. As attractive as the film is on the aesthetic level, its theme appeared outmoded and possibly a remnant of an idea from the bygone days (in the 1950s) of Bulgaria's poetic realism.

One cannot help but speculate on how Bulgarian cinema would have developed had Petrov devoted his considerable talents solely to screenplay writing. Surely, international recognition for Bulgarian cinema in Western countries would have advanced at twice the pace it did over the past two decades.

Yordan Radichkov (born 1929 in Kalimanitsa)

An outstanding writer of novels, short stories, and plays, Yordan Radichkov relates to Bulgarian cinema as an influential outsider, for he seldom is listed as an original screenplay writer. Rather, his stories were adapted to the screen by the choice of others.

Radichkov is sometimes referred to as the "Bulgarian Gogol." Others place him in the tradition of Yordan Yovkov, who, in turn, is also compared to Gogol. Radichkov is a masterful storyteller, one who freely mixes the grotesque with folklore, simply because that's the way he views folk traditions. Parody and satire, metaphorical language and poetic mysticism—these are but a few of the literary devices at his command. His complex symbolic parables make for tense psychological dramas and richly visual film productions.

A prolific output of books has placed Radichkov in the front line of the country's literary scene: *The Heart Beats for the People* (1959), *Simple Hands* (1961), *Topsy-Turvy Sky* (1962), *Mountain Flower* (1964), *Striped Rug* (1964), *Torrid Noon* (1965), *A Fierce Mood* (1965), *Unlit Courtyards*

Binka Zehlyazkova's *The Attached Balloon* **(1967). Screenplay by Yordan Radichkov.**

(1966), *The Goat-Beard* (1967), *Aquarius* (1967), *The Silent Wind* (1968), *We, the Sparrows* (1968), *The Gunpowder Primer* (1969), *A Leather Melon* (1969), *Rock Drawings* (1970), *Chaff and Grain* (1972), *How's This?* (1974), *Reminiscences about Horses* (1975), and *Everybody and Nobody* (1976).

In the 1960s, he began to write plays: *Confusion* (1966), *January* (1973), *Lazaritsa* (1977), and *Attempt to Fly* (1979). The real mingles with the absurd in these dramas of the human spirit, which can be interpreted as philosophical statements on existence in today's increasingly entangled civilization. *Lazaritsa*, for instance, covers the seasons of life from a lonely perch in a tree; the one-man play has immediate associations with the theater of Beckett and Ionesco. *January* received the ultimate compliment in Bulgarian art circles when Stoyan Dukov successfully parodied the play in an animated cartoon, titled *February* (1977).

Attempt to Fly also has a long history behind it. The original short story was adapted by Radichkov for Binka Zhelyazkova's feature film, *The At-tached Balloon* (1967), which had to be withdrawn from circulation shortly after release, owing to the restrictions placed on the arts at that time. Later, for the 1979 Bulgarian Theater Festival in Sofia, no less than four different productions were presented of *Attempt to Fly,* the same story as that in *The Attached Balloon,* this time adapted to the stage.

Another prominent film version of one of his stories, Hristo Hristov's *The Last Summer* (1974) won several international festival awards and critical recognition for everyone creatively involved in the project. It was the first successful Radichkov film and Hristov's best effort to date. The protagonist—a peasant who refuses to leave an abandoned village soon to be flooded owing to the construction of a dam—was played by the late Grigor Vachkov, who also personified Lazaritsa in its long theatrical run at the Satirical Theater in Sofia.

Apparently, theater professionals enjoy Radichkov's work the most. After the debacle of Zhelyazkova's *The Attached Balloon,* actor Naum

Varna Theater production of Yordan Radichkov's *Attempt to Fly,* the stage version of *The Attached Balloon* presented at the 1979 Sofia Festival of Bulgarian Theater and Drama.

Shopov adapted his story "Bread" into a film-novella (1972); the story is from *The Gunpowder Primer* collection, which also served as the source for Todor Dinov's *Gunpowder* (1977). And stage director Krikor Azarian collaborated with the author on a screen adaptation of *Everybody and Nobody* (1978). All things considered, any adaptation of a Radichkov story to the screen is a task that demands the best from the director, for his style of writing does not lend itself readily to narrative filmmaking. The attraction lies in the depth of the language itself.

Nikolai Haitov (born 1919 in Yovorovo)

Storyteller, dramatist, and screenplay writer, Nikolai Haitov was a shepherd and forester in his beloved Rhodope Mountains before turning to writing in the mid-1950s. His books, upon publication, were immediate popular successes: *Rivals* (1957), *Spark from the Hearth* (1959), *Rhodope Unveiled* (1960), *Letters from the Wilderness* (1965), *Elm Leaves* (1966), *Wild Stories* (1967), and *The Prickly Rose* (1969), among others.

In the 1960s, Haitov began to write for the theater. *Locked Spring* (1961) and *Here on Earth* (1963) paved the way for an acclaimed trilogy of one-act plays: *Lanes, Boat in the Forest, Dogs* (1966). The cartoonist Todor Dinov filmed his fairy-tale play *The Dragon* (1974), set in the Middle Ages.

Then, in the 1970s, Haitov found his way to original screenplay writing. He was first discovered by a young Bulgarian student at the Moscow Film School, Georgi Djulgerov, who adapted one of his stories for a graduation project: *The Cooper* (1969), relocated in Armenia instead of the Rhodope Mountains. *The Cooper* won a prize at the Oberhausen Short Film Festival in 1970; this recognition prompted Djulgerov to make a second version, a film-novella titled *The Test* (1971). *The Test*, in turn, was coupled with another Haitov film-novella, Milen Nikolov's *Naked Conscience* (1970), for distribution as a full-length feature film, titled *Colorful World* (1971). At the same time, Nokolov adapted another Haitov story, *The End of the Song* (1971).

Haitov worked on all these scripts. They served as preparation for the most successful film in Bulgarian history: *The Goat Horn* (1972), directed by Metodi Andonov from an original screenplay by Haitov. *The Goat Horn* was viewed by three million Bulgarians, or approximately one-third of the population.

All these films were set in the Rhodope Mountains. The beauty of the Rhodopes was attested to in ancient literature by Ovid, Vergil, and Horace. It was here, in the land of Thrace, that the legend of Orpheus originated; Thracian costumes and folk traditions survive in the area to the present day. The tale of vengeance in *The Goat Horn*, honed to a ballad or legend by centuries of storytelling, may have had its roots in ancient Thrace. In any case, the film's attraction in this part of Bulgaria relates to the impact the "Western" has upon American and European audiences.

The myths and legends, the flair of an unpolished but musical language, the age-old tests of manhood and valor, the rites of nature, the celebrations of spring planting and autumn harvesting, the songs and the dances—this is the lore of the Rhodopes that Haitov brought to mass audiences through the films he scripted for the young film industry.

His next successful screenplay was *Manly Times* (1977), directed by Eduard Zahariev. Beginning with the remark that this is "a very old story," Haitov wove a tale of love and kidnapping that could fit into any historical period of the past. When placed next to Djulgerov's *The Test* and Metodi Andonov's *The Goat Horn*, Zahariev's *Manly Times* gives the impression of being the completion of a Haitov trilogy on the theme of courage and endurance in a time of trial.

Another striking element in Haitov's stories is the author's respect for the outsider—to be more exact, for the loser. Even when the hero is victorious, he has lost something vitally human in the process. An innocent young girl is trained by her father to avenge the murdered mother in *The Goat Horn*. The kidnapper in *Manly Times* suffers the ignominy, and the consequences, of falling in love with his captive. In a story adapted by Hristo Hristov, *A Tree without Roots* (1974), a man of the mountains is lost in the buzz of the city. And in *The Cherry Orchard* (1979), directed by Ivan Andonov from an original Haitov screenplay, a forester in communion with nature cannot win a lonely battle with public officials to save the fruit trees he has easily protected from natural parasites.

Respect for the individual, right or wrong, was a significant contribution by a prominent writer to Bulgarian film as it came of age over the last decade. Nikolai Haitov, so far as his Haiduk tales of the Rhodope Mountains are concerned, will be long remembered as his country's balladeer.

Metodi Andonov's *The Goat Horn* (1972). Screenplay by
Nikolai Haitov.

Georgi Mishev (born 1935 in Yoglav)

Satirist and screenplay writer, Georgi Mishev
is second only to Angel Wagenstein as an artist
who conceives his material in direct relation to
the cinema. All of his film material is original; in
addition, his screenplays are so linked with visual
motifs and typed characters that the viewer is
aware from the start that he is deep in "Mishev
Country."

Mishev studied journalism, and then began
writing children's stories in his spare time, publishing *The Blue-Eyed Fisherman* (1958) at the age
of twenty-three. This was followed by collections
of short stories, novels, and books for youths:
Ossam Stories (1963), *The Adamites* (1966), *Matriarchate* (1967), *Well Dressed Men: Simple Stories from
the Provinces* (1967), *Autumn Carnival* (1970), the
play *The Hypotheses on the Burning of the Bridge at
Lovech, August 3, 1925* (1972). *Moving Away*

(1973), and *Villa Zone (The Garden Party)* (1976).

Born and raised in a village, he often returns
to memories of his youth for story material,
while the clash of village customs and traditions
with an impersonal, anonymous city life in a
changing society serve as the basis for his
screenplays. In general, Mishev has worked with
only three film directors—Eduard Zahariev, Lyudmil Kirkov, and Ivan Andonov—whose collaborations complement each other as the
humorous and questioning sides of his view of
life.

The Zahariev films reveal a satirist with a
penchant for the absurd and the ridiculous in
everyday life among the common people. In
their first effort together, *If the Train Doesn't Arrive* (1967), an absurd hunt takes place in the
night when a stranger, accompanying three village friends on an expedition, suddenly disappears. In *The Hare Census* (1973) an official from

58

Eduard Zahariev's *Villa Zone* (1975). Screenplay by Georgi Mishev.

the city arrives in a village to count the number of wild hares in the district, an absurdity that allows fortunately for a closing picnic on the grass. In *Villa Zone* (1975) it's a family celebration in the backyard that permits Mishev and Zahariev to poke scathing fun at the new class of workers and peasants transplanted to an urban and modernized society. These three films are among the finest produced in Bulgaria; they also are comedies Western audiences can appreciate at face value.

Parallel to the Zahariev films (perhaps influenced by them) Mishev penned a series of screenplays for Lyudmil Kirkov: *A Boy Becomes a Man* (1972), *Peasant on a Bicycle* (1974), *Don't Go Away* (1976), and *Matriarchate* (1977). *A Boy Becomes a Man* and *Don't Go Away* are two parts of the same story—about a youth in a small town who rebels against the stifling mentality around him, and later his further disillusionment as a teacher in similar circumstances. The films can be viewed as ironic, but painfully human, footnotes to the bittersweet satire in the Zahariev series.

Nostalgia for village life, now a reality of the past, impregnates Mishev's screenplays for Kirkov's *Peasant on a Bicycle* and *Matriarchate*. In the first, a city-dwelling worker returns on weekends to the nearby village he was raised in; the adventures he experiences on his bicycle are sobering. The portrait of village life in *Matriachate* is a bit more depressing: all the men have left a village to work in the city, with the absurd result that a matriarchate, that is, a society of abandoned women, collectively manage a collective farm in an environment that is socially meaningless.

His recent scripts for other directors—principally those with Ivan Andonov: *Fairy Dance* (1976) and *Ladies' Choice* (1980)—reveal a looser, lighter satirical style, along the lines of comedies produced at the Satirical Theater in Sofia. There is no question, however, of the major role he has played in the maturing of New Bulgarian Cinema. Indeed, without his types and personalities on the screen—"Georgi Mishev characters"—it would be difficult to imagine a national cinema in this corner of the Balkans.

2
BIOGRAPHIES

(*Note:* In view of the impossibility of recording full biographies of each important filmmaker in Bulgaria, the author has chosen instead a chronological approach with emphasis being placed on only a dozen feature-film directors.)

Zahari Zhandov (born 1911 in Russe)

Although over fifty feature films had already been made in Bulgaria when the documentary filmmaker Zhandov was called in to direct *Alarm* (1951), this was the true beginning for the young film industry. He belonged to the older generation of Bulgarian filmmakers, who learned their trade before and during the Second World War, and had won recognition abroad for his documentaries and short films: *A Day in Sofia* (1946) and *Men amid the Clouds* (1947) (First Prize at the Venice Film Festival), the latter about weather stations. Zhandov then had the distinction of collaborating with Joris Ivens on the Czechoslovakian-Polish-Bulgarian documentary coproduction *The First Years* (1949); he was the cameraman for the Bulgarian sequence. *Alarm*, although restricted by the schematic formulas of the Personality Cult, had a documentary freshness in its portrayal of the antifascist struggle in 1944. Zhandov also had the good fortune to collaborate with the talented screenplay writer, Angel Wagenstein, on *Alarm* and *Septembrists* (1954), and waited nearly twenty years to make the impressive *Master of Boyana* (1981). He is the father

Zahari Zhandov.

figure in Bulgarian cinema.

Two directors who learned their trade in the war years, Boris Borozanov (b. 1897) and Anton Marinovich (b. 1907), made feature films for private companies before the nationalization of the film industry. Borozanov's patriotic flair earned him the distinction of making the first state-subsidized feature film, *Kalin the Eagle* (1950), a national epic in the old style. Marinovich specialized in family-style comedies, thrillers, and entertainment films.

First VGIK Graduates

Bulgarian cinema dates its beginnings from 1950, when the first state film, *Kalin the Eagle,* paired the Socialist movement with the National Revival and the first graduates of the Moscow Film School (VGIK) returned home to revitalize the sleeping national film industry. Directors Dako Dakovski (1919–62), Ducho Mundrov (b. 1920), and Borislav Sharaliev (b. 1922), screenplay writers (and documentary

Borislav Sharaliev.

filmmakers on the side) Angel Wagenstein (b. 1922) and Hristo Ganev (b. 1924), were in the 1950 graduating class. Each contributed to the development of Bulgarian cinema in the crucial period of the Personality Cult and afterward.

Dako Dakovski dutifully adapted the national classic, Ivan Vazov's novel *Under the Yoke* (1952), and thereafter dealt exclusively with contemporary life and issues in a series of films on peasant life, beginning with *The Troubled Road* (1955).

Borislav Sharaliev collaborated with classmate Hristo Ganev on his diploma script, *Song of Man* (1954), about the last days of the revolutionary poet Nikola Vaptsarov (the "Bulgarian Mayakovsky" faced the firing squad in 1942). His best features are the children's film *Knight without Armor* (1966) (a Valeri Petrov script), the youth film *All Is Love* (1979), *The Thrust* (1981) on the liberation of Sofia, and *Boris the First* (1984), the epic scripted by Angel Wagenstein in two parts.

Ducho Mundrov, a partisan fighter who escaped a sentence of death as the war came to a close, collaborated with Nikola Korabov on the documentary *Nikola Vaptsarov* (1952), and with the same director on the feature film celebrating the building of a "city of youth," *People of Dimitrovgrad* (1956). His métier, however, was the "Eastern," films on the resistance movement that were often based on personal experiences (*The Commander of the Detachment,* 1959).

FAMU and Lodz Graduates

Kiril Ilinchev (b. 1921) graduated in the 1951 class at FAMU in Prague. A director with a penchant for the theatrical, he adapted Stefan L. Kostov's classic Gogol-like satire of the Thirties, *Golemanov* (1958).

Yakim Yakimov (b. 1925) studied at the Lodz Film School in Poland. He is best known for a series of films on youth problems and the generation gap, several in collaboration with screenplay writer Pavel Vezhinov (*Troubled Home,* 1965).

More VGIK Graduates

Yanko Yankov (b. 1924) graduated from the Moscow Film School in 1952. He made the first Bulgarian comedy, *It Happened on the Streets* (1956), which signaled a new era in the young industry after the restrictions of the Personality Cult. Some of Yankov's films have proven to be controversial: *Years of Love* (1957), *Confession*

Nikola Korabov.

Hristo Piskov

(1969), and the TV comedy *An Ornery Man* (1970).

Nikola Korabov (b. 1926), also VGIK '52, has a distinct taste for the historical epic (the adaptation of Dimiter Dimov's *Tobacco*, 1962). His change of pace to a contemporary theme, *Vula (Permission to Marry)* (1965), aroused a storm of controversy. Most recently, he has followed Bulgaria's famous basso around the world's opera stages to make the documentary *Nikolai Ghiaurov—50* (1980). His best-known films are *Tobacco, Ivan Kondarev* (1974), and *Destiny* (1983).

Peter Vassilev (b. 1918) specializes in comedy and light entertainment. He made the first detective thriller (*The Traces Remain*, 1956) and a satirical comedy, *The Whale* (1970).

Vladimir Yanchev (b. 1930), the son of political exiles living in the Soviet Union, returned to Moscow to study at VGIK; he graduated in 1955. His genre too is comedy, beginning with *Favorite No. 13* (1958), and he has made several films in coproduction with the Soviet Union.

Irina Aktasheva.

Hristo Piskov (b. 1927) and the Soviet actress Irina Aktasheva (b. 1931) are a husband-wife directorial team who met while studying at VGIK. Piskov was an assistant director to Lev Arnstam on the Bulgarian-Soviet coproduction, *History Lesson* (1957), a biography of Dimitrov; Aktasheva acted in the same film. After she had assisted her husband on a film about the Resistance, *Poor Man's Street* (1960), they made the controversial *Monday Morning* (1966, unreleased) together, the first of a series on contemporary themes.

Rangel Vulchanov (born 1928 in Krivina)

Bulgaria's leading director, Vulchanov studied direction at home in Sofia, acted during his student days in Zahari Zhandov's *Alarm* (1951), and propelled his country's cinematography into the world spotlight with his first feature film, *On a Small Island* (1958). The poetic, philosphical tone of this film heralded a promising "new wave" in Bulgarian cinema, but its international success was the result of a close collaboration of Vulchanov with screenplay writer Valeri Petrov, cameraman Dimo Kolarov, composer Simeon Pironkov, and several of the country's finest actors. The shooting team then collaborated on *First Lesson* (1960) and *Sun and Shadow* (1962), although Vulchanov preferred on these occasions to work with nonprofessional actors (an option he has employed with astonishing success to the present day). He has experimented with various genres, each time with impressive results and few artistic setbacks: *The Inspector and the Night* (1963) (contemporary ethics), *The She-Wolf* (1965) (moral problem with psychological overtones), *Escape to Ropotamo* (1973) (musical), *The Inspector and the Forest* (1975) (documentary realism), *With Love and Tenderness* (1978) (questions of aesthetics), and *The Unknown Soldier's Patent Leather Shoes* (1979) (avant-garde recollections of childhood).

Vulchanov's personal courage as an independent-minded director has also played a role in the development of Bulgarian cinema. When a Bulgarian-Czechoslovakian coproduction, *Aesop* (1970), was delayed in its home release, the director stayed on in Czechoslovakia to make *Face behind the Mask* (1970) and *Chance* (1970). Among his documentaries are the lyrical *Journey between Two Shores* (1967), filmed in North Africa, the folkloric *Bulgarian Rhythms* (1972), and two portraits of composer Lyubomir Pipkov. He also made the experimental monodrama *In Quest of a Remembrance* (1963). For *The Unknown Soldier's*

Rangel Vulchanov.

Patent Leather Shoes Vulchanov received the Golden Peacock at the 1981 New Delhi Film Festival; the prize was well deserved and signaled world recognition for a national cinematography. His latest feature film, *Last Wishes* (1983), a political satire on European royalty during the First World War, has received critical acclaim at international festivals.

Binka Zhelyazkova (born 1923 in Svilengrad)

The second prominent member of the Bulgarian "new wave," Zhelyazkova also studied film direction at the Academy of Dramatic Art in Sofia, graduating in 1953 (a year after Rangel Vulchanov). For several years she worked as an assistant director (Anton Marinovich's *Adam's Rib*, 1956), then made the controversial *Partisans (Life Flows Quietly By)* (1958, unreleased) from a screenplay written by her husband and collaborator, Hristo Ganev, who codirected the film. They collaborated successfully on the interna-

Bulgaria after the passing of the Personality Cult, Sharaliev's *Two Victories* (1956). Besides the collaborative efforts with his wife, Binka Zhelyazkova, Ganev made important documentary films: *Feast of Hope* (1962), on the Algerian War; *Doctor* (1970); *Open at the Letter P* (1975), on the revolution in Portugal; and *The Artist* (1977). He wrote the script for Ivan Vesselinov's cartoon, *Devil in the Church* (1969).

Vulo Radev (born 1923 in Lesidren)

After graduating from the Moscow Film School (VGIK) in 1953 as a cameraman, he worked for Nikola Korabov and Yanko Yankov on various projects, the most significant being Korabov's historical epic based on a popular novel by Dimiter Dimov, *Tobacco* (1962). His breakthrough as a director occurred with his debut film, *The Peach Thief* (1964); he also wrote the screenplay but, surprisingly, did not photograph the film. The international success of *The Peach Thief*, together with films by Rangel Vulchanov and Binka Zhelyazkova, heralded New Bulgarian Cinema and a school of poetic realism. Like

Binka Zhelyazkova.

Vulo Radev.

tional hit *We Were Young* (1961), which embodied her own experiences as a participant in the Resistance. With her next film, *The Attached Balloon* (1967), she was again the center of controversy: the film, based on a story and original screenplay by Yordan Radichkov, was shelved shortly after release. Her reputation as a director of integrity, nevertheless, kept her in the forefront of Bulgarian cinema up to the present, a spotlight shared by her scriptwriter husband, Hristo Ganev. Later films: *The Last Word* (1973), *The Swimming Pool* (1977) (with Ganev), and *The Big Night Bathe* (1980) (with Ganev).

Screenplay writer and documentary filmmaker Hristo Ganev (b. 1924) graduated from VGIK in the same class with Angel Wagenstein in 1950. His diploma script, *Song of Man* (1954), was filmed by another classmate, Borislav Sharaliev; it portrayed the life and death of Nikola Vaptsarov, the revolutionary poet killed by the fascists in 1942. He contributed to one of the first comedies attempted in

The Peach Thief, Radev's next film, *Tsar and General* (1966), a wide-screen production, used a literary source, and its success placed the director in the front ranks of the young national cinematography. His later films, although less impressive, are still striking in visual concept: *The Longest Night* (1967), *Black Angels* (1970), and *Doomed Souls* (1975) (another adaptation of a Dimiter Dimov novel). He has also made documentary films.

Children's Film Directors

It was only natural that children's films should appear on Bulgarian screens shortly after the disappearance of the Personality Cult and schematic formulas. The first attempts at the genre were fumbling and hardly related to the world of children: Peter Vassilev's *The Traces Remain,* a detective story; and Boyan Danovski's *Item One,* scripted by Valeri Petrov and dealing with the experiences of a five-year-old. Petrov returned to the children's film a decade later to correct his mistakes: Borislav Sharaliev's *Knight Without Armor* (1966) is one of the few Bulgarian films that does not show signs of aging.

The first successful director in the genre was Dimiter Petrov (b. 1924), a graduate of the Prague Film School (FAMU). His *The Captain* (1963) was a prizewinner at the Venice Film Festival, and thereafter Petrov devoted his career principally to the children's film: *Porcupines Are Born without Bristles* (1971) and *With Children at the Seaside* (1972), the latter scripted by the Mormarev Brothers, who also specialized in the genre.

Ivanka Grubcheva (b. 1946) was eventually to surpass Petrov's success. She studied at the Potsdam-Babelsberg Film School in the German Democratic Republic, her diploma film being the short feature, *The Brat* (1968), based on a Georgi Mishev story. After trying her hand at the antifascist theme, she returned to the world of children to make three festival prizewinners in a row: the TV film *Children Play Out of Doors* (1972) and *With Nobody* (1975), both based on screenplays by Georgi Danailov, and *Exams at Any Odd Time* (1974), from a script by the Mormarev brothers. Her latest children's film, *The Porcupines' War* (1979), was scripted again by the Mormarev brothers and bears reference to their screenplay for Dimiter Petrov, *Porcupines Are Born without Bristles* (1971).

Marianna Evstatieva (b. 1939) studied at the Polish Film School in Lodz. She makes children's film's with social implications: *The Little Tiger*

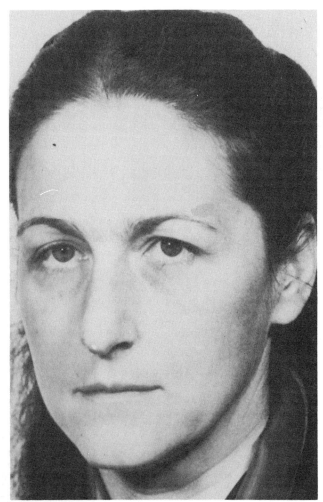
Ivanka Grubcheva.

(1973) and *Moments in a Matchbox* (1979). Another director of promise in the genre is Rashko Ouzunov: *The Dash* (1972) and *Talisman* (1978), the latter a critical view of classroom education in Bulgaria.

Documentary to Feature Film

Zahari Zhandov was not the only documentary filmmaker who graduated to the feature film. Another was Yuri Arnaudov (b. 1917), cameraman and documentary director, who finished Dako Dakovski's *Kaloyan* (1963) upon that director's sudden death during the production. Arnaudov worked as a cameraman on several feature films and directed a historical film on his own: *Tsar Ivan Shishman* (1969). His documentaries on historical themes are particularly notable.

Vassil Mirchev (b. 1927) studied documentary at the Polish Film School at Lodz under Jerzy Bossak and Andrzej Munk. His first feature film, *Men* (1966), after several documentaries, had a distinctive documentary bent. Another Lodz graduate, Vladislav Ikonomov (b. 1938), made a number of documentaries before turning to the feature film (*The Subpoenaed Didn't Come*, 1966).

A husband-wife pair, Yanush Vazov (b. 1927) and Lada Boyadjieva (b. 1927), graduated from the documentary to the feature film. Vazov, the son of the film pioneer Alexander Vazov, studied at FAMU in Prague and made a series of shorts for the documentary and popular-science studios in Sofia on art, history, folklore, and biology. Boyadjieva also studied at FAMU, after completing a course in film journalism at IDHEC in Paris; she also specialized in the "cultural" short, films on icons, Egypt, and famous Bulgarian personalities. They made their first feature film together, the TV production *Return* (1967), then each branched off on his own with feature-film productions in 1972: Vazov's *Ten Days without Pay* and Boyadjieva's TV film *Only Manly Days*.

Another woman documentary filmmaker, Vesselina Gerinska (b. 1938), graduated from VGIK in Moscow in the short film department. She made documentaries and popular-science films before attempting a feature film: *Guilt* (1976).

A cameraman, Todor Stoyanov (b. 1930),

worked for several feature-film directors upon graduating from the Sofia Academy of Dramatic Art in the film department, among them Gencho Genchev (b. 1927) on *Margaritka, Mama and I* (1961). Genchev, who studied documentary at VGIK in Moscow, broadened his experience by working first in Italy, and then turned to the feature film. Stoyanov collaborated on his first feature films with theater director Grisha Ostrovski: *Sidetrack* (1967), *Men on a Business Trip* (1969), and *The Five from the Moby Dick* (1970). His first independent feature was *Strange Duel* (1971).

Cartoon and Acting to Feature Film

Another route that led to directing feature films was the cartoon. Todor Dinov (b. 1919), the father of Bulgarian animation, studied at VGIK in the animation department. His best cartoons weave a simple moral into clear line drawings and they are full of witty gags: *The Lightning Rod* (1962), *Jealousy* (1963), *The Apple* (1963), and *The Daisy* (1965). His first feature film, *Iconostasis* (1969), was made in collaboration with Hristo Hristov, a noted theater director. Dinov directed independently *The Dragon* (1974), based on a Nikolai Haitov story, and *Gunpowder* (1977),

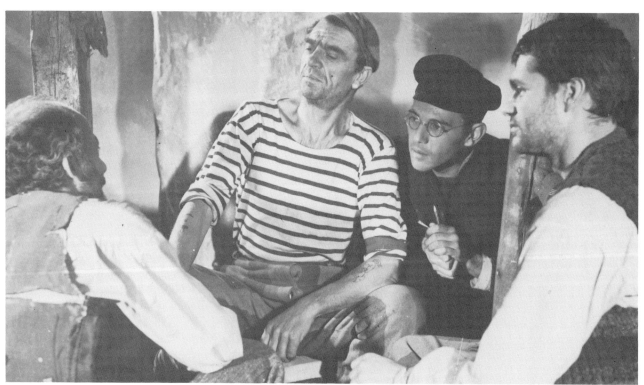

Ivan Andonov as the bespeckled student (third from left) in Rangel Vulchanov's *On a Small Island* (1958).

based on a Yordan Radichkov tale.

Ivan Andonov (b. 1934) was first a popular stage and screen actor (he appeared in Vulchanov's *On a Small Island,* 1958), but a natural talent for drawing led him to the cartoon film and exhibitions of his paintings. Beginning in 1963, he made fifteen cartoons and won prizes at the Locarno festival for *The Shooting Range* (1965) and *Trouble* (1967). His first attempt at a feature film, *A Difficult Love* (1974), in which he also played a lead role, was unimpressive. Then he collaborated with scriptwriter Georgi Mishev on a satire on the art world, *Fairy Dance* (1976), and followed this with a Mishev script, *Ladies' Choice* (1980), and two more equally successful films: *The Roof* (1978) and *The Cherry Orchard* (1979), the latter in collaboration with the writer Nikolai Haitov.

Actor Naum Shopov (b. 1930) ventured into the director's chair on one occasion—the adaptation of a Yordan Radichkov story into a short feature film, *Bread* (1972).

Sofia Dramatic Directors

Not all of Bulgaria's directorial talent studied abroad. Both Rangel Vulchanov and Binka Zhelzazkova, who set standards in New Bulgarian Cinema, studied at home at the Academy of Dramatic Art in Sofia. The Academy had a small film department in a wing of the school until 1973, when the Sofia Film & Television Academy was founded, and offered courses in theater and cinema as related and complementary disciplines. It is for this reason that Bulgarian cinema until today has a strong theatrical character and stylistic trait. Indeed, the stage directors in Sofia had a hand in directing feature films from the very beginning.

Stefan Surchadjiev (b. 1912) was engaged at the National Theater in Sofia when he was called upon to codirect, with Anton Marinovich, *Dawn over the Homeland* (1951) and *Our Land* (1953). He became manager of the newly founded Satirical Theater in 1957, whose directors have turned to cinema on several occasions. Another Marinovich collaborator was Krastyo Mirski (b. 1920), who helped to make the film version of the popular play by Georgi Karaslavov based on his own stage production at the National Theater, *The Daughter-in-Law* (1954).

Boyan Danovski (b. 1899), a National Theater director who became the second manager of the Satirical Theater in Sofia, directed *Item One* (1956), one of the first attempts at a children's

film, based on a script by Valeri Petrov. Danovski also trained future film directors at the Academy of Dramatic Art.

Grisha Ostrovski (b. 1918) studied theater at the Sofia Academy and became a leading stage director at the Satirical Theater before codirecting, with Todor Stoyanov, the international hit *Sidetrack* (1967). They made two more films together, *Men on a Business Trip* (1969) and *The Five from the Moby Dick* (1970), and then Ostrovski made *Incident at Gerlovo* (1970) on his own.

Assen Shopov (b. 1933), a stage director from the Army Theater in Sofia, scored a success with his debut film, *Eternal Times* (1975), but has stayed mostly in the theater since.

Sofia Graduates

Both theater and cinema directors shared teaching posts at the Sofia Academy of Dramatic Art until 1973, when the Film School was founded as an independent institution of higher

Lyubomir Sharlandjiev.

learning. Film directors Lyubomir Sharlandjiev, Zako Heskia, and Peter Donev learned their trade in these mixed surroundings. Boyan Danovski and Yanko Yankov were prominent instructors.

Lyubomir Sharlandjiev (1931–78) graduated from the Sofia Academy in 1956, worked for a number of years at theaters in the provinces, and then made his first feature film, *A Chronicle of Sentiments* (1962), after assisting on productions at the Boyana Studios. Like Yankov, he developed acting talent, and was married to one of the country's foremost actresses, Nevena Kokanova. He made the controversial *The Prosecutor* (1968, unreleased), set in the period of the Personality Cult.

Zako Heskia (b. 1922) graduated in 1952 and worked for a long period as assistant director on feature films. His adventure stories—*The Eighth* (1969), *Dawn over the Drava* (1973) (the first large-scale national epic), and *The Last Battle* (1977)—are arguably the best "Easterns" made in Bulgaria.

Peter Donev (b. 1926), formerly a teacher, studied screenplay writing and then direction at the Sofia Academy. He wrote his first script for Hristo Piskov, *Poor Man's Street* (1960), and is a rarity in Bulgaria as a writer-director: the TV film *Autumn* (1964), *Almanach* (1966), *Set Out Again* (1969), films set in the provinces.

Stefan Dimitrov (b. 1935) made his first feature film, *The Highway* (1975), at the age of forty, coming to the cinema by way of stage productions after graduating from the Sofia Academy under Boyan Danovski. He is principally a TV director.

Hristo Hristov (born 1926 in Plovdiv)

Upon receiving a degree in medicine in his native Plovdiv in 1953, Hristov entered the Sofia Academy to study stage direction, graduating in 1958. He made a name for himself at the theater in Plovdiv before leaving, in 1966, to study film direction at the Moscow Film School (VGIK). Today, after serving for a decade as president of the Union of Bulgarian Filmakers, he teaches film production at the new film school in Sofia. His first feature film, *Iconostasis* (1969), was a collaborative effort with Todor Dinov, the father of the Bulgarian cartoon.

Iconostasis, like Vulchanov's *On a Small Island* (1958) a decade before, can be viewed today as a breakthrough in Bulgarian film history. Some critics have compared it with the best to emerge from East European cinema in the postwar

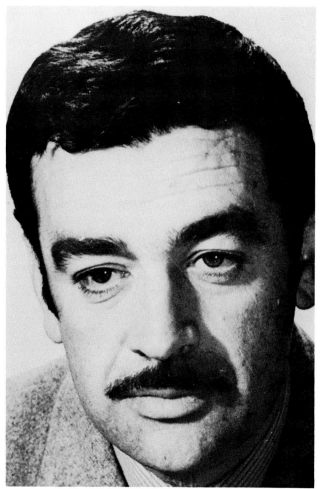

Hristo Hristov.

years. It is also significant that *Iconostasis* was made by another director of the older generation—Hristov, in fact, was born two years before Rangel Vulchanov.

Hristov's next film, independently directed, was *The Last Summer* (1972, released 1974), based on a story by Yordan Radichkov; the director also did the set design, and it is arguably his best film. *The Last Summer* appeared on Bulgarian screens after Hristov had finished *Hammer or Anvil* (1972), an epic film featuring the nation's hero, Georgi Dimitrov, and the Leipzig Trial, a co-production with the German Democratic Republic.

Hristov has nearly always turned to classic and modern literary sources for his film material adapting works by Dimiter Talev, Gencho Stoyev, Yordan Radichkov, Nikolai Haitov, and Pavel Vezhinov. His theatrical training is too often visible in his film direction. Other films include *A Tree without Roots* (1974), *Cyclops* (1976), *Barrier* (1979), *The Truck* (1980), *A Woman at Thirty-three* (1982), and *Question Time* (1985).

Metodi Andonov (born 1932 in Kalishte, died 1974 in Sofia)

After graduating from the Sofia Academy of Dramatic Art, Andonov produced plays at the Satirical Theater for a decade before deciding to direct a feature film, *The White Room* (1968), based on a novel by Bogomil Rainov. This confrontation with Dogmatism in the Stalinist period made him immediately recognized at home and abroad; the film appeared in the same year as Lyubomir Sharlandjiev's *The Prosecutor* (1968, unreleased).

Metodi Andonov next directed a detective story, *There's Nothing Finer Than Bad Weather* (1971), again from a script by Rainov, and then scored the biggest hit in Bulgarian film history at the box office, *The Goat Horn* (1972). The film was seen by three million people at home, and it established scriptwriter Nikolai Haitov as the country's leading movie storyteller. Andonov's last film, *The Great Boredom* (1973), was another detective thriller scripted by Rainov, the special-

ist in the genre. The team of Andonov-Rainov seemed destined for even greater things in the 1970s.

The premature death of this talented director at the age of forty-two in 1974 was a major loss to Bulgarian cinema. He had not only discovered the formula for artistic and commercial success, but was also equally at home in film and theater direction.

Lyudmil Kirkov (born 1933 in Vratsa)

After graduating from the Sofia Academy of Dramatic Art in 1954, Kirkov directed stage productions in the provinces and then enrolled for courses in film direction at VGIK in Moscow, graduating under Mikhail Romm in 1959. His first feature film (*The Last Round*, 1961), was not successful, but his next were strong collaborative efforts with writers Emil Manov (*The End of the Vacation*, 1965), and Nikolai Nikiforov (*Swedish Kings*, 1968). His breakthrough came when he collaborated with screenplay writer Georgi Mis-

Metodi Andonov.

Lyudmil Kirkov.

hev on a series of films: *A Boy Becomes a Man* (1972) and *Don't Go Away* (1976), a portrait of village life in two parts; *Peasant on a Bicycle* (1974) and *Matriarchate* (1977), nostalgic and tragic views of the migration from village to town in an increasingly industrialized country. Kirkov's moral stance can be felt again in *Short Sun* (1979), based on a script by the young, talented dramatist and screenplay writer, Stanislav Stratiev, with whom he also collaborated on *A Nameless Band* (1982) and *Balance* (1983).

The veteran director was formerly the artistic manager of the Suvremenik ("Contemporary") production unit; it was the last organized, in 1978, of the creatively independent groups at the Boyana Studios.

Ivan Terziev (born 1934 in Lovech)

Upon graduating as an actor from the Sofia Academy in 1958, Terziev took an interest in amateur filmmaking and won prizes at interna-

tional festivals. This led to an invitation to study film direction at VGIK in Moscow; his diploma work there, *Fyodor Gai* (1966), was based on a story by the Soviet writer Vassili Shukshin.

After making an unsuccessful debut with a detective story, *Mister Nobody* (1969), Terziev hit his stride with *Men without Work* (1973), a tale of unproductive workingmen that raised ethical questions when events take an unexpected turn. This was followed by *Strong Water* (1975), again about the complex question of idling workingmen on the job. The film won him international attention at its appearance in Locarno. On the strength of these two films alone, Terziev belongs to the vanguard of Bulgarian cinema.

Lyudmil Staikov (born 1937 in Sofia)

Upon graduating from the theater department of the Sofia Academy in 1962, Staikov directed plays in Bourgas, attracting national at-

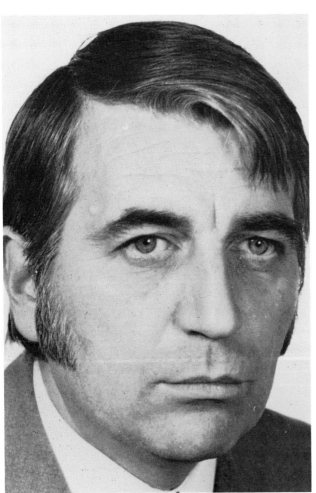

Ivan Terziev.

Lyudmil Staikov.

tention. His modern style immediately won him dramatic prizes, one for direction at the Third National Review of Bulgarian Drama and Theater. He also acted in several roles. Then he won more critical attention by adapting and staging Salinger's *Catcher in the Rye* at the Youth Theater in Sofia. Turning to television, he wrote screenplays and staged plays for a TV theatre, winning prizes again for TV direction in 1965 and 1969, as he broadened his scope by directing musical spectacles and experiments on television. Staikov's debut in the feature film *Affection* (1972) was awarded a prize at the Moscow festival. Other prominent films were *Amendment to the Defense-of-State Act* (1976) and *Illusion* (1980), in addition to his broadcasts and documentaries on music for television (*The Sofia Chamber Orchestra, The Human Voice*). He is also the artistic manager of the Mladost ("Youth") production unit at the Boyana Studios and has crowned his achievements by directing a historical epic to celebrate Bulgaria's 1,300th anniversary as a nation in 1981: *Khan Asparukh* (1981), in three parts.

Eduard Zahariev.

Eduard Zahariev (born 1938 in Moscow)

Upon graduating from the Budapest Film School in 1961, Zahariev made a series of important documentaries (*Rails in the Sky, Salt, Steel, Bulgarian State Railways*) before directing his first feature film from a script by Georgi Mishev: the controversial *If the Train Doesn't Arrive* (1967). The Mishev-Zahariev collaboration on this and two other satires, *The Hare Census* (1973) and *Villa Zone* (1975), are high-water marks in Bulgarian cinema. *The Hare Census* was awarded a prize in Locarno and *Villa Zone* at Karlovy Vary; both have been particularly helpful in making Bulgarian cinema known abroad. Zahariev's latest films star his wife, Marianna Dimitrova, in films of a tragicomic nature: *Manly Times* (1977), from a screenplay by Nikolati Haitov; and *Almost a Love Story* (1980), Georgi Mishev assisting the director on the screenplay. Another side of this talented filmmaker can be seen in *The Sky over the Veleka* (1968), a parable in a documentary vein, and *Elegy* (1982), a tragic tale scripted by Alexander Tomov from his novel.

Georgi Stoyanov (born 1939 at Moscow)

One of the few Bulgarian directors who studied abroad in the West, Stoyanov completed his studies at IDHEC in Paris in 1964, after graduating at home in mechanical engineering

Georgi Stoyanov.

71

in 1959. His first films were documentaries and short features (*Siesta,* 1965), and he worked as assistant director for Vulchanov and Yankov before making his first feature-length film, *The Painlevé Case* (1968), the title derived from one film-novella in a three-part production (the other two were *Music* and *Guests*). Stoyanov's style in the film-grotesque set him aside from directors of the older and younger generations; further, he was to change his style with each film he made. *Birds and Greyhounds* (1969) is a lyric metaphor on the resistance movement; the script was written by a former resistance fighter, Vassil Akyov, who also collaborated with Stoyanov on *Panteley* (1978), the story of an unwilling freedom fighter in the war years. *The Third Planet in the Solar System* (1972) was Bulgaria's first attempt at a science-fiction film, a failure that commands respect in view of the limited studio facilities for such a genre. Stoyanov collaborated with screenplay writer Nikola Russev on three features: *Houses without Fences* (1974), *A Cricket in the Ear* (1976), and *Constantine the Philosopher* (1983), the last a superspectacle for the 1,300th anniversary, on Saint Cyril. Stoyanov is the artistic manager of the Sredets (the Slav name for today's Sofia) production unit at the Boyana Studios, and in 1982 he was elected president of the Union of Bulgarian Filmmakers.

Georgi Djulgerov (born 1943 in Bourgas)

Upon winning a prize at the Oberhausen Short Film Festival for his VGIK diploma film, *The Cooper* (1969), Djulgerov returned home and shot the same story by Nikolai Haitov in the author's native Rhodope Mountains (the Moscow Film School version had been shot in Armenia). The remake, *The Test* (1971), appeared as a film-novella together with Milen Nikolov's Haitov adaptation, *Naked Conscience,* in the two-part feature film *Colorful World* (1971). The young director then made a feature film on the "lost generation" during the resistance movement, *And the Day Came* (1973), based on a screenplay and the personal experiences of Vassil Akyov. After working for a time in television (*The Wardrobe*), he won the prize for direction at the Berlin festival for *Advantage* (1977), the story of a petty con man living on the edge of society during the Stalinist years. His next film, *Swap* (1978), continued his aesthetic and sociopolitical research into the same period, that of the Personality Cult. Djulgerov crowned these achievements with the spectacular three-part *Measure for Mea-*

Georgi Djulgerov.

sure (1981), set in Greek Macedonia at the time of the Ilinden Uprising of 1903. As a teacher at the Sofia Film Academy, he, with his cameraman Radoslav Spassov, has molded a new generation of filmmakers. Djulgerov is the artistic manager of the Suvremenik ("Contemporary") Film Unit.

More Graduates Abroad

Ivan Nichev (b. 1940) graduated from the Polish Film School in 1967. His prolific output of documentaries and TV-produced short features led to three feature films concerned with the world of art: *Memory* (1974), *Stars in Her Hair, Tears in Her Eyes* (1977), and *Boomerang* (1979). He tends to work with recognized writing talent (Svoboda Buchvarova, Angel Wagenstein) and is one of the promising talents in Bulgarian film and theater direction today. His collaborator, the poet-scriptwriter Svoboda Buchvarova, is the artistic manager of the Haemus production unit (named for a mountain range).

Milen Nikolov (b. 1938) graduated from FAMU in Prague and made his film debut with the short feature *The White Horse* (1968), which was later paired with another Aleksi Naidenov story adaptation, Lyudmil Kirkov's *Armando,* to make the two-part feature film *Armando and The White Horse* (1969). This impressive beginning led to another film-novella, his adaptation of Nikolai Haitov's story, *Naked Conscience* (1970), which was paired later with Georgi Djulgerov's adaptation of Haitov's *The Test* to make the feature-length film *Colorful World* (1971). Meanwhile, he had already adapted another Haitov story, *The End of the Song* (1971). Later attempts at comedy (*Indian Summer,* 1973) and satire (*The Fortress Guard,* 1974) were not as impressive as his earlier films.

Margarit Nikolov (b. 1945) graduated from VGIK in Moscow in 1970. His diploma film, *Verses* (1970), was later released as a film-novella in the two-part feature film *At Daybreak* (1972), thus pairing his adaptation of a Pavel Vezhinov story with another story of the same writer adapted by Ivan Nichev, *The Human Heart* (1972). His first full-length feature film was *Daylight* (1974), and he is best known for a four-part TV production, *On the Tracks of the Missing* (1976), dealing with the fateful year 1925, when a military regime replaced elected public officials and a reign of terror began that was later to encompass all of Europe.

More Native Directors

Todor Andreikov (b. 1933), a critic by profession, ventured into the director's chair on one occasion—to make the successful *Sunday Matches* (1975), based on an original screenplay. He was also for a time the director of the Bulgarian Film Archive in Sofia.

Nikola Russev/Nikola Lyubomirov (1943) are one and the same person: in order not to be confused with the screenplay writer and dramatist with the same name, Nikola Russev (the director) changed his professional identity to Nikola Lyubomirov. Thus, as the records now show, Nikola Russev wrote the scripts for Georgi Stoyanov's *Houses without Fences* (1974), *A Cricket in the Ear* (1976), and *Constantine the Philosopher* (1982)—while Nikola Lyubomirov (Russev) directed *Where Did We Meet?*(1976), scripted by Valeri Petrov, and *A Unique Morning* (1978), scripted by Kamen Kalchev.

New Generation Directors

Kiran Kolarov (b. 1946) was the first graduate of the Sofia Film Academy (VITIS), founded in 1973, to make a name for himself abroad. He wrote and directed *Status—Orderly* (1978) and *The Airman* (1980), and contributed the screenplay for Assen Shopov's *Is the Bagpipe an Instrument?* (1978). He is considered by critics to be the most talented among the "new generation" directors in Bulgaria.

So far as the other debut directors are concerned, their work appeared just as this book was going into print (toward the end of 1984). Svetla Ivanova, a critic for *Bulgarian Films* (1981/5), listed the "new generation" of VITIS graduates as follows:

Evgeni Mihailov and Elly Mihailova, a husband-wife and director-camerawoman team, attracted international attention when their *Home for Lonely Souls* (1981) appeared at the Moscow and San Francisco film festivals. The screenplay for this mature film on the psychological problems facing an actress in the provinces was scripted by the veteran Boyan Papazov *(Strong Water, All Is Love)* and stars the remarkably gifted Plamena Getova.

Ivan Pavlov and Plamen Hinkov, another director-cameraman team, made their joint debut from VITIS with *Mass Miracle* (1981), starring a young actor, Dimiter Ganev, as the son of a plant director trying to pass the entrance exams into the Sofia Film Institute with an amateur film of his own making.

Iskra Yossifova and Malina Petrova codirected the children's film *The Journey* (1980), set in 1944 in war-torn Sofia, as a social revolution took place.

Ognyan Gelinov shows signs of becoming a capable director of social comedies: his *The Flying Machine* (1981), set at the turn of the century, is absurd and witty.

Anri (Henri) Kuler made the impressive *Death of the Hare* (1982), a poetic view of childhood in an experimental vein. The director's previous experience was at the Sofia Animation Studio, where he wedded a graphic style to intellectual irony and sophistication.

Documentary Filmmakers

In addition to the aforementioned Zahari Zhandov, Eduard Zahariev, and other directors named in the "Documentary to Feature Film" section, here are a few more documentary filmmakers who have seldom, if ever, ventured away from their chosen calling:

Hristo Kovachev (b. 1929) was a camera assistant before making his first documentary: *Our Own Steel* (1954), a film he later recalled with irony and humor in *Builders* (1974); the former film had followed the usual schematic formula for Socialist Realism during the period of the Personality Cult. He won the Second Prize at the Moscow festival for *Men and Lights* (1961), the Lion of St. Mark at Venice for *From One to Eight* (1966), two Golden Doves at Leipzig for *Builders* (1974) and *Agronomists* (1977), and the Grand Prix at Lille for *Shepherds* (1979). His documentaries tend to be warm, human, and filled with touches of humor.

Nevena Tosheva (b. 1928) began as a film editor and later found her way to the documentary film. Her portraits of people and the social problems they face, presented in a natural manner without fanfare, have won her critical praise and international film prizes. Her best-known

films are *Summer of Hopes* (1974) and *The Teacher* (1975).

Yuli Stoyanov (b. 1930) graduated from FAMU in Prague. He is noted for the poetic, concise quality of his documentaries, and has a string of prizes for his historical treatments, such as *Days* (1964), and contemporary themes, such as *Friendly Meeting* (1965). He made the feature-length documentary, *The Appeal* (1972), to celebrate the ninetieth anniversary of Georgi Dimitrov's birthday.

In general, the reputation of the two documentary film studios for cinema theaters and television is very high among European countries. The same is true of the Studio for Popular Science Films.

Cartoons and Puppets

Todor Dinov (b. 1919) and Ivan Andonov (b. 1934) have been treated under "Cartoon and Acting to Feature Film." It is to Dinov's credit

Hristo Kovachev.

Todor Dinov.

Donyo Donev.

that Bulgarian cinema first became known abroad at international festivals; his style of synthesizing time and space in an intellectual, philosophizing cartoon placed him closer to UPA graphics and Zagreb Studio's "reduced animation" techniques. His best-known cartoons were made at the beginning of the 1960s: *The Lightning Rod* (1962), *Jealousy* (1963), *The Apple* (1963), and *The Daisy* (1965).

Ivan Andonov, whose cartoons were awarded prizes at Locarno, specialized in satires of an equally philosophical nature: *Esperanza* (1967), *Trouble* (1967), *Melodrama* (1971).

Donyo Donev (b. 1929) studied graphic art in Sofia and worked as a caricaturist on a newspaper for a time, then studied for a year (1960) at the animation studio in Moscow after experimenting in the cartoon to his dissatisfaction. His humorous, gag-filled cartoons blend folklore with ironic twists and surprise endings. Best known for his series beginning with *The Three Fools* (1970), he developed a cartoon of gentle, sagacious ridicule aimed at the foibles of the human species: *De Facto* (1973), *The Musical Tree* (1976), and *Causa Perduta* (1977). He has also directed puppet films.

Ivan Vesselinov (b. 1932) excels in an intellectual cartoon of sarcasm and barbed wit (*The Devil in the Church,* 1969). Zdenka Doicheva (b. 1926) and Radka Buchvarova (b. 1918) raised the children's cartoon to a high level of art and entertainment. Stoyan Dukov (b. 1931) collaborated with Todor Dinov on his early international success, *The Apple* (1965), and, working independently, then developed a satirical collection of parables that place him as a caricaturist on a level with Dinov and Donev: *Fortress Houses* (1967), *Mini* (1971), and *February* (1977). Hristo Topusanov (b. 1930) has made every variety of cartoon, from children's fairytales to parodies and satires, and has collaborated on Ivan Vesselinov's projects; his skills as a producer, scriptwriter, and director have received awards at several international festivals of animation.

The latest generation of animators, more graphically oriented and given to a sense of intellectual irony, number Anri (Henri) Kuler, Slav Bakalov, Nikolai Todorov, Rumen Petkov, Velislar Kazakov, and Assen Münning.

3
CINEMA IN BULGARIA

Bay Ganyu Country

The river traffic on the Danube brought the cinematograph to Bulgaria.

The first demonstrations of the Lumière invention took place in the port town of Russe in February or March of 1897. By the time the novelty had arrived in Sofia, the cafés were already buzzing with the exploits of a fictional character of satirist Aleko Konstantinov—*Bay Ganyu* (published in 1895) featured a lovable, impertinent Bulgarian in typical peasant garb commenting on affairs of state in European capitals. A quarter-century later, "Bay Ganyu Country" was thematic material for a successful motion picture.

In the meanwhile, newsreel cameras recorded the Ilinden Uprising of 1903 in the section of Macedonia still occupied by the Turks. The streets of Sofia and the national shrine at the Rila monastery were photographed, but since the new nation was still eighty percent agrarian, film production companies were still a possibility for the future. The first native photographers simply ordered cameras from abroad and began shooting; among these were Vladimir Petkov and Hristodor Arnaudov. A neighbor, Milton Monaki of Macedonia, went into business in 1905 by simply writing to his brother, Yanaki, in London; his mail-order address for historical doings in and around Bitola, a crossroads city in Turk-occupied territory on the Via Egnatia, required only "Monaki, Macedonia" to reach him.

The Balkan uprisings and wars before that fatal shot at Sarajevo resulted in a continuous flow of national production of newsreels, enough to guarantee the construction of the Modern Theater in 1908 and the inauguration of a "Kino Journal" in 1913. Sofia's movie house also featured the latest Max Linder comedy, which made its way from the Pathé Studios in Paris by way of Berlin and Vienna, and then down the Danube to the Balkan countries.

The proprietor of the Modern Theater, Vassil Gendov, had to do something to save his business once the Great War broke out in 1914, thus drying up his supply from the West. The only answer was to go into film production himself. He produced and directed *The Bulgarian Is Gallant* (1915), starring none other than Vassil Gendov in a role borrowed from a Linder comedy. It was a smash hit—so far as a limited, but faithful, home audience was concerned. With only a thin line between Gendov-Film and bankruptcy, this intrepid pioneer was to produce, direct, star in, distribute, and exhibit eleven feature films between 1915 and 1937, the majority of which also costarred his wife, Zhanna Gendova, as the female lead.

The titles alone of the Gendov-Film produc-

Vassil Gendov acting in *The Bulgarian Is Gallant* (1915), which he also produced and directed.

apparently all of the Gendov films were lost in 1944 during an air raid over Sofia.

Gendov-Film had competitors—in fact, a total of fifty-five feature films were produced in the thirty-five years before the first fiction film, *Kalin the Eagle,* was made under a nationalized industry in 1950. The private companies—Rila-Film, Slav-Film, Balkan-Film, Kubrat-Film, and Rex-Film—survived on guts and determination and an ability to make do under the most primitive conditions imaginable. Though it would appear to be wishful thinking to hope for a minor masterpiece among those that have been preserved in the Bulgarska Nacionalna Filmoteka in Sofia, in fact there is one: *After the Fire over Russia* (1929).

Boris Grezhov's *After the Fire over Russia* was "discovered" by the film world in 1979 at a FIAF (International Federation of Film Archives) symposium in Lausanne. With good reason: Grezhov (1899–1967) had died in Switzerland, and his career as a filmmaker was appreciated by key film historians attending the Lausanne symposium. The Bulgarian-born director had worked as an assistant for Robert Wiene and other German directors in Berlin between 1917 and 1921. Upon serving this apprenticeship, he returned to Sofia to make seven feature films in Bulgaria, from 1923 to 1947.

Maiden Rock (1923) was the first, a folktale in the literary tradition, followed by *Bulgaria Allegra* (1928). Then came *After the Fire over Russia* (1929), a story of White Russians who immigrate to Bulgaria to work in the mines. The film is remarkable for its restrained acting and psychological realism, as well as its rather controversial subject matter in the wake of the 1917 Revolution. Equally controversial for home audiences was his next film, *Graves without Crosses* (1931), lamenting the victims of the White Terror in 1923. His subsequent films also bear intriguing titles: *For Our Country* (1940), *Tittle-Tattle* (1941), and *Atonement* (1947). The career of Boris Grezhov has yet to be fully estimated.

A Bulgarian critic associated with the Sofia archive, Alexander Alexandrov, credits Nikolai Larin's *Under the Old Sky* (1922) with being the country's first "art film"; it features actors from the National Theater in a filmed version of Tsanko Tserkovski's drama. Alexander Vazov's *Cairn* (1936) was a box-office hit; the director had adapted a popular poem of his uncle, Ivan Vazov. And Yossip Novak's *Strahil the Voyvoda* (1938), scripted by Orlin Vassilev, was the last high-water mark in the interregnum period; it deals with the exploits of a legendary outlaw

tions tell the story: *Love Is Madness* (1917), *The Devil in Sofia* (1921), *Maneuvers in Peacetime* (1922), *Bay Ganyu* (1922), *The Man Who Denied God* (1927), *The Street of the Lost* (1928), *Idols of the Street* (1929), *Tempest of Youth* (1930), *The Revolt of the Slaves* (1933), and *The Scorched Earth* (1937). The most popular of these was *Bay Ganyu,* starring the popular stage actor, Stoyan M. Popov. Nothing else can be determined with accuracy, as

Boris Genzhov's *After the Fire over Russia* (1929).

ture at best. The first sound film was, appropriately, Peter Stoychev's *Song of the Mountains* (1934); with *Land* (1930) the writer-director had earlier adapted Elin Pelin's historical tragedy published under the same title in 1922. Boris Grezhov's *Maiden Rock*, Vassil Gendov's *Bay Ganyu*, Vassil Poshev's *The Faithful Guard* (1929) (based on a Yordan Yovkov novel, adapted in collaboration with the author), and Alexander Vazov's *Nastradin Hoggia and Sly Peter* (1939), among others, were pure literary adaptations.

Boris Genzhov's *Maiden Rock* (1923).

hero in the struggle against the Turks. Vassilev adapted his own novel for the film production, and it's significant that his screenplay for Boris Borozanov's *Kalin the Eagle* (1950), twelve years later, introduced the new nationalized film industry while covering much of the same patriotic ground as before.

Owing to the rural nature of the country, these first features by private companies relied principally on legends and folktales, or national litera-

Boris Genzhov's *Graves without Crosses* **(1931)**

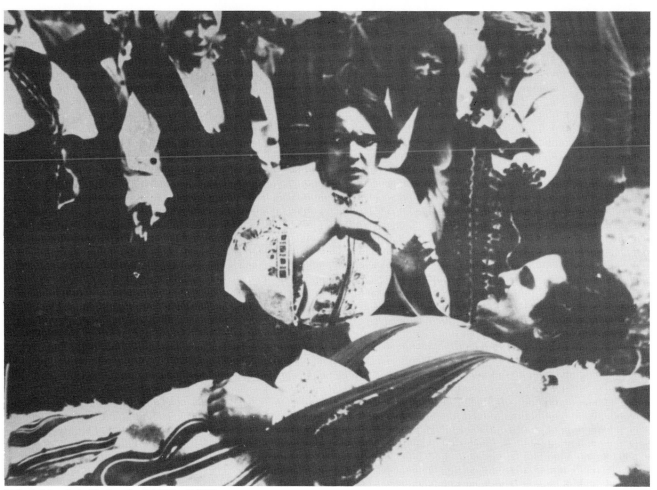

Nikolai Larin's *Under the Old Sky* **(1922).**

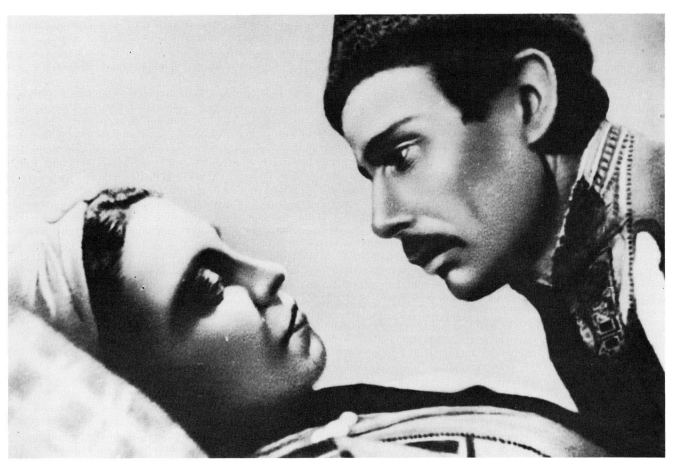

Yossip Novak's *Strahil the Voyvoda* **(1938).**

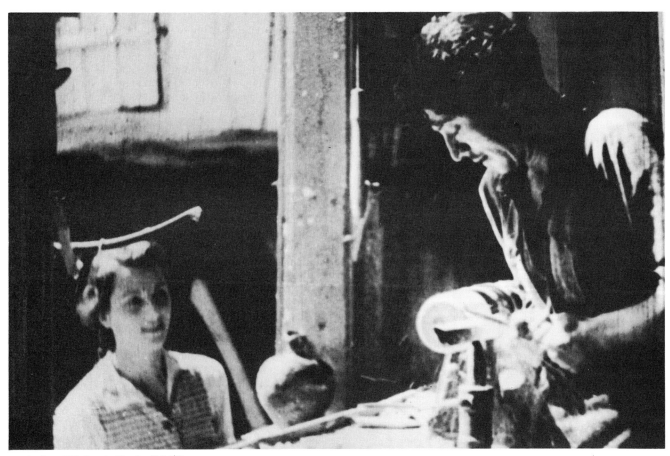

Dimiter Minkov's *Boyka* **(1947).**

The National Revival of the previous century was still fresh in the minds of most prewar moviegoers.

Military themes took stage center as Bulgaria entered the war on the side of Germany. But as in Italy, the same directors who contributed patriotic pictures of rather innocent entertainment content were there with more meaningful messages when the war was over. Boris Borozanov, who was given the assignment to make the first official film of the new government, *Kalin the Eagle* (1950), had previously made *Bulgarian Eagles* (1941), about Bulgarian aviators. Another wartime director, Anton Marinovich, made the first feature of the postwar years, *New Days Will Come* (1945), paralleling in content the subject matter of documentaries of the day following the Socialist revolution of 9 September 1944. Other optimistic feature films in the immediate postwar period were Ivan Fichev's *The Struggle for Happiness* (1946) and G. Bogoyavlenski's *Return to a New Life* (1947), whose titles are self-explanatory.

So far as the quality of the eight feature films produced in the postwar years before the nationalization of the film industry in 1948, only two are considered to be standouts, according to Alexander Alexandrov at the Bulgarian Film Archive. Both were directed by newcomer Dimiter Minkov: *Bulgarians of Ancient Times* (1945), based on Lyuben Karavelov's classic novel, and *Boyka* (1947), a film adaptation of Dimiter Gemidjiski's popular play.

Of much more value to film historians are the documentary treasures in the film archive at Sofia. Not only are there newsreels dating back to the Balkan Wars and World War I, but one can also find footage on the interregnum years of major political and historical significance. A particularly long documentary is the account of the bombing of the Church of Saint Nedelya in Sofia in 1925 and the subsequent trial and execution of the accused revolutionaries—a morbid page in Bulgarian history.

Under Way

When Bulgarian partisans descended from the mountains in late 1944, Zahari Zhandov was there to greet them with his camera. The Uprising of 9 September 1944 was the subject matter of the first Patriotic Newsreel, released on 25 September 1944, featuring footage of the first hours of the combined liberation and revolution. A reproduction of the footage found in Zhandov's and other cameramen's newsreel-documentaries of the day forms the thematic content of Borislav Sharaliev's *The Thrust* (1981), one of the spectacular feature films commissioned for the 1,300th anniversary of Bulgaria's birth.

Zhandov, son of a noted stage actress (Elena Kranova), became a cameraman at an early age. He was working for a private company, Finaco, when the war came—whereupon he began to cover the action on the fronts, as the fascists gave way to the partisans. His first documentary short for the new government, *A Day in Sofia* (1946), won a prize at Marianske Lazne. The Venice international festival awarded him a further prize for *Men amid the Clouds* (1947), a report on weather stations.

At that time considered Bulgaria's best known filmmaker, Zahari Zhandov joined the Dutch director Joris Ivens in the making of an omnibus documentary, *The First Years* (1949), coproduced by Poland, Czechoslovakia, and Bulgaria. Ivens, after making *Indonesia Calling* (1946), had settled in East Europe for a decade as documentary filmmaker and supervisor; it was Zhandov in Bulgaria (as well as Ivan Frič in Czechoslovakia and Wladislaw Forbert in Poland), however, who did most of the actual shooting for *The First Years*. The story of the making of the Bulgarian segment, about peasants from the village of Raduilovo forming a cooperative to seek a common water source for land irrigation, was reviewed twenty years later by Ivens's scriptwriter and assistant, Marion Michelle: her *The Masters of the Rain* (1969) documents the reactions of people in the same village, as they see themselves once again constructing a reservoir to help bring progress to the area.

Both films together offer the possibility of understanding the revolutionary changes that have taken place in Bulgaria over the past thirty-five years. Before 1945, this was a primarily agricultural country of small holdings. After 1946, a land reform allowed peasants to till their own individual land, permitting the new owners up to a maximum of fifty acres for private use and a share in the fruits of the collective farms, according to Party regulations. This land reform was as momentous to the average Bulgarian as his previous liberation from the Turkish yoke.

By the same token, Dako Dakovski's feature films on village life—*The Troubled Road* (1955), *The Secret Supper of the Sedmaks* (1957), and *The Lindens of Stublen* (1960)—are historic chronicles on folk traditions and land reform; viewed together, they offer a collective portrait of village

Boris Borozanov's *Kalin the Eagle* (1950).

life already fading before the camera as industrialization became Bulgaria's main concern.

It is important to understand how these short and feature-length documentaries paved the way for the Bulgarian feature film of the future. For, as Zhandov noted in an interview, there was little in the way of equipment in 1950 to start a national film industry: only two or three Arriflex cameras, poor sound gear, miserable laboratories, and few theaters to show the new productions. Any kind of prior know-how was viewed as expertise in the young film industry.

But this fresh approach had its rewards as well.

The first feature film officially produced in Socialist Bulgaria was Boris Borozanov's *Kalin the Eagle* (1950)—started under the aegis of a private company, but finished under the state industry. Zahari Zhandov's *Alarm* (1951), however, was the real beginning.

Zhandov—he both directed and shared the camera duties—was given a screenplay adapted directly from a play by the author himself, Orlin

Vassilev. But since *Alarm* focused on the Resistance movement in 1944 and the division of loyalties in a close family circle, the story was a part of every Bulgarian's memory, and thus few errors could surface in the narrative. Only polish was missing.

That ingredient was added to the script by a new graduate from the Moscow Film School: Angel Wagenstein, who was to become one of the ablest talents in the Bulgarian cinema. In addition, a young actor from the Sofia Academy of Dramatic Art, Rangel Vulchanov, played one of the bit roles in the film; as a director, he was to lift his country's cinema to world acclaim only a few years later.

Alarm, despite its theatrical weakness and schematic formula, can be viewed today as a semidocumentary on the last days of the Second World War, when the fascist dictatorship was crumbling. It can be faulted for embodying some of the principles of schematism propagated during the period of the Personality Cult, but it is certain that the home audiences did not mind this simplistic style of cinema, which was practically synonymous with the theatrical traditions of the day. Further, in view of the minuscule film production in the early 1950s—one film in 1950, two in 1951, two in 1952, one in 1953, four in 1954, two in 1955—every feature film to appear was greeted as one of the year's major events!

The only other film to match the importance of *Alarm* during this initial period was *Septembrists* (1954), made by the team of director Zhandov and screenplay writer Wagenstein; it was, in fact, Angel Wagenstein's diploma script at VGIK, the Moscow Film School.

Once again, it was a story of heroes and revolution, the kind of film the public both wanted and appreciated as a document on the recent past. It dealt with the uprising in September 1923 against the imposed dictatorship of the military, an historical moment drenched in the blood of patriots. Besides eyewitnesses who provided an authenticity to the story and its filming, the cameraman, Vassil Holiolchev, had served in

the Spanish Civil War while living in exile, one of many Bulgarians driven from their homeland to fight abroad for a common cause. *Septembrists*, made in the immediate aftermath of Stalin's death in 1953, carried a universal message and signaled the search for a national cinematic style.

The Bulgarian feature film had to wait a few more years before this national style appeared in Vulchanov's *On a Small Island* (1958). The change in the wind, however, could be detected earlier in the newly reorganized animation-and-puppet studio in Sofia. Within weeks after the reorganization had begun, Todor Dinov, a newspaper caricaturist, made the cartoon *Brave Marko* (1953, released in 1955), which awakened the country's artists to the possibilities of the film medium.

Brave Marko presented a readily recognizable national character in a graphic form taking its inspiration from Bulgarian folklore, songs and dances, the very customs of the common people. The break with the Disney-like entertainment models at the Soyuzmultfilm Studio for anima-

Zahari Zhandov's *Alarm* **(1951).**

tion and puppet films in Moscow was unmistakable. In fact, instead of adhering to Soviet animator Ivan Ivanov-Vano's stereotyped anthropomorphic characters, Dinov's "Marko" had more in common with Yugoslav cartoonist Dušan Vukotić's "Kićo." In Vukotić's *How Kićo Was Born* (1951) this mustached Chaplinesque character roams the country as a national hero righting wrongs; Marko was also a heroic type. Both Dinov and Vukotić came to the animated cartoon from work as caricaturists for satirical journals: *Starshel* ("Prickles") in Sofia and *Kerempuh* in Zagreb.

Owing to the nature of their medium, cartoon and puppet filmmakers had the jump on feature-film directors so far as new forms, styles, and themes were concerned. The Czech puppeteer, Jiří Trnka, was world famous shortly after the Cannes Film Festival began in 1946, first through his cartoons and then his puppet films. The UPA Studio in Hollywood was founded in 1945 by talented graphic artists who had broken with Walt Disney. Vukotić and the Zagreb "school" were developing the principles of "reduced animation" at the beginning of the 1950s. Todor Dinov was well aware of these new trends on the horizon and acted accordingly.

When Dinov's *Brave Marko* left the drawing board in 1953, the Bulgarian animated cartoon was on the way to becoming one of the best in Socialist Europe.

Lessons in Style

Within a decade after the founding of a state film industry, Bulgaria awakened to worldwide acclaim for a national style—poetic cinema.

In 1953, as the schematic principles of Socialist Realism under the Stalinist Personality Cult gave way to new theoretical platforms in East Europe, cartoonist Todor Dinov turned to native folk traditions to create a distinctly national character in the animated film *Brave Marko* (also known as *Marko the Hero*). Two years later, upon release, *Brave Marko* was saluted at both national and international film festivals, together with Dinov's *Kino Prickles No. 1* (1955), a graphic form of animation based on his drawings in the satirical magazine *Prickles*.

Then came Dinov's *The Careful Little Angel* (1956), a cartoon metaphor on war and peace that was not only a confirmation of a personal style, but also a short that commanded respect and attention at the 1956 Karlovy Vary Film Festival, where it was shown out-of-competition.

Dinov was to become as well known at home as Jiří Trnka in Czechoslovakia, Dušan Vukotić in Yugoslavia, and Walerian Borowczyk and Jan Lenica in Poland—each of whom drew direction and inspiration from native forms of art and folk traditions in the same way as Dinov did. Later, in the 1970s, another Bulgarian cartoonist, Donyo Donev, raised the folk cartoon to even higher expressions of folk art—*The Three Fools* (1970), *A Clever Village* (1972), *De Facto* (1973), *The Musical Tree* (1976), *Causa Perduta* (1977)—but it was Todor Dinov who first showed the way.

In the feature film, where the production machinery moves slower (it takes an average of two years for an approved script to reach its film premiere), the reorganization begun in 1953 was noticeable, first of all, in increased production, directorial debuts, and a variety of new genres with entertainment value (comedies, thrillers, action films). In comparison with the lone feature film produced in 1953, four appeared in 1954, two in 1955, and eight in 1956. The Twentieth Party Congress in 1956 then set down new guidelines under Khrushchev for film production throughout the Socialist countries, which were to have as immediate positive results in Bulgaria as anywhere else in East Europe.

The first hint of a "poetic cinema" occurred in 1954. Two graduates of the Moscow Film School, director Borislav Sharaliev and screenplay writer Hristo Ganev, collaborated on Ganev's diploma script, *Song of Man* (1954), the story of the poet Nikola Vaptsarov, the "Bulgarian Mayakovsky," who faced a firing squad in 1942 for his part in the resistance. The young poet (born 1909) was a national hero, whose fiery revolutionary verses also pleaded for human dignity and compassion for one's fellow man. *Song of Man*, despite weaknesses as a finished film, honored a national hero and planted the seeds of a national film style.

The attempts at comedies, children's films, and detective thrillers in 1955–56 set the stage for a breakthrough film following the April Plenum of the Bulgarian Communist Party. Two projects were approved in 1956, Binka Zhelyazkova and Hristo Ganev's *Partisans* and Rangel Vulchanov's *On a Small Island,* and they were completed at about the same time in 1957. After a heated discussion, *Partisans* never saw the light of day, while *On a Small Island* was an international hit upon its release in 1958.

Partisans (also titled *Life Flows Quietly By*) reviewed the period of the Personality Cult in a critical light. An important film in the mid-1950s, it may still be included in a historical retrospective as something more than a curiosity. In any case, the husband-wife team of Ganev-Zhelyazkova guaranteed quality, as their later film, *We Were Young* (1961), confirmed; it became one of the outstanding examples of Bulgarian poetic realism. One wonders, though, what might have been accomplished had *Partisans* gone into general release.

Vulchanov's *On a Small Island* owes its reputation primarily to a poet, Valeri Petrov, although the debut director contributed as much, and perhaps more, to the film's success as anyone else involved in its making. One of the remarkable factors about the project was how quickly it was made, far away from studio interference: the film was shot in less than thirty days on an island in the Black Sea. It was an astonishing debut for Vulchanov—who has maintained his position in the forefront of Bulgarian cinema up to the present. As for Petrov, he is acclaimed today as Bulgaria's "national poet."

On a Small Island takes place just after the September 1923 uprising, at a time when hundreds of suspected opponents of the military dictatorship are imprisoned on Sveta Anastasia, an isolated island in the Black Sea. Petrov describes the fate of four individuals—a fisherman, a student, a carpenter, and a doctor—each of whom makes an escape attempt that results in his own death. Since these individuals are all types and the story works as a parable or metaphor, the film is open to various interpretations—in fact, it is possible, via the fate of the principal figures, to weigh the destiny of Bulgaria itself as an independent country. Further, this is, in essence, a tragedy—better still, an epic poem—a convention that did not fit easily into the prior precepts of Socialist Realism, but is wholly acceptable and appropriate within the country's rich literary tradition.

Those who worked on the film—Rangel Vulchanov, Valeri Petrov, cameraman Dimo Kolarov, composer Simeon Pironkov—formed a production unit for two more feature films, *First Lesson* (1960) and *Sun and Shadow* (1962). Together with *On a Small Island* the films form a trilogy that epitomizes the "poetic cinema"

Rangel Vulchanov's *On a Small Island* (1958).

Rangel Vulchanov's *First Lesson* (1960).

the film is less a narrative story than a lyrical, abstract, avant-garde poem.

The theme of young people required to forfeit their lives during the Second World War occupied other directors in this period of feverish activity. The East German director Konrad Wolf collaborated with a VGIK classmate, scriptwriter Angel Wagenstein, on a coproduction between Bulgaria and the German Democratic Republic: *Stars* (1959), a love story between a Jewish girl and a German soldier, which stands today as one of the finest films made on the Jewish Question in East Europe. Binka Zhelyazkova directed a script by Hristo Ganev, *We Were Young* (1961), about young partisans active in the Resistance; the film drew from the same source as Ganev's screenplay for Sharaliev's *Song of Man*—that is, personal experiences, for the most part.

These six films—directed by Vulchanov, Zhelyaskova, and Wolf, and written by Petrov, Ganev, and Wagenstein—form the nucleus of Bulgaria's "breakthrough" films of the late 1950s and early 1960s. Their common style, poetic realism, has been compared with Italian Neorealism and the poetic cinema of Marcel Carné and the prewar French directors, but such a comparison overlooks the realities of making

Binka Zhelyazkova's *We Were Young* (1961).

movement in Bulgaria of the late 1950s and early 1960s. *First Lesson*, set during the Resistance in 1942 (the time of Vaptsarov's death), is the most direct of the three, a tragic love story with comic touches and disarming performances by two young nonprofessionals in the lead roles. Two young people appear again in *Sun and Shadow*, presumably a Bulgarian boy and an American girl who are mutually concerned about the threat of a nuclear disaster; although the scare becomes a reality in the closing scene,

Rangel Vulchanov's *Sun and Shadow* (1962).

Konrad Wolf's *Stars* (1959).

personal films in a Socialist production system. A parallel movement in Polish cinema, for instance, is more appropriate for purposes of study and analysis, as is Soviet cinema of the same time. Poland's Andrzej Wajda and Andrzej Munk, Mosfilm's Mikhail Kalatozov, Hungary's Zoltan Fabri, and even Czechoslovakia's puppet-master, Jiří Trnka, pointed the way to some extent.

In fact, however, the reaction against the schematism of Socialist Realism in the early 1950s produced poetic cinema in Bulgaria as elsewhere in East Europe, although it should be added that the aforementioned films were the exceptions to the production rules at the time of their making. Moreover, when Vulchanov's *On a Small Island* appeared on Bulgarian screens, Sergei Eisenstein's shelved *Ivan the Terrible, Part II* was released in the Soviet Union; and when Wolf's *Stars* was released in Bulgaria and East Germany, the times were ripe for a national film style in Bulgaria.

Then came a chain of politically related events during the early 1960s, each effecting a change in Bulgaria's cultural climate. The changes appeared at the same time as the Vulchanov-Petrov avant-garde experiment, *Sun and Shadow*. Poetic cinema, however, continued its course in Bulgaria for a time, as the issues were being officially discussed in the state film office. Vulchanov, a master at drawing outstanding performances from actors and nonprofessionals, extracted from veteran actor Georgi Kaloyanchev the very essence of a complicated ethical hero in the psychological whodunit, *The Inspector and the Night* (1963), a peculiar and distinctly original contribution to the popular *ciné noir* genre. His second "black film," *The She-Wolf* (1965), confirmed his new status as one of the leading psychological directors working in East Europe: once again, he took an ordinary detective story and imbued it with poetic nuances and a personal vision of the times in which he was working.

By the mid-1960s, as the climate for creative film expression changed radically in East Europe, Vulchanov, whose *The Inspector and the Night* had been acclaimed at Cannes, Karlovy

Rangel Vulchanov's *The She-Wolf* (1965).

88

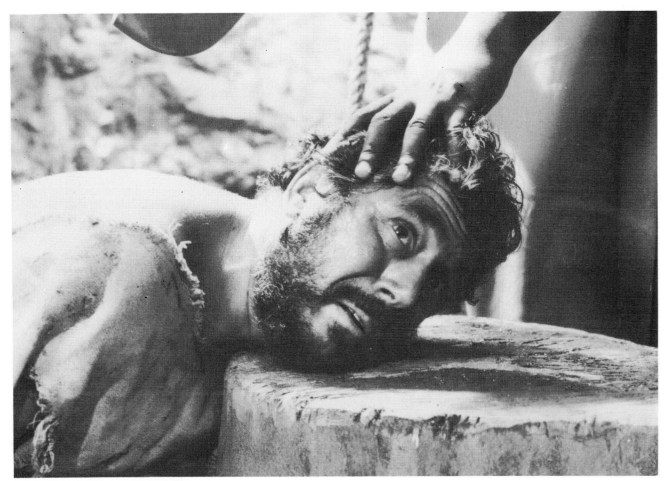

Rangel Vulchanov's *Aesop* (1968).

Vary, San Francisco, and Los Angeles, left for North Africa to make the lyrical documentary *Journey between Two Shores* (1967), his most personal film, which reflected a state of restless wandering. In 1968, after he had finally settled in Czechoslovakia, Vulchanov made a coproduction with Bulgaria, *Aesop,* from a script by Angel Wagenstein; it was released at home in 1970. Two other projects, *The Face behind the Mask* (1970) and *Chance* (1970), were made in Czechoslovakia before he decided to return to Bulgaria with his reputation intact as a director.

The times changed for poet Valeri Petrov too. After the team of Vulchanov-Petrov separated, he collaborated on two films with director Borislav Sharaliev: *Knight without Armor* (1966), a children's film that raised that genre to new heights in its realistic approach to the world of a six-year-old; and *Vaskata* (1967), a TV essay on the heroes of the Resistance. Then he abruptly left the film studios to work in theater and complete a monumental translation of Shakespeare into modern Bulgarian. When Petrov returned to

cinema, it was in collaboration with Rangel Vulchanov again on *With Love and Tenderness* (1978), a lyrical, philosophical reflection on sacrifice and the nature of art; the central figure, an individualistic sculptor, has much in common with Shakespeare's flawed heroes.

Angel Wagenstein, who had proven himself to be one of the country's major film talents after the success of Konrad Wolf's *Stars* at the Cannes festival, also left Bulgaria for an extended period in the mid-1960s. He collaborated with Wolf again on the TV film *The Little Prince* (1966), an East German–Bulgarian coproduction; with Vulchanov on *Aesop* (1970), a Czechoslovakian-Bulgarian coproduction; with Wolfgang Staudte on *Little Secrets* (1969), a West German–Bulgarian coproduction; and with Wolf on *Goya,* an East German–Soviet coproduction based on Lion Feuchtwanger's novel and filmed in Bulgaria. Wagenstein's preference for a lyrical, emotional story of delicate human relationships is felt in even the 70mm spectacle, *Goya.*

Binka Zhelyazkova's *We Were Young,* scripted

by Hristo Ganev, won a Gold Medal at the 1961 Moscow Film Festival. Thereafter, Ganev turned to making documentary films on the political conditions in other countries: *Feast of Hope* (1962), on the Algerian War; and *Open at the Letter P* (1975), on the April Revolution in Portugal. He also wrote scripts for cartoons, the best known being Ivan Vesselinov's *The Devil in the Church* (1969). Zhelyazkova's next project after *We Were Young, The Attached Balloon* (1967), became a center of controversy and was withdrawn from circulation shortly after its release.

The Attached Balloon has had a remarkable history. Based on a story by Yordan Radichkov, with an original screenplay by the same author, the film is packed with absurd humor—indeed, the situation itself is absurd. A group of peasants discover a loose Lamorisse-style balloon, and all climb aboard. Once in the balloon, however, their dreams of escaping to new lands in a fantastic voyage are left unrealized, for the balloon is tied to the ground. The same story was reworked for a successful stage play, *Attempt to Fly,* by Radichkov; it appeared in multiple productions at the 1979 Bulgarian Drama & Theater Festival in Sofia. A year later, Mladen Kisselov's production at the National Theater in Sofia was invited to the Berliner Festtage in the German Democratic Republic.

Zhelyazkova and Ganev wiped the slate clean years later in a collaborative effort, *The Swimming Pool* (1977); the film appeared in the same production season as the Vulchanov-Petrov *With Love and Tenderness* (1978). Thus, in retrospect, a decade had to pass before the leading directorial and screenplay-writing talent could comment in a metaphorical manner on the first creative chapter in Bulgarian film history. Meanwhile, Binka Zhelyazkova wrote and directed the autobiographical *The Last Word* (1973), on woman partisans active in World War II.

The trend was upward in Socialist cinema throughout the 1960s. Setbacks in one area led to progress in another. The important gain in the late 1950s and the early 1960s was that a lyrical, poetic style had replaced the schematic formulas of the Stalinist years. By some quirk of fate Albert Lamorisse's *The Red Balloon* (1956) and *Trip in a Balloon* (1960) inspired Andrei Mikhalkov-Konchalovsky's *The Boy and the Pigeon* (1961) (a diploma short film at VGIK) and Mikhail Kalik's *Man Following the Sun* (1961); these films, in turn, may have been the inspiration for Binka Zhelyazkova's *The Attached Balloon*

Binka Zhelyazkova's *The Attached Balloon* **(1967).**

90

Binka Zhelyazkova's *The Last Word* **(1973).**

some years later. And at the same time as
Lamorisse was enjoying his popularity, Saint-
Exupéry's aviation fable, *Le Petit Prince*, inspired
adaptations: Wolf and Wagenstein's *The Little
Prince* (1966), for East German television; and
Arunas Zhebrunas's *The Little Prince* (1967), at
the Lithuanian Film Studio. As a result of this
widespread interest in lyrical, poetic, avant-
garde forms of film expression, the fable, parable, and moral tale entered into the lexicon of
Socialist cinema.

Bulgarian cinema had found its national
style—a poetic cinema. The next step was to
reap a cinematic harvest from a rich cultural
heritage.

Green Years

After the soaring promise of the late 1950s,
the 1960s can best be described as the "green
years" of Bulgarian cinema.

It was the same across East Europe. Still, in
retrospect, a number of remarkable films were
made in that period, despite the inactivity of the
country's finest directorial talent.

Dimiter Petrov's *The Captain* (1963), for instance. In its own way, *The Captain* achieved
somewhat the same recognition as the critical
films of the late 1950s. It was, first of all, an
international hit, appealing to both children and
adults, and thus confirming Petrov as a promising director with a deft hand for a difficult
genre. The main roles were children, the theme
was friendship, and the formula was to secure
Bulgaria a position in the forefront of the children's film genre.

Vulo Radev's *The Peach Thief* (1964). Often
cited as a prime example of "poetic realism" in
Bulgarian cinema, it was made by a cameraman-
turned-director. The film's main attraction today
lies in the romantic love story, exceptionally well
played by Nevena Kokanova as the Bulgarian
officer's wife and Rade Marković as the Yugoslav
prisoner of war. The period is the First World
War, and the location backdrop is the

Dimiter Petrov's *The Captain* **(1963).**

Vulo Radev's *The Peach Thief* **(1964).**

Vulo Radev's *Tsar and General* (1966).

Hristo Piskov and Irina Aktasheva's *Monday Morning* (1966).

magnificent fortress city of Turnovo.

Vulo Radev's *Tsar and General* (1966). For the first time, King Boris is presented on the screen in Bulgarian cinema's first wide-screen historical epic. The tsar's opponent during the Second World War was General Tsaimov, and they are matched in several dialogue scenes penned by writer-historian Lyuben Stanev.

Hristo Piskov and Irina Aktasheva's *Monday Morning* (1966). This controversial film is set in a provincial city and focuses on the experiences of two young people, one a postman, who awaken to the reality that the world is not as idealistic as they were led to believe. Shelved upon completion, it's not yet in release.

Borislav Sharaliev's *Knight without Armor* (1966). This Valeri Petrov screenplay may have been designed for Rangel Vulchanov's talents—nevertheless, its view of hypocrisy among grown-ups through the eyes of a questioning lad received a warm box-office reception.

Borislav Sharaliev's *Knight without Armor* (1966).

Grisha Ostrovski and Todor Stoyanov's *Sidetrack (Detour)* (1967). In this first Bulgarian film to deal openly with the mistakes of the Stalinist years, flashbacks are triggered by a chance meeting between an engineer and an archaeologist who were lovers in the past. The film marks the debut of stage director from the Satirical Theater (Ostrovski) and a veteran cameraman (Stoyanov); Nevena Kokanova and Ivan Andonov, two of Bulgaria's most popular actors, play the couple painfully recalling a past that disrupted their lives and separated them forever.

Eduard Zahariev's *If the Train Doesn't Arrive* (1967). First released and then withdrawn from circulation, it marked the debut of director Zahariev and his first collaboration with scriptwriter Georgi Mishev, another master of satirical, absurd comedy. The film begins with three friends, joined by a stranger, on a hunt; when the stranger disappears, the hunting expedition carries into the night and from one senseless situation to another. The Zahariev-Mishev team were to make more popular films at a later date, but this is arguably the best of their witty, barbed social satires.

Lyudmil Kirkov's *Swedish Kings* (1968). Kirkov's second film proved controversial, and thus placed him too in the front ranks of Bulgarian directors. It deals with a steelworker who on a lark decides to spend his vacation at the Black Sea tourist resorts, believing that his highly paid job will allow him to live as a "Swedish King" (thus the teasing twist in the title) if he so chooses. The confrontation between his world and the life on the Balkan Riviera provides the social context that sets this film apart from others before it—the working hero is a complex, complicated figure in a changing society.

Peter Vassilev's *The Whale* (1970). Released for a short run, this comedy begins with a crew of fishermen sending a false report after a fruitless night of trawling—the small catch is reported big enough to fulfill a quota plan, which, in turn, is reported by the next station as bigger in size to fulfill another quota. In the end the catch has reached the size of a whale—in the Black Sea, of all places!

Lyubomir Sharlandjiev's *The Prosecutor* (1968). Another honest view of Personality Cult mistakes, this filmed version of a controversial play by Georgi Djagarov was never released. It's the story of an innocent who is falsely accused, thus setting the stage for a confrontation between the prosecutor and the investigator, which also spills over into a private family affair. The play was presented at the 1979 Bulgarian Drama & Thea-

Grisha Ostrovski and Todor Stoyanov's *Sidetrack* **(1967).**

Eduard Zahariev's *If the Train Doesn't Come* **(1967).**

Lyudmil Kirkov's _Swedish Kings_ (1968).

ter Festival in Sofia, thus ending the controversy
and underscoring the progress made in over-
coming the past since the April 1956 Plenum of
the Central Committee in Bulgaria.

Metodi Andonov's _The White Room_ (1968).
Another hotly discussed film dealing with the
period of the Personality Cult. The tragic hero is
an intellectual, a scientist, whose research
doesn't fit into the dogmatic beliefs of the day;
he enters a hospital for infectious diseases and
dies of his illness shortly thereafter. Based on
Bogomil Rainov's novel, _Roads to Nowhere_
(Rainov also wrote the screenplay), it was an impressive debut for Andonov, up to then a stage
director at the Satirical Theater in Sofia. _The
White Room_ marked the beginning of Bulgarian
cinema's abiding interest in the sociopolitical
theme. It won the Golden Rose at the 1968
Varna Festival of Bulgarian Feature Films.

Todor Dinov and Hristo Hristov's _Iconostasis_
(1969). Another milestone in Bulgarian film history, this epic on a religious theme was the debut
film of animator Todor Dinov and stage director
Hristo Hristov (who had just finished his studies
in film direction at the Moscow Film School). Its
literary source is Dimiter Talev's historical novel
on the Bulgarian Renaissance at the end of the
nineteenth century, but inspiration may also
have come from Andrei Tarkovsky's historical
biography of the renowned medieval icon-
painter, _Andrei Rublev_ (written 1964, filmed
1966, shown as a Special Event at Cannes in

Lyudmil Sharlandjiev's _The Prosecutor_ (1968)

1969). Although Talev's novel and the film center on a conflict between a liberal painter and a conservative matriarch, *Iconostasis* breathes a life of its own when the painter enters the Bachkovo monastery near Plovdiv to inspect the magnificent frescoes painted on the refectory walls in 1606.

Georgi Stoyanov's *Birds and Greyhounds* (1969). For the first time, the antifascist Resistance is treated in a comic vein by a writer, Vassil Akyov, who was a partisan fighter and drew accordingly from his personal experiences. Stoyanov, a graduate of IDHEC in Paris, adds absurd, grotesque touches to the story of a group of sixteen-year-old boys imprisoned for not embracing Bulgaria's common cause with the Germans in the Second World War.

Vulo Radev's *Black Angels* (1970). Set in 1942–43, this attempt at a polit-thriller (another was Radev's earlier *The Longest Night*, 1967) received wide support as a new form of Eastern adventure film. A group of young partisans are given the daring task of killing a dangerous Bulgarian fascist. It was one of several attempts to recast the war years into entertainment formulas for the young public.

Georgi Djulgerov's *The Test* (1971). The first successful film adaptation of a Nikola Haitov story, it introduced a director who broke completely away from the "theatrical tradition" in Bulgarian cinema that had hindered an international breakthrough from the very beginning. Djulgerov had first turned to the Haitov story for his diploma film at VGIK, filming *The Cooper* (1969) in Armenia instead of the original's Rhodope Mountains, then returned home and shot the same story all over again as a film-novella in a two-part Haitov feature, titled *Colorful World* (1971) (the other half, *Naked Conscience*, was directed by Milen Nikolov). *The Test* refers to a traditional ritual for the testing of manhood, also of a cooper's profession.

To these fifteen films should be added Binka Zhelyazkova's *The Attached Balloon* (1966, released briefly in 1967). The story of that controversial film had been covered in the previous chapter. Suffice it here to say that the Yordan Radichkov story was the most discussed film project of the decade—and beyond. When the same story appeared as a tragicomedy on the stages of Bulgaria more than ten years later, it was an instant success in several complementary

Metodi Andonov's *The White Room* (1968).

97

Hristo Hristov's *Iconostasis* **(1969).**

Georgi Stoyanov's *Birds and Greyhounds* **(1969).**

Vulo Radev's *Black Angels* **(1970).**

Binka Zhelyazkova's *The Attached Balloon* **(1967).**

Georgi Djulgerov's *The Test* (1971).

productions. Since then, *Attempt to Fly* has been received with the same enthusiasm by audiences in Berlin (GDR) and Bratislava, and Radichkov has been hailed as one of the leading literary figures in Socialist Europe.

There is thus much to be said for waiting for the right moment. Some stories, and some films, seem to ripen on the vine.

And a footnote: a retrospective of all of Bulgaria's feature-film productions (including the above) was presented during the 1,300th anniversary celebrations at the Bulgarska Nacionalna Filmoteka in Sofia.

Another Breakthrough

Another, quite genuine, breakthrough in Bulgarian cinema occurred on the world film stage during the late 1970s. It can be conveniently marked by international awards won at festivals in Moscow and Teheran in 1977, and Berlin in 1978.

Binka Zhelyazkova's *The Swimming Pool* (1977) discussed the past in an open and frank manner; it won a Gold Medal in July 1977 at the Moscow Film Festival. The next winner was Eduard Zahariev's *Manly Times* (1977); a few months after Moscow, in November 1977, the acting prizes at the Teheran Film Festival were awarded to Marianna Dimitrova and Grigor Vachkov. Then came the Silver Bear for Direction at the Berlin Film Festival, awarded to Georgi Djulgerov's *Advantage* (1977) in March 1978.

Within the brief period of eight months, Bulgarian films had captured major festival prizes as though apples were being picked from overloaded trees. By contrast, Bulgarian cinema under general directors of the 1960s—Alexander Dunchev (1964–67), Georgi Karamanev (1967–68), Filip Filipov (1968–69), and Hristo Santov (1969–71)—had failed to arouse such enthusiasm on the world scene.

The turning point, in 1971–72, occurred under a new general director: Pavel Pissarev began his official duties by inviting the filmmakers themselves to have a say in the production of the state film industry. At that time, it meant that three independent production units—Haemus, Mladost, and Sredets—would share the responsibility for what went on the nation's screens; they were formed for the 1973–74 season, and a fourth unit, Suvremenik, was added in 1978–79. Finally, a Film Academy was founded in Sofia in 1973.

The results of this change in policy were immediately noticeable.

In 1972, Metodi Andonov's box-office winner, *The Goat Horn*, appeared. This was a feature film that went to the roots of Bulgarian life and culture. Based on a story by Nikolai Haitov, who also wrote the script, *The Goat Horn* was a tale of revenge set during the time of the Turkish Occupation. Not only was this a narrative that transferred easily to the cinema, but it was also a tragedy—a genre which is rare in Socialist cinema as a whole.

The Goat Horn won a vast audience to Bulgarian cinema at home, but also secured the reputation of "folk writers" in Bulgarian letters. Haitov and others with established names as "storytellers"—Yordan Radichkov, in particular—found that their unusual tales drawn from the lives of the people were now acceptable to the front office at the Boyana Studios; in fact, they were increasingly in demand. Satirist Georgi Mishev began to write comedies that were unthinkable but a decade before. Pavel Vezhinov, one of Bulgarian cinema's prolific

Metodi Andonov's *The Goat Horn* (1972).

Hristo Hristov's *Hammer and Anvil* (1972).

screenplay writers, broke away from scripts in a realistic vein to experiment with science fiction and fantastic themes.

The key production year was 1972. In addition to *The Goat Horn* (seen by three million viewers in Bulgaria), Hristo Hristov made a historical epic on Georgi Dimitrov and the Leipzig Trial, *Hammer or Anvil,* and completed *The Last Summer* (released in 1974), based on a Yordan Radichkov story. Lyudmil Kirkov began his fruitful association with the scriptwriter and humorist Georgi Mishev, in the first of a two-film series about life in the provinces, *A Boy Becomes a Man* (followed in 1976 by *Don't Go Away*). Georgi Stoyanov attempted the first science-fiction film in Bulgaria, *The Third Planet in the Solar System,* in collaboration with screenplay writer Pavel Vezhinov. And Lyudmil Staikov made *Affection.*

The most important of these productions, now a classic in Bulgarian film history, was Hristov's *The Last Summer,* which was discussed at length before approval was given for its release in 1974, two years after its completion. Radichkov as a writer did not fit into a readily defined literary mold, nor was his screenplay for Binka Zhelyazkova's *The Attached Balloon* (1967) much appreciated in official circles, because of the portrait of the 1950s and 1960s contained in the film, albeit in a metaphorical application of folkloric symbols and modes of expression. In the Hristov-Radichkov *The Last Summer,* the plight of

Hristo Hristov's *The Last Summer* (1974).

Hristo Hristov's *The Last Summer* (1974).

Hristo Hristov's *The Last Summer* (1974).

a villager who refuses to abandon his home (and traditional way of life), although a newly constructed dam will shortly submerge the area under water, is made manifest via stream-of-consciousness passages, surrealistic fantasies, and monologues set against visual juxtapositions. The film thus offers a social analysis of the village-to-town migration, as well as seemingly siding with a primitive free spirit (Grigor Vachkov, the leading exponent of Radichkov on stage and screen) who refuses to comply with the dubious gains of a land reform that wantonly destroys ancient traditions.

Stoyanov's *The Third Planet in the Solar System* was typical of several experiments undertaken at the Boyana Studios throughout the 1970s, principally by allowing directorial talent to make "novellas" that could be released for the theaters in an omnibus film and aired on television in separate episodes. The three stories in this case—"Eden," "The Stranger," and "My First Day," all penned by Pavel Vezhinov—focus on the past, present, and future in an H. G. Wells

time-machine atmosphere, each story containing a subtle twist of irony at the end. It was a project, however, that badly needed the services of a special-effects expert.

Light humor and bitter irony pervaded *A Boy Becomes a Man*, Kirkov's attack on the narrow-mindedness of provincial life made in collaboration with satirist Georgi Mishev. It is the moral position that gives the film its sharp edge, but this is tempered with the realization that the agrarian society is passing. Regret and nostalgia sweeten the cup of bitterness.

Staikov's *Affection*, as the title hints, could have immersed itself in sentimentality. As boy became man in the Kirkov film, so here a girl becomes a woman by refusing to make the compromises her parents have made; she belongs to an established family in urban Sofia and her ideals receive only lip service. Staikov uses flashbacks and visionary effects to dig below the surface of contemporary Bulgarian society, a daring search by a gifted debut director.

In 1973 Rangel Vulchanov and Binka Zhelyaz-

Lyudmil Kirkov's *A Boy Becomes a Man* **(1972).**

Lyudmil Staikov's *Affection* **(1972).**

Ivan Terziev's *Men without Work* (1973).

kova returned to the front ranks of Bulgarian cinema. Vulchanov's *Escape to Ropotamo* was an attempt at a musical in a Czech vein, and Zhelyazkova's *The Last Word* (a Cannes entry) placed the antifascist Resistance movement on an abstract plane. Neither film compared with the advances made by the younger generation: Ivan Terziev's *Men without Work*, Eduard Zahariev's *The Hare Census,* and Georgi Djulgerov's *And the Day Came.*

Terziev's *Men without Work* offered a new portrait of the workingman. The script was by Nikolai Nikiforov, who wrote the screenplay for the much discussed *Swedish Kings* (1968), directed by Lyudmil Kirkov. As in *Swedish Kings,* the story evolves around workers in their free time—on this occasion, during a forced layoff. This was Terziev's second film, and it established him as a director with a sensitivity to the problems of the laborer.

Zahariev's *The Hare Census,* scripted by Georgi Mishev, is an absurd tale from start to finish—indeed, it appears to take up where the pair had

previously left off: on a hunting expedition. The joke revolves around the arrival of an official "statistician," whose duties are to count the number of hares in the area surrounding a village. The male members of the village council turn out for the occasion; a tramp across the fields in autumn leads to an outdoor picnic; and, although nary a hare is found to "count," the public official (played to the hilt by a gifted comic actor, Itzak Fintzi) returns to the city in a car stuffed with cabbages!

Djulgerov's *And the Day Came* completely reworked the formula of the action-packed "Eastern" (the "Western" in a war setting). The script was written by Vassil Akyov, who wrote the screenplays for Georgi Stoyanov's offbeat partisan films, *Birds and Greyhounds* (1966) and *Panteley* (1978). For the first time, the tragic condition of young people fighting in the Resistance movement is rendered in painful, nonheroic terms—the magnificence of their deeds is not diminished, only the glory that brings with it a loss of youth and, if necessary, the sacrifice of life

Eduard Zahariev's *The Hare Census* **(1973).**

Georgi Djulgerov's *And the Day Came* **(1973).**

Georgi Djulgerov's *And the Day Came* **(1973).**

Hristo Hristov's *A Tree without Roots* **(1974).**

for an ideal. This is a tender salute to the lost generation. Its lyrical beauty also owes much to the camera of Radoslav Spassov, who worked with Djulgerov on *The Test* (1971) and was destined to become the country's leading photographer with a flair for supple movement and the visual nature of the medium.

In 1974, a year of fermentaton, more directors (Ivan Nichev, Ivanka Grubcheva) and scriptwriters (Nikola Russev, Stanislav Stratiev)

made their film debuts as Bulgarian cinema began to attract admirers abroad. The big film of the year was the delayed release of Hristov and Radichkov's *The Last Summer* (shot in 1972), but Hristo Hristov's *A Tree without Roots* and Lyudmil Kirkov's *Peasant on a Bicycle* combined with *The Last Summer* to offer a collective and rather definitive statement on the deepest problem in Bulgarian society: the migration from the villages to the towns and the serious problems resulting from this drastic change.

Hristov's *A Tree without Roots,* scripted by Nikolai Haitov, is a tragic story about an old man from the village who doesn't fit in with his son's family, now living in modern Sofia. Yet the old man has dignity, and he is understood by his grandchild as a man alienated by the break in the family structure. In comparison with Hristov's primitive fighter in Radichkov's story *The Last Summer,* this Haitov version of the same tragic hero is mild and sentimental in Hristov's hands—reverse sides of the same coin.

Kirkov's *Peasant on a Bicycle,* scripted by Georgi Mishev, adds salt and pepper to the same story. This time, a rustic type abandons the city on weekends to return to the nearby village of his youth on a bicycle, simply because he has not been able to break the bonds with the past and a traditional way of life. During his regular trips back to the village, however, he falls fatally in love with a young girl who is temporarily employed there. He ends up making a fool of himself—the tragic hero reduced to the court jester.

In 1975, the migration problem culminated on the screen, while new critical films on the workingman posed questions that required more complicated answers. The migration films were Assen Shopov's *Eternal Times* and Eduard Zahariev's *Villa Zone;* the worker films were Ivan Terziev's *Strong Water* and Todor Andreikov's *Sunday Matches.* Each refused to pull its punches, and was thus acclaimed abroad for the integrity of its statement.

Assen Shopov's *Eternal Times,* as the title hints, moves with the snail's pace of a Greek tragedy. A forester tries to keep the villagers from abandoning their homes until he is left like an aging monarch unable to stem the tide. And in Zahariev's *Villa Zone* we see exactly what will ruin the innocent in the material world of consumption and vanity if he does not flee—which the young man does in the film. Georgi Mishev's script for *Villa Zone* is sardonic and unrelentingly critical of the new urban class in Socialist society, epitomized by the couple (Itzhak Fintsi and Katya Paskaleva) who elbow aside anyone and anything standing in the way of status in the new suburban community.

Lyudmil Kirkov's *Peasant on a Bicycle* (1974).

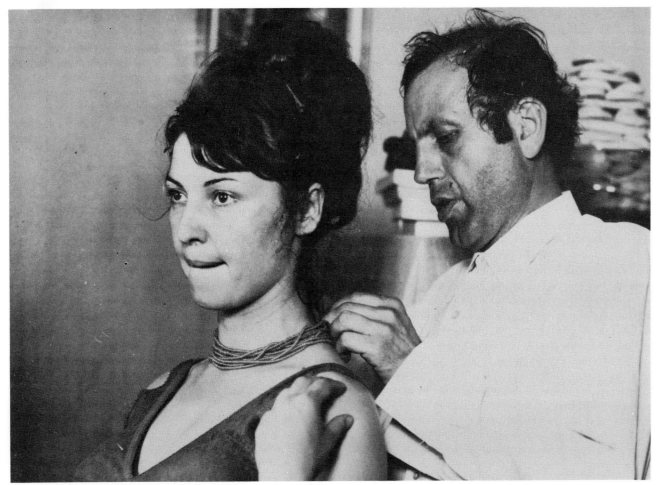

Eduard Zahariev's *Villa Zone* (1975).

The film critic Todor Andreikov has made only one film to date: the maturely weighed and open-ended *Sunday Matches*, set in a mining district. The film is comprised of two episodes (novellas) that both complement and contradict each other as a situation of compromise is both confirmed and denied. The same kind of decision tinged with doubt and resignation is to be found in Terziev's *Strong Water*: once again, he analyzes the plight of workers without work, driven by idleness to question the state of things about them. The plight of the central figure, Chico, is critical at the beginning, but the final resolution is to give up the search for water, which obviously doesn't exist, just for the security of a well-digging job that keeps everyone busy doing nothing of importance, any way you look at it.

It was in 1976 that Bulgaria gained international recognition. Lyudmil Kirkov completed his two-film portrait of village life in collaboration with Georgi Mishev, *Don't Go Away* (the first was *A Boy Becomes a Man* in 1972). Rangel Vulchanov also tied his present to his past work: *The Inspector and the Forest* recalled his earlier *The Inspector and the Night* (1963), and once again featured a remarkable acting performance in Bulgarian film history—Sonya Boshkova, in the role of a country girl trapped into committing the crime of murder.

Two newcomers solidified their positions as front-line directors. Ivan Andonov, a former actor (he played the student in Vulchanov's *On a Small Island* in 1958 and the male lead in Grisha Ostrovski and Todor Stoyanov's *Sidetrack* in 1967), made *Fairy Dance* in collaboration with Georgi Mishev; the satire on the art world and the related provincial consumer mentality was fresh, and reflected a sophisticated scene in the bohemian quarters of the country. Lyudmil Staikov's *Amendment to the Defense-of-State Act* succeeded in recapturing the aura of the 1920s as well as describing the historical events of the time.

Todor Andreikov's *Sunday Matches* **(1975).**

Ivan Terziev's *Strong Water* **(1975).**

Rangel Vulchanov's *The Inspector and the Forest* (1975).

Finally, two directors, Hristo Hristov and Georgi Stoyanov, continued on the path of experiment with notable results. Hristov's *Cyclops* was a *tour de force:* he directed, wrote the script, and contributed the decor in a philosophical statement on war and destruction set inside an underground submarine. It was the first time an "author's film" had been attempted in a film industry that relies heavily on artistic collaboration. Stoyanov's *A Cricket in the Ear,* too, was off the beaten path: its comic situations had an absurd, almost Beckettian ring. Here is a weird tale of two chums at a crossroads who stop-and-go in a tangle of events that puzzle but never daunt them.

During the 1977–78 season, Bulgarian cinema reached an artistic level that matched the best emerging at that time from Socialist cinematographies. Eight films attested to the maturity and promise of its directors: Georgi Djulgerov's *Advantage* (1977), Eduard Zahariev's *Manly Times,* Binka Zhelyazkova's *The Swimming Pool,* (1977) Rangel Vulchanov's *With Love and Tenderness* (1978), Ivan Andonov's *The Roof* (1978), Lyud-

Rangel Vulchanov's *The Inspector and the Night* (1963).

111

Ivan Andonov's *Fairy Dance* (1976).

Lyudmil Staikov's *Amendment to the Defense-of-State Act*
(1976).

Hristo Hristov's _Cyclops_ (1976).

mil Kirkov's _Matriarchate_ (1977), Georgi Stoyanov's _Panteley_ (1978), and Ivan Nichev's _Stars in her Hair, Tears in her Eyes_ (1977), in addition to gains made in the documentary field, the genre of the children's film, and the animated cartoon.

Djulgerov's _Advantage_, the Berlin festival winner, chronicles the legendary feats of a con man and pickpocket in the 1950s during the period of the Personality Cult. Its loose, improvisational style appealed to international festival audiences in particular, for it offered a great deal of information on past East European and Bulgarian political history. Perhaps _Advantage_ has to be seen in conjunction with other films made in Socialist countries at this time—for example, Pal Gabor's _Angi Vera (Vera's Training)_ (Hungary,

1978)—to be comprehended to the fullest, but as an individual statement by a talented director it also tells more about Bulgaria's past than any film made in the country. Djulgerov wrote the screenplay, and Spassov was the cameraman.

Zahariev's _Manly Times_, scripted by Nikolai Haitov, draws its strength and inspiration from folk traditions. It's an ancient story of a kidnapped girl falling in love with her abductor during the course of a journey across rugged mountain terrain. In the end, the laws of the Rhodope Mountains decide the outcome in the same manner as the customs of Thracians and Greeks formulated the destiny of Orpheus in the Underworld. Once again, Radoslav Spassov is the cameraman, and the film's actors, Marianna Dimitrova and Grigor Vachkov, received awards at Teheran.

Dialogue plays a role in communicating the nuances in Zhelyazkova's _The Swimming Pool_ and Vulchanov's _With Love and Tenderness_, the screenplays for which were written, respectively, by Hristo Ganev and Valeri Petrov. This was the first occasion that the Zhelyazkova-Ganev and Vuchanov-Petrov teams collaborated on projects in more than a decade: consequently, conscious references to the past are felt in a between-the-lines approach to the subject matter.

Screenplay writer Angel Wagenstein also contributed significantly to the "breakthrough" in 1977. His script for Ivan Nichev's _Stars in Her Hair, Tears in Her Eyes_ caught the yearning for a national identity at the turn of the century: the story of a traveling troupe of actors is sensitively directed with a romantic touch.

Georgi Stoyanov teamed again with scriptwriter Vassil Akyov in another story on the partisan years, _Panteley_. The absurd story of an unwilling Resistance fighter drawn into the conflict because he has lost his identity papers recalls Beckett and Pinter. It underscores the director's efforts to wed his training at IDHEC in Paris to Socialist forms; in fact, the comic antihero romps through the film wearing a Chaplinesque black derby.

The social analysis of an uprooted agrarian society continued in Lyudmil Kirkov's _Matriarchate_, scripted by Georgi Mishev. This searing account of a village abandoned by the men and inhabited only by the women, owing to the necessity of finding work in factories for one sex while still maintaining the collective farms by the other, had its counterpart in a documentary made the same year by Hristo Kovatchev, _Agronomists_ (1977). The two films together form a definitive statement on contemporary Bulgaria

113

Georgi Djulgerov's *Advantage* **(1977).**

Eduard Zahariev's *Manly Times* **(1977).**

Binka Zhelyazkova's *The Swimming Pool* **(1977).**

Georgi Stoyanov's *Panteley* **(1978).**

Lyudmil Kirkov's *Matriarchate* **(1977).**

Ivan Andonov's *The Roof* **(1978).**

as an emerging industrial country breaking with a rural and pastoral past.

Ivan Andonov's *The Roof* is equally honest and perceptive in analyzing the construction of private dwellings with illegally obtained building materials. It is, however, the brittle love story between two outsiders that lifts the film above the ordinary—that and the fluid narrative style that singled the director out as a skilled hand on the visual side of the medium.

The icing on the cake came at festivals awarding prizes and featuring retrospectives of short films. The Golden Dove was awarded at Leipzig in 1978 for Hristo Kovachev's *Agronomists* (1977); he had won the same prize there two years earlier for *Builders* (1974), and was to win the Grand Prix at Lille in 1980 for *Shepherds* (1979). Kovatchev ranks today as one of the leading documentary filmmakers in East Europe.

In 1974, Donyo Donev won the First Prize at the Oberhausen Short Film Festival for the animated cartoon *De Facto* (1973). He was honored with a retrospective of his cartoons at the 1977 festival; the series included two of his finest philosophical fables: *The Musical Tree* (1976) and *Causa Perduta* (1977). Bulgarian animation was being hailed by critics as the best in East Europe.

Bulgarian cinema had come into its own.

Reviving the Past

Bulgaria took great pride in the 1,300th anniversary of the birthday of its state, celebrated on 20 October 1981.

The date coincided with the Second World Animated Film Festival at Varna (October 17–24), an event drawing thousands of visitors to the resort city on the Black Sea. During that same week, the first feature in the three-part spectacle, *Khan Asparukh*, directed by Lyudmil Staikov, was released simultaneously in all the major cities—the entire multimillion-dollar production in wide-screen Eastmancolor had its world premiere on the previous weekend in the newly dedicated Culture Palace in Sofia. Asparukh welded the Bulgars, the Slavs, and the Thracians in the Danube basin into a state in 681.

The world joined in the celebrations. The 1981 Nobel Prize for Literature was awarded to Elias Canetti, a native Bulgarian (born 1905 in Russe). Canetti, a British citizen who writes in German and lives in Vienna, recorded his childhood impressions of Russe in an autobiographical book, *The Tongue Set Free* (published in 1977).

In the years just prior to the anniversary, the artistic forces of the country were massed to capture international attention for a heritage and a culture. There was much to offer, but the task was not easy. Treasures like the Thracian Gold Exhibit, the Old Slavonic Manuscripts, and the Bulgarian Orthodox Icons could be recalled for the occasion, but others had to be brought to Sofia via diplomatic channels—for instance, that priceless illuminated manuscript of the fourteenth century, the *Gospels of Tsar Ivan Alexander* (British Museum, London). Nothing within reason and possibility was spared to revive the past.

The Bulgarian film industry was also mobilized under Pavel Pissarev, now First Vice President of the Committee for Culture, and Nikolai Nenov, the new General Director of the Bulgarian Cinematography State Corporation. Since the first Grand Prix of the celebration year was garnered by Rangel Vulchanov's *The Unknown Soldier's Patent Leather Shoes* (1979), at New Delhi in January 1981, it's appropriate to start our survey there.

Vulchanov also opened the 1979 London Film Festival with this project, originally planned in 1963 but not completed until fifteen years later. The lyric poem about a childhood in a village between the wars is triggered, in the film, by Vulchanov's filming of the Changing of the Guard in London. Beautifully photographed (by Radoslav Spassov) and narrated by the director himself, the film ranks as one of the highest achievements in Bulgarian film history.

Hristo Hristov won one of the First Prizes at the 1979 Moscow Film Festival for *Barrier*. Starring Soviet actor Innokenty Smoktunovsky, this is another film of fantasy and imagination: a composer, on the verge of a nervous breakdown, meets a blithe spirit who is clairvoyant and can teach him "how to fly." The encounter eventually leads to his death. The superbly lensed flying scenes are Chagall-like and earned photographer Atanas Tassev recognition as one of the country's top cinema talents.

Ivan Nichev's *Boomerang* (1979) never reached a festival, but deserved a chance to compete on the international market. The story is about trying to get ahead by using persuasion of every kind, no matter what the consequences. The twist in this tale of corruption is that the go-getter is a student from the School of Journalism, who doesn't want to be assigned to the provinces for his first job upon graduation; there's also an old writer whose partisan stories are no

Rangel Vulchanov's *The Unknown Soldier's Patent Leather Shoes* (1979).

Rangel Vulchanov's *The Unknown Soldier's Patent Leather Shoes* (1979).

Hristo Hristov's *Barrier* **(1979).**

Hristo Hristov's *Barrier* **(1979).**

longer in favor. The "deals" in this critical view of the writer's world are never fully explained, but a certain desperation running through the film hints of what goes on behind the scenes.

Another disarmingly honest film was Lyudmil Kirkov's *Short Sun (A Ray of Sunlight)* (1979), scripted by Stanislav Stratiev. The director's moral stance was never more definite and on the side of the just than in this quiet, revealing story of corruption. Once again, it's a student in the foreground, who is working with a crew on digging a well for a property owner in Sofia's "villa zone." While digging, the crew comes upon human bones, and the question arises whether these belong to freedom fighters who gave their lives in opposing the military coup d'état in 1923 and 1925. This finding also prompts revelations in the personalities of the well-diggers. In order to keep the student from spreading the news, and thus stopping the construction of the well, the villa's owner rigs an accidental death.

A third powerful film of this year also related to youth: Kiran Kolarov's *Status—Orderly* (1978).

It made history of a sort by being the first feature made by a graduate of the new Sofia Film Academy. Kolarov, a student of Hristov and Djulgerov, was ably assisted by cameraman Radoslav Spassov in this ironic, bitter description of the lives of peasant-born orderlies serving amoral officers at the turn of the century under the new monarchy. The film was entered in the 1978 Paris Film Festival.

Georgi Djulgerov's *Swap* (1978), entered in the 1979 Rotterdam Film Festival as part of the Djulgerov retrospective, takes up where his earlier *Advantage* (1977) left off. Using actual footage shot during the period of the Personality Cult, Djulgerov employs flashbacks to recount the errors a journalist made in the past, as he is confronted in the present by a girl whose face both captivates him and releases pent-up feelings of guilt and betrayal. Although complicated in its structure, *Swap* has its rewards as a primer in history.

Eduard Zahariev's *Almost a Love Story* (1980) reunites the stars of his earlier *Manly Times*, this

Lyudmil Kirkov *Short Sun* (1979).

Kiran Kolarov's *Status—Orderly* **(1978).**

Georgi Djulgerov's *Swap* **(1978).**

Eduard Zahariev's *Almost a Love Story* **(1980).**

time in the story of a working girl rejected by a prospective father-in-law on the grounds that the bridegroom should finish his studies at the university first. Again, a kidnapping takes place to get the girl out of the way—her determination, however, wins the battle, only to lose her boyfriend's fleeting love as he notices the pasture is full of pretty flowers. It's a sentimental love story, rescued at times by comic situations that recall the director's collaboration with Georgi Mishev.

Ivan Andonov's *The Cherry Orchard* (1979) also features the same actor starring in his successful *The Roof* (1978): Peter Slabakov, playing a forester in a Nikolai Haitov story, fighting for funds to keep an orchard alive. The loner loses out to personal gain in the end, but his untimely death unites the villagers to his spirit if not his cause.

Another film imbued with social principles and moral ideals was Borislav Sharaliev's *All Is Love* (1979). The bad boy in this tale of juvenile delinquency is saved by a good girl's love—not in itself enough to satisfy the older generation and officials at a correctional institution.

Lyudmil Staikov's *Illusion* (1980) represented Bulgaria in the competition at the 1980 Karlovy Vary Film Festival. A lyrical poem on the September Uprising in 1923, the film is a companion to the director's earlier *Amendment to the Defense-of-State Act* (1976). Here was another example of the current interest in the formal, experimental elements in filmmaking.

The Berlin entry, Hristo Hristov's *The Truck* (1980), was another strong production during the anniversary year, appearing at the February festival only weeks after Vulchanov's *The Unknown Soldier's Patent Leather Shoes* won the Grand Prix in January at New Delhi. This metaphorical sketch on contemporary Bulgaria as a land transformed from a rural society into an industrial nation draws on an Henri-Georges Clouzot classic, *The Wages of Fear* (1953), for its strong narrative line and stylistic traits—yet, it should be added, the social microcosm is packed with motifs, symbols, and images from Hristov's prior masterful portraits of a society in the throes of change.

In spring 1981, the first of the commissioned

Ivan Andonov's *The Cherry Orchard* (1979).

Borislav Sharaliev's *All Is Love* (1979).

Lyudmil Staikov's *Illusion* (1980).

Hristo Hristov's *The Truck* (1980).

Zahari Zhandov's *Master of Boyana* (1981).

superspectacles could be seen in Sofia. Zahari Zhandov's *Master of Boyana* (1981), presented at the theater of the Bulgarian Filmmakers' Union thirty years after the director's own *Alarm* (1951), was a major event for several reasons, the principal one being that the lovely Boyana Church (close to the Boyana Film Studios) had recently been declared a cultural monument under UNESCO protection. Zhandov had also waited some fifteen years to make this fictionalized biography of the unknown painter who did the frescoes in 1259, fully two generations before Cimabue and Giotto in Italy introduced naturalism into religious painting in the West.

A documentary, *Nikolai Ghiaurov—50* (1980) directed by Nikola Korabov, was included in the celebrations. The viewer is taken on a tour of the world's operatic and concert stages to see another Bulgarian son, Ghiaurov, one of the world's great bassos, perform in several famous roles. The documentary was well chosen, if for no other reason than to demonstrate Bulgaria's continuing contribution to the arts.

The Cannes entry in 1981, in the "Certain Regard" section, was Binka Zhelyazkova's *The Big Night Bathe* (1980). Scripted by Hristo Ganev, this historical parable is best appreciated by those viewers familiar with the country as an archaeological treasure-store, for there are references to a Thracian ritual and a moral responsibility of the living for the heroic deeds of the past.

Then there is Georgi Djulgerov's *Measure for Measure*, completed just in time for the official October feast day. Another three-part spectacle, this chronicle of the historic Ilinden Day Uprising in Macedonia in 1903 might appear to some to be a provocation, in light of the ongoing "Macedonian Question" on the current political stage. The setting, however, is Greek Macedonia (rather than Yugoslavia or Bulgaria), and the source of the narrative is records and eyewitness accounts of how Macedonia eventually freed herself from Turkish occupation under very trying circumstances. In any case, this is one of the most significant achievements in Bulgarian film history.

Nikola Korabov's *Nikolai Ghiaurov—50* (1980).

Binka Zhelyazkova's *The Big Night Bathe* (1980).

Georgi Djulgerov's *Measure for Measure* (1981).

Georgi Djulgerov's *Measure for Measure* (1981).

Georgi Djulgerov's *Measure for Measure* (1981).

Lyudmil Staikov's *Khan Asparukh* (1981).

Lyudmil Staikov's *Khan Asparukh* (1981).

Lyudmil Staikov's *Khan Asparukh* (1981).

Ludmil Staikov's *Khan Asparukh* (1981).

Lyudmil Staikov's *Khan Asparukh* (1981).

Lyudmil Staikov's _Khan Asparukh_ (1981).

Georgi Stoyanov's _Constantine the Philosopher_ (1983).

Georgi Stoyanov's *Constantine the Philosopher* (1983).

Borislav Sharaliev's *Boris the First* (1984).

Yevgeni Mihailov's *Home for Lonely Souls* (1981).

Lyudmil Staikov's monumental *Khan Asparukh—the* feature film for the 1,300th anniversary celebration—is six hours in length and was programmed in Bulgarian theaters as three separate films. It's the story of the arrival of Khan Asparukh and his migrating horde of Proto-Bulgars from the steppes of Central Asia to the Danube region in the twenty years or so before 681, the year the Bulgars united with the Slavs and other peoples in the area to form a new state. The film features hundreds of extras, an enormous layout of costumes, and action scenes on a spectacular scale worthy of Hollywood.

By the end of 1983, Georgi Stoyanov's *Constantine the Philosopher* was completed—and then held back for release until Part Two could be made by the same director. Another two-part spectacle, set for a premiere in November 1984, is Boris Sharaliev's *Boris the First.* The former deals with the missionary activities of the brothers Cyril and Methodius, while the latter treats the conversion of the Bulgarian monarch to Christianity in the year 865.

A number of quality debut films have recently appeared upon the scene, heralding the flurry of activity in all the arts throughout the early 1980s. The "new generation" directors and their films include Evgeni Mihailov's *Home for Lonely Souls*

Ivan Pavlov's *Mass Miracle* (1981).

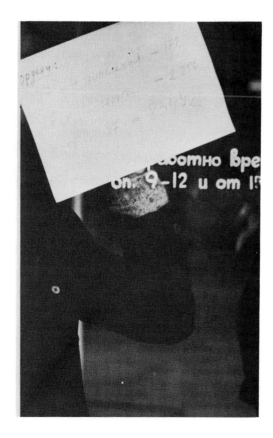

Kiran Kolarov's *The Airman* (1980).

(1981), Ivan Pavlov's *Mass Miracle,* (1981), Og-nyan Gelinov's *The Flying Machine,* Iskra Yos-sifova and Malina Petrova's *The Journey* (1980), and Kiran Kolarov's *The Airman* (1980).

Finally, a word should be said about the first feature-length cartoons to be made at the Sofia Animation Studio. Donyo Donev's *We Called Them Montagues and Capulets* (1985) was more than a year on the drawing board. Rumen Petkov's *Treasure Planet* is a variation on Robert Louis Stevenson's classic *Treasure Island.* And Slav Bakalov's *Close Distance* combines animation and live action in a science-fiction context. Without doubt, animation has made giant strides in the past few years.

The important factor for the pioneers of Bulgarian film and for the state industry was to produce films that everyone would understand. This preference for dramatic realism may have been naïve in the beginning, and it can be viewed as an irritating birthmark today, but Bulgaria's attendance figures are still among the highest in Europe. So long as one out of every two Bulgarians keeps queuing for the formula movie of old, directors will continue to make little distinction between jobs in the theater and at the studio.

Bulgarian cinema, as this short introduction has tried to illustrate, has come a long way in thirty years. It is a vibrant and folk-oriented cinema. Those who appreciate the films cannot help but love the people.

Inside Boyana

The Boyana Studios at the foot of Mount Vitosha turn out a feature film a week for cinemas or television.

The annual breakdown is about equal: twenty-five for movie screens, and the same for the TV tube. This is in addition to another twenty-five animated films, and over two hundred shorts and documentaries. There are approximately thirty-six hundred cinemas in the country. Each moviegoer is reckoned to attend the movies on an average of ten to thirteen times a year.

When one considers that as late as 1953 only one feature film was produced a year, the growth of the Bulgarian film industry is astonishing, to say the least. The statistics also show that the quality of the films rose with the increased sophistication of the home audience. Thus, it was quite natural that each decade demonstrated

134

improvement in both style and content.

A sprawling complex, the Boyana Studios are referred to as "film city" by the local population. Nearly all of the technical facilities are housed under one roof, the staff including over nine thousand qualified employees. The headquarters of Bulgarian Cinematography are also located at Boyana, save for branch offices in the center of Sofia on Rakovski Street.

The Bulgarian Cinematography has five distinct sections: the Boyana Feature Film Studio, the Sofia Animation Film Studio, the Vremé Popular Science and Documentary Film Studio, the Film Laboratory, and Bulgariafilm. Bulgariafilm, the import-export and public-relations service, prints eight times annually a news bulletin, *Bulgarian Films* (the English-language version). The Bulletin appears in English, Spanish, French, and Russian. Bulgariafilm has also published in English two booklets on Bulgarian cinematography.

Until 1983, the Boyana Studio was composed of four creative groups: Haemus, Mladost (Youth), Sredets, and Suvremenik (Contemporary), each with its own artistic director. Film directors had a choice of joining any of these groups, while each unit, in turn, had a council to assess scenarios and decide on the merits of a project. Specific themes and genres were preferred by separate groups for various reasons. Beginning in 1983, a new policy was introduced: the four creative groups were disbanded, and feature film production was placed under a double management: the first unit is headed by Zako Heskia, the second by Lyudmil Kirkov.

The setting of the Boyana Studios and the all-in-one character of the complex have proven an attraction for foreign producers. More than twenty coproductions have been made in the past with Bulgariafilm. The film lab now is on a level with others in Socialist Europe, with possibilities of handling Eastmancolor, Sovcolor, Fujicolor, and Orwocolor, as the case may be. The Sofia Animation Film Studio is a part of the "film city" at Boyana.

So far as information on Bulgarian cinema is concerned, the Bulgarian Film Archive is presently preparing a documentation on the full history of the feature films and important shorts and documentaries produced in the country since the turn of the century. Until that documentation is ready, the faulty and incomplete filmography at the back of this book will have to do. Other recommended sources are three books on Bulgarian cinema: Sergio Micheli's *Il Cinema Bulgaro* (Padua: Marsilio Editori, 1971),

Albert Cervoni's *Les écrans de Sofia* (Paris: Film éditions, Pierre L'Herminier, Editeur, 1976), and Maria Ratschewa and Klaus Eder's *Der bulgarische Film* (Frankfurt: Kommunales Kino, 1977). Sergio Micheli has also published *Cinema di Animazione in Bulgaria* (Bologna: Cappelli editore, 1975), and a complete issue of *Cinema,* the Swiss film quarterly, has been dedicated to a study and survey of Bulgarian cinema (*Grenzüberschreitung—Bulgarien / Nouveau cinéma bulgare,* No. 4/1976).

Despite the impossible task every film historian faces in trying to see the important feature films made in a certain country, I am pleased to say that all the doors were opened at the Boyana Studios, as well as the branch offices on Rakovski Street, to see, and research, whatever I wished. Nevertheless, even a decade of repeated visits to Sofia, plus the hours spent inside Boyana, was hardly enough to produce an impartial, yet factual, history of the Bulgarian cinematography.

The author takes full blame for glaring mistakes, particularly those that reach beyond the borders of the country.

Animation

During VARNA '81—the Second World Animated Film Festival—the critic Alexander Grozev detailed the history of Bulgarian animation in four brief articles published in the festival bulletin. This is how the story goes:

Back in 1915, the cartoonist Raiko Alexiev made the first fumbling attempt at an animated film based on his own drawings; he failed. It wasn't until the 1930s that the "trick" of animating a film was tried again—this time by Vassil Bakardziev on his film *The Fly.* Similar experiments by the painter Dimiter Todorov to make drawings on paper "move" were without notable success.

After the Socialist revolution (9 September 1944), the enthusiasm of artists for all genres of filmmaking spread to the field of animation, and a section for the animated cartoon was included in the plans for a State Cinematography. The first Bulgarian animated cartoon was made in 1949: *It Serves Him Right,* which was soon forgotten by the collective artists in charge. Others followed—*Wolf and Lamb* (1950) and *Republic in the Woods* (1952), in addition to the puppet-oriented *The Dangerous Bomb* (1951), *Master Manol* (1952), *Incident in the Kindergarten* (1953), *Under Pike's Orders* (1953), and *The Little Painter*—as the foundation of an animation school was constructed around the talents of Radka Buchvarova, Zdenka Doicheva, Petko Slavov, and Stefan Topaldzikov.

It wasn't until the return of Todor Dinov from the Moscow Film School, where this talented cartoonist had studied under Ivan Ivano-Vano, that Bulgarian animation truly came to life. Dinov freely mixed Disney-style animation (the standard Moscow formula) with Bulgarian folk traditions in style and content—and the result was *Brave Marko* (1953), based on a script by Hristo Santov. He had created a national figure, one imbued with the mythic and philosophical dimensions of a legendary Balkan hero.

Dinov then turned to a series of *Kino Prickles*, drawn from a contemporary satirical magazine between 1955 and 1957, and proved himself to be an innovative artist with the creation of *Little Annie* (1958) and *Prometheus* (1959). It was *Prometheus* that brought him international recognition, for it broke entirely from the naturalism of the Disney model and entered the real world of pen-and-ink drawings. It was only a step thereafter to the success of *The Story of the Pine-Tree Branch* (1960), *Duet* (1961) (codirected by Donyo

Donev), *The Lightning Rod* (1962), *Jealousy* (1963), *The Apple* (1963) (codirected by Stoyan Dukov) and *The Daisy* (1965). It is to Dinov's credit that collaborators Donev and Dukov were added as "codirectors" to projects under Dinov's inspiration and direction, for he preferred to foster talent, rather than minimize it, within the realm of his own creative genius.

Todor Dinov's cartoons sparkled with his dry wit, a graceful line, warm characters, and a surprise twist to a conventional story. Some of them—*Jealousy*, for instance—are as fresh today as when first released by the Sofia Animation Studio.

The "Dinov School" rapidly developed into a "Bulgarian Animation School," consisting of individualists with ranging interests and talents: Donyo Donev, Stoyan Dukov, Hristo Topuzanov, Pencho Bogdanov, Radka Buchvarova, Zdenka Doicheva, Ivan Vesselinov, Ivan Andonov, Proiko Proikov, Gencho Simeonov, Georgi Chavdarov, Asparukh Panov, Anri Kulev, and more recently still others. The "Golden Age of the Bulgarian School" is generally dated from the second half of the 1960s, shortly after Todor Di-

Todor Dinov's *Jealousy* (1963).

Todor Dinov's *The Daisy* (1965).

Donyo Donev's *The Clever Village* (1972).

nov won the first major prizes abroad at Oberhausen and Annecy, Cracow and Mamaia, and several other festivals with entry space for cartoons.

The philosophical parable became the trademark of the Bulgarian school. It could be found in children's films as well as in cartoons for grown-ups. Donyo Donev, who reached full maturity as a cartoonist at the beginning of the 1970s, created a series of masterful cartoons to guarantee his place in the annals of film animation: *The Three Fools* (1970), *The Clever Village* (1972), *Three Foolish Hunters* (1972), *De Facto* (1973), *The Three Fools and the Cow* (1974), *The Musical Tree* (1976), and *Causa Perduta* (1977).

With a Dinov as teacher and a Donev as pupil, it was only natural that a Dukov should also enter the picture. Stoyan Dukov did not imitate the clear line of Todor Dinov, nor did he try to equal the comic wizardry of Donyo Donev—he chose, instead, intellectual irony for his calling card. His best cartoons exhibit a variety of both style and execution to fit a precise theme: *Houses Are Forts* (1967), *Mini* (1971), *En Passant* (1975), *A Musical Story* (1976), and *February* (1977).

Ivan Andonov and Ivan Vesselinov were other festival winners during the late 1960s. Andonov won prizes at the Locarno festival for *The Shooting Range* (1964) and *Trouble* (1967). Vesselinov was a regular guest at Oberhausen at the same time with *Tightrope Walker* (1969), *The Devil in the Church* (1969), and *The Heirs* (1970).

Today, the Sofia Animation Studio is producing its first feature-length cartoons, among twenty-five cartoons and puppet films annually. Donyo Donev's *We Called Them Montagues and Capulets,* Rumen Petkov's *Treasure Planet,* and Slav Bakalov's *The Close Distance* were inspired by enthusiastic supporters, the thousands of Bulgarians, old and young, attending the biannual Varna Animation Festival. Here, in Varna, the formation of a new school is being honed to a fine edge.

A retrospective of Bulgarian animated films was organized for the 1979 Leipzig Film Festival by Krassimira Gercheva. It deserves to go on tour with the rest of Bulgaria's art treasures.

PART II

FILMOGRAPHY (1915–1985)

Key: Sc: Scenario; Dr: Director; Ass't Dr: Assistant Director. Ph: Photographer; Set: Set Design; Mu: Music; Cast: only principal actors. Dates are years of release unless otherwise noted; Prem: Premiere. Important and relevant films are in boldface.

1915

BALGARAN E GALANT / The Bulgarian Is Gallant. / Sc & Dr: Vassil Gendov. Ph: Chatanov. Cast: Vassil Gendov, Mara Lipina, Angelov, Metodi Stanoev.

Although disputed as the first feature film produced in Bulgaria, this was certainly the most popular of its time. Gendov copied a Max Linder comedy.

1917

LYUBOVTA E LUDOST / Love Is Madness. Sc & Dr: Vassil Gendov. Ph: Yossif Raifler. Cast: Vassil Gendov, Manol Kirov, Zhanna Gendova, Maria Toromanova-Hmielik.

A surviving segment of the original print in the Bulgarian Film Archive reveals Gendov to be a quite proficient actor and director. His wife, Zhanna, is equally charming in this delightful comedy, that may have been inspired by Lubitsch.

DEZATA NA BALKANA / The Sons of the Balkans. Sc: Stoyan Milenkov. Dr: Kevork Kuyumdjian (Peter K. Stoychev) Ph: Kevork Kuyumdjian (Minko Balkanski). Cast: Teodorina Stoycheva, Krastyo Sarayov, Yordan Minkov, Minko Balkanski.

A love story set in the mountains. Dragan and Neda triumph in their devotion to each other over every adversity. The background of the Balkan Wars lends patriotic fervor to the story. Noted actors from the National Theater in Sofia made their first screen appearances in this melodrama, directed by actor Peter K. Stoychev under a pseudonym.

1921

LILIANA. Sc: Konstantin Saghaev. Dr: Dimiter Panchev, Nikolai Larin. Ph: Charl Keneke. Cast: Svetoslav Kazandjiev, Zvetana Odzhakova, Ivan Zachev.

A tragic love story. The peasant Kamen is in love with the beautiful Liliana. When she dies, he commits suicide by leaping from a cliff.

DIAVOLAT V SOFIA / The Devil in Sofia. Sc & Dr: Vassil Gendov. Ph: Yossif Raifler. Cast: Vassil Gendov, Zhanna Gendova, Ivan Popov, Medy Mihailova, Georgi Sotirov, Elena Snezhina.

A comedy about the devil loose in Sofia, the leads played by Vassil and Zhanna Gendov. Iram Popov, one of the pioneers of Bulgarian theater, makes his screen appearance, as does the noted actress Elena Snezhina.

VINOVNA LI E? / Is She Guilty? Dr: Nikolai Larin. Ph: Charl Keneke. Cast: Petko Chirpanliev, Raina Nobotkova, Yordan Karafermanov, Vassil Bakardjiev, Georgi Ivanov, Johan Rosenblat.

A melodrama spiced with criminal intrigue.

1922

VOENNI DEISTVIA V MIRNO VREME / Maneuvers in Peacetime. Sc & Dr: Vassil Gendov. Ph: Yossif Raifler. Cast: Vassil Gendov, Drago Alexiev, Georgi Sotirov, Alexander Kreps, Zhanna Gendova.

A caper about foreign agents and secret documents, starring Vassil and Zhanna Gendova.

BAY GANYU. Sc & Dr: Vassil Gendov, based on a novel by Aleko Konstantinov. Ph: Yossif Raifler. Cast: Stoyan M. Popov, Stoycho Hristov, Ivan Kasabov, Yordan Karafermanov, Peter Zhishkov, Dimiter Staikov, Racho Rachev, Zhanna Sladkareva-Yakovleva.

A comic classic. The "Bay Ganyu stories" were well known in both literary circles and cabaret theaters in Sofia. The Gendov adaptation set standards in Bulgarian cinema.

POD STAROTO NEBE / Under the Old Sky. Sc: Tsanko Tserkovski, based on his drama with the same title. Dr: Nikolai Larin. Ph: Charl Keneke. / Cast: Ivan Popov, Nikola Balabanov, Petko Chirpanliev, Slatan Kasherov, Bela Ouzheva, Mila Savova.

Reckoned to be the first "art film" in Bulgarian cinema, owing to the full participation of stage personalities from the National Theater, this adaptation of Tsanko Tserkovski's drama, with Ivan Popov playing the lead, was a sensation.

1923

MOMINA SKALA / Maiden Rock. Sc & Dr: Boris Grezhov. Ph: Charl Keneke. / Cast: Mihail Gorezki, Katya Stoyanova, Yordan Minkov, Dimiter Sotirov, Boris Grezhov, Dimiter Keranov, Vera Salplieva-Staneva, Ivan Stanev, Petko Chirpanliev.

Based on a folk legend, it's the story of a poor shepherd in love with the daughter of the village mayor. This first film by a gifted director, Boris Grezhov, was made shortly after his return from the Ufa studios in Berlin.

1924

CHARLIE CHAPLIN NA VITOSHA / Charlie Chaplin on Vitosha. Sc & Dr: Vassil Bakardjiev. Ph: Hristo Konstantinov. Cast: unknown (apparently this was a montage film edited for a celebration).

A comedy made for a film ball in the Military Club of Sofia, spliced together from actual and archival footage.

1925

COVARNATA PRINZESSA TURANDOT / The Malicious Princess Turandot. Dr: Rayko Alexiev. Ph: Hristo Konstantinov. Cast: Zoya Zharankova, Rayko Alexiev, Nikola Tanev.

The story of the Princess Turandot and the quest of three suitors for her hand.

1927

CIOVEKAT, KOITO ZABRAVI BOGA / The Man Who Denied God. Sc & Dr: Vassil Gendov. Ph: Hristo Konstantinov. Cast: Vassil Gendov, Zhanna Gendova, Mitko Gendov, Sashko Kiprov, Milka Lambreva, Stavruda Frateva, Stella Dakova, Ketty Milenkova, Lyuben Georgiev.

A melodrama about an honest man whose passion for gambling leads to domestic tragedy, the imprisonment of his wife, and the brief loss of his child—until he reforms and rights the wrongs he has committed. Vassil and Zhanna play the leads in this Gendov tale-of-tears, also featuring their son Mitko.

V NOKTITE NA POROKA / In the Clutches of Sin. Sc & Dr: Johan Rosenblat (Johan Rosev). Ph: Walter Anders. Cast: Johan Rosenblat, Nadya Zaharieva, Ivan Kasabov, Racho Rachev, Yordan Karafermanov, Georgi Vassilev, Peter Damov.

A happy family idyll is ruined by the tragic death of the couple's first child. Then, after a stormy flirtation with sin

and vice, the birth of a second child brings peace back to the family hearth.

1928

PUTIAT NA BESPUTNITE / The Street of the Lost. Sc & Dr: Vassil Gendov. Ph: Hristo Konstantinov. / Cast: Vassil Gendov, Milka Erato, Zhanna Gendova, Bistra Fol, Mate Todorov, Vladimir Trandafilov, Nikola Balabanov, Docho Kasabov, Mitko Gendov.

The daughter of a poor but honest cobbler bears an illegitimate child; then, to stay alive, she has to turn to plying a trade on "the street of the lost." A neighbor's son, however, secretly loves her. A Gendov melodrama, with the acclaimed stage actor Vladimir Trandafilov in a supporting role.

VESSELA BULGARIA / Bulgaria Allegra. Sc: Dimiter Panchev. Dr: Boris Grezhov. Ph: Walter Anders. Cast: Boris Rumenov, Zvetana Rumenova, Kokon Harizanov, Mimi Balkanska, Ivan Stanev, Kosta Armyanov, Dimiter Todorov, Atanas Nikolov, Boris Pozharov, Nikola Balabanov, Ivan Kostov.

A dream comes true when a national lottery is won. It allows two friends to live a life of ease, until a charming lady enters the scene.

1929

BELOVARHA VITOSHA / Snow-Capped Mt. Vitosha. Sc & Dr: Georgi Deyanov. Ph: Franz Vut. Cast: Georgi Deyanov, Olga Ivanova, Kosan Belev, Boyan Antonov, Vera Georgieva, Manfred von Satin, Franz Vut, G. Pirev, Georgi Vassilev.

A sentimental love story set at the foot of Mt. Vitosha, the snow-capped peak located in the vicinity of Sofia where the Rila and Rhodope mountain ranges coverge.

ULICHNI BOGESTVA / Idols of the Street. Sc & Dr: Vassil Gendov. Ph: Hristo Konstantinov. Cast: Vassil Gendov, Zhanna Gendova, Vladimir Trandafilov, Kosta Hadjiminev, Bistra Fol, Peter Gabrowski, Docho Kasabov, Mitko Gendov, Ivan Slavov, Hristo Hristov.

The story of an honest worker duped by a former friend. He goes to prison, while the guilty party goes on to become a rich merchant. The Gendovs, Vassil and Zhanna, triumph over evil in the end.

SLED POSHARA W RUSSIA / After the Fire over Russia. Sc: Pancho Mihailov. Dr: Boris Grezhov. Ph: Vladimir Termen. Cast: Tacho Kolarov, Dimiter Keranov, Baronesa Loudon, Titty Tarnovskaya, Konstantin Kissimov, Vladimir Karpov, Docho Kasabov, Ivan Kasabov, Rayna Chukleva.

This masterful silent film by gifted Boris Grezhov was "rediscovered" recently in a Lausanne archival tribute to the director (he had died in Switzerland). It's a tale of love and intrigue, the protagonist being an émigré White Russian officer working now in a Bulgarian mine.

NAI VIARNATA STRAZHA / The Faithful Guard. Sc: Yordan Yovkov, Vassil Poshev, based on Yovkov's novel with the same title. Dr: Vassil Poshev. Ph: Franz Vut, Vladimir Termen. Cast: Vassil Poshev, Vladimir Trandafilov, Elena Mihailova, Elena Hristova, Mitrofan Poshev, Peter Goryanski, Peter Pavlov, Peter Kyuchukov, Peter Popov, Ivan Kasabov, Georgi Deyanov, Hristo Lesizki.

This tale of bravery, sacrifice, and patriotism was adapted to the cinema by the author of the novella himself, Yordan Yovkov, the leading Bulgarian storyteller of his day, whose fine prose set accepted standards of modern style.

LYUBOV I PRESTAPLENIE / Love and Crime. Sc: Georgi Ivanov. Dr: Nisim Koenson, Georgi Ivanov. Ph: Walter Anders. / Cast: Christina Georgieva, Yanka Yaneva, Nadya Ivanova, Angel Popov, Peter Andreyev, M. Plahov, V. Dimitrova.

A story of love and jealousy. The trouble begins when a poor young painter is taken in by a rich lady, only to fall in love with his patroness's daughter.

NA TAMEN KRASTOPAT / On a Dark Crossroad. Sc & Dr: Vassil Bakardjiev. Ph: Franz Vut. Cast: Vassil Bakardjiev, Lyuba Kokova, Tseno Nenkov.

Two rivals fight for the heart of a village beauty, the winner to be determined by his virtue and bravery.

PLENNIKAT / The Prisoner. Sc & Dr: Mihail Slavov, based on Konstantin Mutafov's drama *The Prisoner of Trikers*. Ph: Hristo Konstantinov. Cast: Mihail Slavov, Pascal Dukov, Mara Penkova, Stella Dukova, Assen Kamburov, Bogomil Andreyev, Stefan Kirov, Peter Gabrovski.

When two friends go off to war, only one returns—to fall in love with the betrothed of his friend, who is believed dead. Instead of dying, he had been taken prisoner, only to return home in peacetime and sacrifice himself for the new lovers.

1930

BURYA NA MLADOSTA / Tempest of Youth. Sc & Dr: Vassil Gendov. Ph: Hristo Konstantinov. Cast: Zhanna Gendova, Vassil Gendov, Mizho Leviev, Kosta Hadjiminev, Peter Gabrovski, Bistra Fol.

The son of a rich impresario falls in love with a lowly working girl. The father attempts to sidetrack the love affair, but all ends well at the altar.

ZEMYA / Land. Sc & Dr: Peter K. Stoychev, based on Elin Pelin's novel with the same title. Ph: Hristo Konstantinov. Cast: Pascal Dukov, Nina Stoycheva, Vessela Manafova, Teodorina Stoycheva, Peter K. Stoychev, Bogomil Andreyev, Angel Chavdarov.

This was the first adaptation of Elin Pelin's novel (published in 1922) dealing with a patriarchal peasant family's decline. The Sofia countryside was the author's favorite setting, the characters humorous and true to life.

POD ORLOVOTO GNESDO / Under the Eagle's Nest. Sc & Dr: Petko Chirpanliev. Ph: Minko Balkanski. Cast: Petko Chirpanliev, Ivan Kasabov, Georgi Ivanov, Konstantin Kiuvchiev, Zheni Prokepieva, Vassil Tanchev, Varvara Vorotinska, Ivan Popov, Nasko Chirpanliev, Spas Totev.

A love triangle. The young lovers are threatened by a rich man who also loves the girl. Falsely accused, the boy lands in prison; distraught, the girl enters a convent. But all works out well in the end via an act of bravery.

1931

KRAZHATA V EXPRESA / Robbery on the Express. Sc & Dr: Vassil Bakardjiev. Ph: Simeon Simeonov. Cast: Vassil Bakardjiev, Simeon Simeonov, Viola Yordanova, Bogomil Ivanov, Vassil Tanchev.

A rich heiress traveling from France to Istanbul on the Orient Express is robbed, setting off a chain of events in this thriller, Bulgarian style.

BESKRASTNI GROBOVE / Graves without Crosses. Sc: Boncho Nestorov, based on his novel. Dr: Boris Grezhov. Ph: Hristo Konstantinov. Mu: V. Bovchevski. Cast: Vladimir Trandafilov, Zorka Yordanova, Konstantin Kissimov, Ivan Dimov, Krastyo Sarafov, Hristo Kodjiabachev, Stefan Savov, Elena Snezhina, Nikola Balabanov, Bogomil Andreyev, L. Yordanova.

An elegy lamenting the victims of the White Terror of 1923. It was Bulgarian cinema's first sound film, and another artistic success for Boris Grezhov. The film featured leading stage personalities of the day.

1933

FAMOSNIAT KILIM / The Famous Carpet. Sc & Dr: Vassil Bakardjiev. Ph: Simeon Simeonov. Cast: Vladimor Stoyanov, Stefka Stancheva, Melina dell'Orso.

A short feature made for an advertising agency, the story of which is borrowed from a children's fairytale about a famous carpet stolen for purposes of reproducing its wonders on a commercial basis.

BUNTAT NA ROBITE / Revolt of the Slaves. Sc & Dr: Vassil Gendov. Ph: Minko Balkanski. Cast: Vassil Gendov, Zhanna Gendova, Micho Leviev, Mila Savova, Bistra Fol, Mihail Popov, Hristo Hristov, Kosta Hadjiminev, Peter Topalov.

Patriotic film based on the writings of historian Dimiter Strashimirov (brother of writer Anton Strashimirov) and the memoirs of Dimiter Kazev-Burski, as well as eyewitness accounts of the Macedonian uprisings against the Turks at the turn of the century.

1934

PLANINSKA PESEN / Song of the Mountains. Sc & Dr: Peter K. Stoychev. Ph: Yossip Novak. Mu: Nikola Atanassov. Sound: Stoyan Mishkovich. Cast: Peter K. Stoychev, Nina Stoycheva, Teodorina Stoycheva, Bistra Fol, Anna Todorova, Bistra Zvetanova, Plamen Charov, Bogomil Andreyev, Nikola Balabanov, M. Tihinova, Lyubomir Tsolotovich, Stefan Peychev, Kost Stoyanov, Atanas Hristov, Maria Kasakova, Angel Chavrarov, Nevena Docheva.

A peasant lad leaves the village for the city, where fortune smiles upon him: he receives an education and becomes a famous violinist. A torment of the soul brings him back to the place of his birth, which then inspires him in his music. The first "musical" produced in Bulgaria.

PRED OTECHESTVOTO DA SABRAVIM OMRASATA SI / Let's Forget Our Conflicts for the Sake of the Fatherland. Sc & Dr: Vassil Bakardjiev. Ph: Simeon Simeonov. Cast: Vassil Bakardjiev, Lyuba Dokova, Tseno Nenkov, Peter Dokov.

A more ambitious variation on his earlier *On a Dark Crossroad* (1929), the film has a patriotic tone to resolve differences among warring political parties under a dictatorial monarchy.

1936

GRAMADA / Cairn. Sc & Dr: Alexander Vazov, based on a

poem with the same title by Ivan Vazov. Ph: Stoyan Mishkovich. Sound: Georgi Parlapanov. Cast: Stefan Savov, Nevena Milosheva, Konstantin Kissimov, Elena Snezhina, Hristo Kodjiabashev, Nikola Balabanov, Assen Kamburov, B. Stoyanov, Panteley Hranov, Dimiter Peshev, Stefan Peychev.

Based on a famous poem by Ivan Vazov, the poet laureate of the National Revival, the film was directed by the writer's nephew and became a commercial hit. Its patriotic fervor accounted for much of the success: scenes of Bulgarian suffering under the Turkish yoke, heroism in the fight for liberation, and the matching of word and image in dramatizing verses known by heart to most of the audience. The title refers to a pile of stones erected as a monument on a roadside.

1937

ZEMIATA GORI / The Scorched Earth. Sc & Dr: Vassil Gendov. Ph: Simeon Simeonov. Sound: Robert Hetman. Cast: Vassil Gendov, Zhanna Gendov, Diana At. Hristova, Vicho Raykov, Ivan Arzhentinski, Viara Belcheva.

The Gendovs' eleventh and last film in over twenty years of producing, writing, directing, editing, and acting in their homemade features, this one about a drunkard who mistreats his wife and daughter but repents in the end.

1938

STRAHIL VOYVODA / Strahil the Voyvoda. Sc: Orlin Vassilev, based on his novel. Dr & Ph: Yossip Novak. Mu: Vesselin Stoyanov. Cast: Ivan Dimov, Ruzha Delcheva, Bogomil Andreyev, Dimiter Peshev, Assen Kamburov, Ivan Popov, Rosho Rishov, Kosta Rainov, Boris Kirchev, Leo Konfortov, Boris Borozanov.

Based on Orlin Vassilev's romantic novel *The Haiduk Who Couldn't Take Care of His Mother*, this was the writer's first screenplay; it's the story of a legendary outlaw hero during the period of the Turkish oppression.

1939

NASTRADIN HOGGIA I HITAR PETER / Nastradin Hoggia and Sly Peter. Sc & Dr: Alexander Vazov. Ph: Hans Tayer. Sound: Georgi Parlapanov, Kiril Popov. Cast: Assen Kamburov, Stoyan Buchvarov, Vesselin Simeonov, Vladimir Keranov.

A humorous folkloric tale about the relationship of a Turk with a Bulgarian adept at pulling the wool over the eyes of his adversary.

1940

ZA RODINATA / For Our Country. Sc: Collective of writers and artists (Boris Grezhov). Dr: Boris Grezhov. Ph: Stefan Petrov. Mu: Nikola Tsonev. Sound: Georgi Parlapanov, Kiril Popov. Cast: Vladimir Trandafilov, Dimiter Keranov, Simeon Simeonov, Lily Topalova, Vessela Baltadjieva, Ivan Charachiev, Stefcho Kirov.

A patriotic film about two friends who go willingly to the front as the Second World War breaks out, to fight for God and country.

TE POBEDIHA / They Were Victorious. Sc & Dr: Boris Borozanov. Ph: Yossip Novak, Hristo Konstantinov. Mu: Georgi Antonov, Ivan Kavaldjiev. Cast: Rusha Delcheva,

Petko Atanassov, Nadezhda Kostova, Hristo Kodjiabashev, Stavruda Frateva, Ivan Kirchev, Lily Popivanova, Nikola Kazandjiev, Panteley Hranov, Boris Ganchev, Georgi Savov, Vesselin Simeonov.

The rivalry between two suitors for the hand of a lovely maiden stretches even to the battlefield—where one saves the life of the other, and they become friends forever. The film was patriotically dedicated to Tsar and Fatherland during the war.

1941

BALGARSKI ORLI / Bulgarian Eagles. Sc & Dr: Boris Borozanov. Ph: Peter Yurizin. Mu: Georgi Antonov. Sound: Georgi Parlapanov, Kiril Popov. Cast: Irina Tasseva, Nikola Ikonomov, K. Vassilev, K. Kasabov, Zora Ogneva, Yordan Seykov, Marin Toshev, Alexander Stoyanov, Stoyan Evgeniev, Kasta Naumov.

Another patriotic war film by a director adept at action and melodrama, this one dealt with the feats of Bulgarian pilots.

STOINE U KOSTENURKA / Stoine the Tortoise. Sc & Dr: Boris Borozanov. Ph: Georgi Parlapanov. Sound: Kiril Popov. Cast: Panteley Hranov, Asparukh Temelkov, Nadya Kostova, Ivan Popov.

The third patriotic film in a row by Boris Borozanov, this one about a young man's adventures in military camp as he trains to fight on the front.

SCIUSCIU-MUSCIU / Tittle-Tatle. Sc: P. K. Chinkov. Dr: Boris Grezhov. Ph: Stefan Petrov. Cast: Stefan Savov, Panteley Hranov, Dimiter Chavdarov, D. Abadjiev, Kasta Naumov, A. Petrov, V. Krayevski, S. Stanchev, H. Nikolov, E. Kozey.

A thriller involving a police inspector on a train and a fast-talking swindler, the moral of which is to keep government officials informed on the activities of thieves and agents in the country.

LYUBOVTA NA SEMCARIA / The Rake's Love. Sc, Dr & Ph: Spas Totev. Cast: Georgi Djivilekov, Zhanna Bayzhanova, Dimiter Daskalov, Ivan Bishev, people of Pazardjik.

A patriotic film about a boy in love with a girl whose father insists that he must prove himself as a man first—so the "rake" goes to the front and thus wins the hand of his love. Moral: thus the country is guaranteed proud soldiers.

1942

ISPITANIE / The Test. Dr: Hrisan Tsankov. Ass't Dr: Anton Marinovich. Ph: Hezhi. Mu: Peter Fenish, Georgi Antonov. Cast: Ivan Dimov, Nadya Nozharova, Krastyo Sarafov, Stoyan Kolarov, Lily Popivanova, Boris Ganchev, Rumen Gherchev, Ekaterina Sableva.

A melodrama about love and deception. A rich man suspects his wife of being unfaithful, but when the wife is put to a test to prove her love, peace is restored to the marriage.

1943

SVATBA / Marriage. Sc: Dimiter Simidov, based on his story with the same title. Dr: Boris Borozanov. Ph: Boncho Karastoyanov. Mu: Parashkev Hadjiev. Sound: Georgi Parlapanov, Kiril Popov. Cast: Manya Bizheva, Assen Kamburov, Stefan Peychev, Simeon Simeonov, Stefan Savov, Vesselin Simeonov.

A melodrama based on a well-known story, made by the most active film director of the war years, Borozanov, whose flair for theatricality placed him in the front of the struggling national film industry.

IVA SAMODIVA / Iva the Fairy. Sc & Dr: Kiril Petrov. Cast: Dorina Illeva, Lyubomir Zhelyazkov, Asparukh Temelkov, Sijka Petrova, Maria Yaznikova, Zoya Zharankova, M. Popov, Vesselin Simeonov, Pateley Hranov, Nikola Ikonomov.

A triangle of jealousy develops during an ocean cruise, involving a young girl, an older man, and a young boy. The title refers to the legend of the fairy Iva: she infatuated men as does the girl in the film.

BULGARSKO-UNGARSKA RAPSODIA / Bulgarian-Hungarian Rhapsody. Dr: Boris Borozanov, Frigyes Ban. Ph: Georgi Parlapanov. Cast: Magda Kolzhakova, Hristo Kodjiabashev, Dorita Boneva. A coproduction with Hungary.

A Bulgarian-Hungarian coproduction, also known as *Encounter on the Beach*. The scene is a music conservatory in Budapest, where two girls from Bulgarian villages are studying. They meet a pair of Hungarian students, marry in a double wedding, and settle in Bulgaria.

1944

ROSIZZA. Sc & Dr: Boris Borozanov. Ph: Georgi Parlapanov. Cast: L. Popov, Elena Snezhina, Lyubomir Zhelyazkov, Maria Kirova, Panteley Hranov, Andrei Chaprazov, Olga Kircheva, Katya Dimova.

A detective thriller. A young man of means is engaged to a rich girl, but is infatuated with a young chambermaid. When he is falsely accused of committing a murder, the engagement is off—it's Rosizza who stands by him until the mystery is solved, whereupon they marry.

1945

SHTE DOIDAT NOVI DNI / New Days Will Come. Sc: Anton Marinovich, Stefan Topaldjikov, Dr: Anton Marinovich. Ph: Boncho Karastoyanov. Mu: B. Leviev. Sound: Georgi Parlapanov, Kiril Popov. Cast: N. Dikov, T. Gecheva, Assen Kamburov. M. Gencheva, M. Germanova, Asparukh Temelkov, M. Dayrova, Stoyan Kuyumdjiev. A Juzhe-Film production.

Released in May 1945 just as times were changing, this is a story of peasants revolting against rich landowners to obtain their rights and herald the coming of a new day. The first film produced after the September 1944 Revolution.

BULGARI OT STARO VREME / Bulgarians of Ancient Times Sc, Dr & Ph: Dimiter Minkov, based on a novel by Lyuben Karavelov. Mu: N. Terziev. Cast: Stoyan Buchvarov, Elena Hranova, Petko Atanassov, A. Andonova, V. Vachev, N. Galabova, E. Tugarov. A Balkan-Film production.

A popular hit in the postwar months, this combination of a well-known literary source and favorite stage actors sets a pattern for Bulgarian cinema in the years to come.

1946

MENE ME, MAMO, SMEY LYUBI / Mama, a Dragon

Loves Me. Sc, Dr & Ph: Vassil Bakardjiev. Mu: Georgi Antonov. Sound: Georgi Parlapanov, Kiril Popov. Cast: Z. Vassileva, K. Georgiev, Eugenia Kozareva, L. Dyelyekanova, L. Angelov, Istilian Krastev, M. Krasteva, M. Stanoev. A Bazhra-Film production.

A light comedy. The story was taken from a motif supplied by a popular song, titled *Rada and the Monster*.

OGNENA DIRYA / Traces of Fire. Sc: Boris Borozanov, K. Popov, P. Pirinski. Dr: Boris Borozanov. Ph: Georgi Parlapanov, Vassil Holiolchev. Mu: Parashkev Hadjiev. Sound: Georgi Parlapanov, Kiril Popov. Cast: Lyubomir Zhelyazkov, M. Stoyanova, Nikola Popov, Stefan Petrov, M. Seymankova, P. Vitanov. A Film-Front production.

A patriotic tale set in the times of the Turkish Oppression. The resistance is led back then by the *haiduks*, outlaw bands under an elected leader, called a *voivoda*. A love interest also surfaces.

BORBA ZA SHASTIE / The Struggle for Happiness. Sc: Vladimir Yurizin. Dr: Ivan Fichev. Ph: Simeon Simeonov. Cast: Lyubomir Zhelyazkov, Helena Chakirova, Vassil Kirkov, Eva Ficheva, Lina Veleva, Marta Myankova, D. Pavlov, D. Bochev, K. Kyurkchiev. A Slav-Film Production.

A political thriller set on the eve of the 1944 Revolution. A composer suspects his girl of having a relationship with a sculptor, for whom she acts as a model. In truth, the sculptor is a member of the Communist Underground. A shootout with the police takes place: some Communists are taken prisoners, then comes the liberation in the nick of time to save them.

1947

OTNOVO IVI GIVOTA / Return to a New Life. Sc: Stoyan Topaldjikov, Georgi Bozhoyavlenski, Stefan Z. Daskalov, A. Vulchanov, Nikola Ikomonov. Dr: Georgi Bozhoyavlenski. Ph: Yossip Novak. Mu: Pancho Vladizhgerov. Cast: K. Yankov, Av. Kazarova, M. Mancheva, V. Grozeva, V. Dimitrova, Assen Kamburov, Nikola Popov, Petko Atanassov. A Rila-Film production.

A violinist returns from the war as an invalid having lost his hands. But his true love and friends stand by him, and he overcomes his pessimism to join in the building of a new society.

BOYKA. Sc, Dr & Ph: Dimiter Minkov, based on Dimiter Gemidjinski's popular play with the same title. Mu: N. Terziev. Cast: Stoyan Buchvarov, L. Lambrev, M. Makedonski, Elena Hranova, Marta Myankova, Petko Atanassov, Stoyan Stoychev, M. Gemidjiyska. A Balkan-Film production.

"Boyka" is the name of a female *Voivoda*, the leader of an outlaw band of *Haiduks* in the time of the Turkish Oppression. Outlawry was an accepted form of resistance, and this legendary song and folk-drama features a famous woman outlaw.

ISKUPLENIE / Atonement. Sc & Dr: Boris Grezhov. Ph: Vassil Holiolchev. Cast: Boris Mihalilov, Elena Hranova, Maria Yaznikova, Hristo Rukov, Tsvetana Yanakieva. A Balkan-Film production.

A complex tale of shame and expiation. A merchant is assaulted and robbed of funds entrusted to his keeping. The shame leads him to fake his death, so that his relatives in the village now believe he's dead. Returning home in disguise, however, he takes note of the wrong he has committed, and decides to leave his homeland forever to atone for the deception. (In the original script, the story ends differently: he is recognized by his relatives, who rejoice that he is still alive.)

A Footnote

Of the fifty-five feature films listed above, many of the silent ones were lost in the Second World War during a bombing raid on Sofia. After the Liberation in September 1944, private companies continued to produce eight more films on their own—then, in 1948, the film industry was nationalized. One of the productions begun by a private company, Boris Borozanov's *Kalin the Eagle* (1950), was released as the first of the newly established Bulgarian State Film Industry—officially correct, but hardly the real beginning of modern Bulgarian cinema. It makes more sense to close the chapter of "Early Film History" in Bulgaria with *Kalin the Eagle.* Zahari Zhandov's *Alarm* (1951) opens a new era.

Only recently, a retrospective of the early feature films produced in Bulgaria was programmed at the Bulgarian Filmotheque in Sofia. The fifty-five features made by private companies in the years before 1950 were presented in chronological order, so far as copies (or excerpts of copies) survived and could be preserved for archival exhibition. The series was succeeded by a presentation of the more than 350 feature films produced by the Bulgarian State Cinematography since 1950. Thus every film made in the country for the general entertainment of the population could be viewed by the public in conjunction with the anniversary celebration in 1981 of the founding of Bulgaria 1,300 years ago. It was a national event welcomed by both critics and historians, as well as a chronicle of a national cinema from birth to full maturity.

So far as wide-screen and color productions are concerned (other than those made in coproduction with foreign countries), the major advances were made in the mid-1960s. Vulo Radev's *Tsar and General* (1966) was the first definitive use of wide-screen cinematography, its success at home equalled abroad by Grisha Ostrovski and Todor Stoyanov's *Sidetrack* (1967). The first color wide-screen production was Nikola Korabov's *Freedom or Death* (1969), surpassed in quality by Vulo Radev's *The Black Angels* (1970). The first large-scale spectacle to make full use of modern cinematography's technology was Lyudmil Staikov's *Khan Asparukh* (1981). Color was the rule by 1973.

1950

KALIN ORELAT / Kalin the Eagle. Sc: Orlin Vassilev. Dr: Boris Borozanov. Ph: Vassil Holiolchev. Set: Ivan Penkov, Alexander Milenkov. Mu: Parashkev Hadjiev. Cast: Ivan Dimov, Petya Lambrinova, Boris Ganchev, Stefan Petrov, Konstantin Kissimov. 93 mins. Prem: March 20.

The wedding of Bulgarian patriotic cinema to the Socialist schematic formula. The rebel Kalin, nicknamed "Eagle," returns to his homeland after fifteen years in exile as a Turkish prisoner. Now he finds that the struggle must go on—against the new exploiters of the peasants.

1951

TREVOGA / Alarm. Sc: Orlin Vassilev, Angel Wagenstein. Dr: Zahari Zhandov. Ph: Emil Rashev, Zahari Zhandov. Set: Assen Shopov. Mu: Lyubomir Pipkov. Cast: Stefan Savov, Nadya Stanislavska, Gancho Ganchev, Karolina Gancheva, Rangel Vulchanov. 119 mins. Prem: February 19.

A major breakthrough in Bulgarian cinema, due to the cooperative efforts of director Zhandov (a documentary filmmaker) and screenplay writer Wagenstein (fresh from the Moscow Film School) in adapting Vassilev's drama of a family conflict to the screen. A father with two sons, one a Fascist loyalist and the other a Communist partisan, is faced with a difficult decision of taking sides. Prizewinner at Karlovy Vary.

UTRO NAD RODINATA / Dawn over the Homeland. Sc: Kamen Kalchev. Dr: Anton Marinovich, Stefan Surchadjiev. Ph: Boncho Karastoyanov, Konstantin Yanakiev. Set: Hristo Velkov, Mony Aladjemov, Lyuben Tapkov. Mu: Todor Popov. Cast: Lyubomir Kabakchiev, Ivan Stefanov, Zheni Bozhinova, Apostol Karamitev. 88 mins. Prem: October 22.

Schematic formula film on the construction of a new Bulgaria.

1952

DANKA. Sc: Krastyo Belev. Dr: Ivan Fichev, Boris Borozanov, Kiril Ilinchev. Ph: Vassil Holiolchev, Boncho Karastoyanov. Set: Ivan Penkov. Mu: Dimiter Saghaev, Georgi Ivanov. Cast: Milka Tuykova, Ivanka Dimitrova, Miroslav Mindov, Ivan Kumanov. 90 mins. Prem: March 24.

Story of a girl named Danka growing up during the antifascist resistance period.

POD IGOTO / Under the Yoke. Sc: Pavel Spassov, Georgi Kransov, based on the novel with the same title by Ivan Vazov. Dr: Dako Dakovski. Ph: Boncho Karastoyanov. Set: Georgi Popov, Stoyan Sotirov. Mu: Filip Kutev. Cast: Miroslav Mindov, Lily Popivanova, Petko Karlukovski, Vassil Kirkov, Nikola Popov. 123 mins. Prem: November 10.

A literary adaptation of the most famous novel by the Bulgarian national poet, Ivan Vazov. The novel had already been dramatized for the stage, and this appears to be a supportive source in the making of the film. Nevertheless, Dako Dakovski proved to be an adept chronicler of village life. The epic tale is set in Bulgaria under the Turks before the April 1876 Rebellion.

1953

NASHA SEMYA / Our Land. Sc: Angel Wagenstein, Chaim Oliver. Dr: Anton Marinovich, Stefan Surchadjiev. Ph: Emil Rashev. Set: Assen Grozev. Mu: Konstantin Iliev, Alexander Raichev. Cast: Apostol Karamitev, Milka Tuykova, Peter Dimitrov, Georgi Kaloyanchev. 95 mins. Prem: January 5.

Schematic formula film on family relations in the years of change in new Bulgaria.

1954

PESSEN SA CHOVEKA / Song of Man. Sc: Hristo Ganev. Dr: Borislav Sharaliev. Ph: Emil Rashev. Set: Peter Nikolov, Georgi Penchev, Yordan Yordanov. Mu: Georgi Ivanov. Cast: Dinko Dinev, Stefan Karalambov, Ivan Bratanov, Ivan Tonev, Nikolina Lekova. 115 mins. Prem: January 11.

Set in the period of the antifascist struggle, the film is a tribute to poet Nikola Vaptsarov, who was executed by a firing squad in 1942. A step in the right direction by two graduates of the Moscow Film School, Ganev and Sharaliev.

SEPTEMVRIYTSI / Septembrists. Sc: Angel Wagenstein. Dr: Zahari Zhandov. Ph: Vassil Holiolchev. Set: José

Sancha. Mu: Lyubomir Pipkov. Cast: Asparukh Temelkov, Boris Ganchev, Lyuboslav Stefanov, Ivan Bratanov, Ani Damyanova. 123 mins. Prem: April 26.

Warm, human portraits mark a new trend in Bulgarian cinema. The bonds of Socialist schematic principles are broken in presenting a historically researched account of the uprising in September 1923.

GRANIZATA / The Border. Sc: Gencho Stoev. Dr: Nikola Minchev. Ph: Georgi Karayordanov. Set: Mony Aladjemov. Mu: Emil Georgiev. Cast: Kunka Baeva, Ivan Bratanov, Bozhidar Milushev. 117 minutes. Prem: June 1.

Formula film along schematic principles set down in Socialist cinema.

SNAHA / The Daughter-in-Law. Sc: Georgi Karaslavov, based on his play with the same title. Dr: Krastyo Mirski, Anton Marinovich. Ph: Boncho Karastoyanov. Set: Georgi Karakashev, Assen Grozev. Mu: Boyan Ikonomov. Cast: Peter Dimitrov, Margarita Duparinova, Vera Kovacheva, Peter Stoychev, Milka Yanakieva. 116 mins. Prem: September 6.

Literary adaptation of a well known theater play. The theater director Krastyo Mirski collaborated with the film director Anton Marinovich on the production.

1955

GEROITE NA SCHIPKA / The Heroes at Shipka Pass. Sc: A. Perevenzev. Dr: Sergei Vassilev. Ph: Mihail Kyrilov. Set: Mihail Bogdanov, Genadi Myasnikov, Georgi Popov. Mu: Nikolai Kryukov, Filip Kutev. Cast: Ivan Pereversev, Victor Avdyushko, Apostol Karamitev, Petko Karlukovski, Evgeni Samoilov, Zheni Bozhinova, Katya Chukova. (Coproduction with the Soviet Union). 138 mins. Prem: April 25.

Epic color production directed by Soviet veteran Sergei Vassilev. It covers a heroic chapter in the Bulgarian struggle for independence from Turkey. During the Russo-Turkish War of 1877–78, a Bulgarian Corps of Volunteers assisted the Russians in the defense of the Shipka Pass in central Bulgaria.

NESPOKOEN PAT / The Troubled Road. Sc: Stoyan Daskalov. Dr: Dako Dakovski. Ph: Emil Rashev. Set: Naiden Petkov. Mu: Filip Kutev. Cast: Ivan Bratanov, Tsvetana Nikolova, Stefan Savov, Georgi Georgiev-Gets. 116 mins. Prem: May 23.

With this film Dako Dakovski established himself as the leading exponent of the Bulgarian peasant and village life in general in the new national film industry. This is arguably the best film of the six he made on the theme.

1956

TOVA SE SLUCHI NA ULIZATA / It Happened on the Streets. Sc. Pavel Vezhinov. Dr: Yanko Yankov. Ph: Georgi Karayordanov. Set: Assen Grozev. Mu: Alexander Raichev. Cast: Apostol Karamitev, Petya Lambrinova, Zheni Bozhinova, Stefan Paychev, Lyubomir Sharlandjiev, Andrei Chaprazov. 87 mins. Prem: March 3.

A contemporary theme with comic elements. It featured a love story and was remarkable for the realistic elements that lent credibility to the tale. A tie to Italian neorealism has been noted by critics.

DIMITROVGRADISI / People of Dimitrovgrad. Sc: Buryan Enchev. Dr: Nikola Korabov, Ducho Mundrov. Ph: Valo Radev. Set: Simeon Chalachev. Mu: Stefan Remenkov.

Cast: Georgi Kaloyanchev, Maria Russalieva, Ivan Dimov, Boris Chirkov, Ina Makarova. 112 mins. Prem: April 30.

The building of a new city, Dimitrovgrad, and a new Socialist society.

SLEDITE OSTAVAT / The Traces Remain. Sc: Pavel Vezhinov, based on his novella "Incident on a Quiet Street." Dr: Peter Vassilev. Ph: Boncho Karastoyanov. Set: Tsenko Boyadjiev. Mu: Parashkev Hadjiev. Cast: Krassimir Medarov, Vera Drazhostinova, Stefan Danailov, Georgi Naumov. 100 mins. Prem: November 3.

A "film for youth" with an adventurous detective story to carry it along. A remake of the same Vezhinov story was produced in 1981 under the title *Crime in Yellow*, directed by Marianna Evstatieva.

REBRO ADAMOVO / Adam's Rib. Sc: Angel Wagenstein. Dr: Anton Marinovich. Ph: Emil Rashev. Set: Slatka Dabova. Mu: Konstantin Iliev. Cast: Emilia Radeva, Georgi Popov, Lyubomir Kabakchiev, Nikola Popov. 98 mins. Prem: October 1.

A contemporary theme on equal rights for women, it treats of Muslim women in the Rhodope Mountains still wearing the veil.

EKIPAZHAT NA NADEZHDA / The Crew from Nadezhda. Sc: Vesselin Hanchev. Dr: Kiril Ilinchev. Ph: Konstantin Yanakiev, Trendafil Zahariev. Set: Slatka Dabova. Mu: Georgi Ivanov. Cast: Nikola Marinov, Vesselin Marinov, Hristian Russinov, Stefan Gadularov, Sashka Ignatieva, Andrei Chaprazov. 97 mins. Prem: November 3.

In Autumn 1918, the crew of the Bulgarian cruiser *Nadezhda*, anchored in the port of Sevastopol in the Ukraine, refused to obey orders in an action against the Bolsheviks shortly after the October Revolution.

EDNA BULGARKA / A Bulgarian Woman. Sc & Dr: N. Borovishki, based on Ivan Vazov's novella with the same title. Ph: Konstantin Yanakiev. Set: Peter Nikolov. Mu: Dimiter Seghaev. Cast: Penka Vassileva, Lyubomir Bovchevski, Stefan Peychev. 22 mins. Prem: November 26.

A short feature on the challenge facing the new Bulgarian woman.

TOCHKA PARVA / Item One. Sc: Valeri Petrov. Dr: Boyan Danovski. Ph: Vassil Holiolchev, Dimo Kolarov. Set: José Sancha. Mu: Peter Stupel. Cast: Rumyana Chokoyska, Vesselin Boyadjiev, Stefan Dimitrov, Zheni Bozhinova. 80 mins. Prem: November 26.

A children's film directed by a theater personality and adapted from a stage production. This was Valeri Petrov's first screenplay.

DVE POBEDI / Two Victories. Sc: Angel Wagenstein, Vesselin Hanchev, Hristo Ganev. Dr: Borislav Sharaliev. Ph: Georgi Georgiev. Set: Georgi Popov, Peter Nikolov, Assen Grozev. Mu: Emil Georgiev, Peter Stupel. Cast: Nikola Popov, Assen Milanov, Nikolina Lekova, Pencho Petrov. 92 mins. Prem: December 31.

A contemporary comedy, in a light vein.

1957

ZEMYA / Land. Sc: Vesselin Hanchev, based on Elin Pelin's novel with the same title. Dr: Zahari Zhandov. Ph: Boncho Karastoyanov. Set: José Sancha. Mu: Lyubomir Pipkov.

Anton Marinovich's *Adam's Rib* (1956).

Lev Arnstam's *History Lesson* (1957).

Cast: Bogomil Simeonov, Ginka Stancheva, Slavka Slavova, Stefan Petrov. 102 mins. Prem: March 4.

A remake of Peter K. Stoychev's silent film adaptation of the same novel in 1930.

TAYNATA VECHERYA NA SEDMATSITE / The Secret Supper of the Sedmaks. Sc: Stoyan Daskalov. Dr: Dako Dakovski. Ph: Emil Rashev. Set: Tsenko Boyadjiev. Mu: Boyan Ikonomov. Cast: Ivan Bratanov, Nikola Boychev, Dimiter Buynozov. 99 mins. Prem: March 18.

Peasants and village life, with added comic elements.

UROK NA ISTORIYATA / History Lesson. Sc & Dr: Lev Arnstam. Ph: Alexander Shelenkov, Yolanda Chen-Yu-Lan. Set: Alexander Parchomenko, Assen Grozev. Mu: Kara Laraev. Cast: Stefan Savov, Tsvetana Arnaudova, Ivan Tonev, Georg Yudin. (Coproduction with the Soviet Union.) 91 mins. Prem: May 27.

An epic Soviet-Bulgarian coproduction based on the records of the Leipzig Trial in 1933, in which Georgi Dimitrov played a heroic role.

LEGENDA ZA LYUBOVTA / LEGENDA O LÁSCE / Legend of Love. Sc: Václav Krška, Jaroslav Beránek, based on a play by Turkish poet Nazim Hikmet. Dr: Václav Krška. Ph: Ferdinand Pečenka. Set: Georgi Popov. Mu: Vesselin Stoyanov. Cast: Apostol Karamitev, Zheni Bozhinova, Emilia Radeva, Andrei Chaprazov, František Smolik, Otilia Benšikova, Zdenka Kampf, Frantisek Kovarčik, with Přemysl Kočí. (Coproduction with Czechoslovakia.) 81 mins. Prem: August 26.

Lyrical approach in color to a romantic theme, directed and photographed by a Czech team.

LABAKAN. Sc: Václav Krška, Jaroslav Beránek, based on a fairy tale by Wilhelm Hauff. Dr: Václav Krška. Ph: Ferdinand Pecauenka. Set: Bogomil Kulič. Mu: Jaromil Burghauser. Cast: Eduard Cupák, Jana Rybářová, Karel Fiala. (Coproduction with Czechoslovakia.) 75 mins. Prem: September 30.

Actually filmed before *Legend of Love* and released in Czechoslovakia in 1956, this was a second coproduction with a Czech team. A fairy tale filmed in color.

GODINI ZA LYUBOV / Years of Love. Sc: Vesselin Hanchev. Dr: Yanko Yankov. Ph: Vulo Radev. Set: Simeon Halachev. Mu: Alexander Raychev. Cast: Stefan Dobrev, Ruzha Delcheva, Antonia Cholcheva, Lyubomir Sharlandjiev, Nevena Kokanova. 79 mins. Prem: December 16.

A controversial film, dealing with problems of love and matrimony. The screenplay was written by the Bulgarian poet, Vesselin Hanchev, and Nevena Kokanova made her first appearance in a bit role. The cameraman, Vulo Radev, was to make a variation on the same theme, *The Peach Thief* (1964).

1958

HAYDUSHKA KLETVA / The Oath of the Haiduks. Sc: Orlin Vassilev. Dr: Peter Vassilev. Ph: Dimo Kolarov. Set: Slatka Dabova. Mu: Alexander Raychev. Cast: Apostol Karamitev, Ginka Stancheva, Stefan Peychev. 96 mins. Prem: January 6.

A legend about the outlaw bands, the *Haiduks*, fighting against Turkish oppression in Ottoman times.

GERATSITE / The Gerak Family. Sc: Hristo Santov, based on Elin Pelin's novel with the same title. Dr: Anton Marinovich. Ph: Trendafil Zahariev. Set: Naiden Petkov. Mu: Constantin Iliev. Cast: Georgi Stamatov, Angelina Sarova, Ivan Dimov, Gancho Ganchev. 96 mins. Prem: February 10.

A literary adaptation of Elin Pelin's epic story (written in 1911), about the tragic downfall of a patriarchal landowner, Yordan Gerak, and his family.

PARTIZANI (ZHIVOTAT SI TECHE TIHO) / Partisans (Life Flows Quietly By). Sc: Hristo Ganev. Dr: Binka Zhelyazkova, Hristo Ganev. Ph: Vassil Holiolchev. Set: Assen Grozev. Mu: Georgi Ivanov. Cast: Bogomil Simeonov, Georgi Georgiev-Gets, Emilia Radeva, Ivan Bratanov, Dimiter Buynozov, Ivanka Dimitrova, Ivan Kondov, Lyubomir Dimitrov, Nikola Dadov, Kunka Baeva, Adriana Andreyeva. 106 mins. Prem: restricted release only.

Never officially released, *Partisans*—or as it was also titled, *Life Flows Quietly By*—told the story of political careerists and touched upon the lives of former partisan heroes. It was shot at the same time as Rangel Vulchanov's *On a Small Island*, and merits being reviewed together with the latter as a key film in the postwar era.

NA MALKIYA OSTROV / On a Small Island. Sc: Valeri Petrov. Dr: Rangel Vulchanov. Ph: Dimo Kolarov. Set: Hristo Neykov. Mu: Simeon Pironkov. Cast: Ivan Kondov, Stefan Peychev, Konstantin Kotsev, Ivan Andonov, Naycho Petrov. 98 mins. Prem: May 5.

A milestone in Bulgarian (and East European) film history. The film was shot in a month's time and owes much of its poetic character to screenplay writer Valeri Petrov, who collaborated with director Rangel Vulchanov from the start. The historical theme of the 1923 uprising is raised to a universal plane.

SIROMASHKA RADOST / Poor Man's Happiness. Sc & Dr: Anton Marinovich, based on an Elin Pelin story. Ph: Trendafil Zahariev. Set: Naiden Petkov, Tsenko Boyadjiev. Mu: Konstantin Iliev. Cast: Ivan Dimov, Georgi Stamatov, Emilia Radeva, Kosta Tsonev, Ivan Bratanov. 82 mins. Prem: July 28.

Uninspired adaptation of an Elin Pelin story. The writer—Elin Pelin was a pseudonym for Dimiter Ivanov—was highly estimated in the postwar years.

ZAKONAT NA MORETO / Law of the Sea. Sc: Chaim Oliver, Angel Wagenstein. Dr: Yakim Yakimov. Ph: Georgi Karayordanov. Set: Alexander Djakov. Mu: Ivan Marinov. Cast: Georgi Georgiev-Gets, Ani Damyanova, Bogomil Simeonov. 95 mins. Prem: September 22.

Set during the Second World War, it's the story of a German warship in the Bulgarian harbor of Sozopol.

GOLEMANOV. Sc & Dr: Kiril Ilinchev, based on a satirical play by Stefan L. Kostov with same title. Ph: Trendafil Zahariev. Set: Slatka Dabova. Mu: Ivan Marinov. Cast: Nikola Popov, Andrei Chaprazov, Penka Ikonomova, Penka Vassileva. 85 mins. Prem: October 27.

More than likely, the inspiration for Stefan L. Kostov's satirical play came from Gogol, although Aleko Konstantinov's fictional character, Bay Ganyu, paved the way for this memorable character. The comedy, penned in 1927, is a perennial on Bulgarian stages, and this film adaptation remains faithful to the original.

LYUBIMEZ TRINAJSET / Favorite No. 13. Sc: Lyuben Popov, Vladimir Yanchev. Dr: Vladimir Yanchev. Ph: Georgi Georgiev. Set: Nedelcho Nanev. Mu: Peter Stupel. Cast: Apostol Karamitev, Ginka Stancheva, Pencho Petrov, Petko Karlukovski, Georgi Karev. 88 mins. Prem: December 15.

A fresh comedy by a director who was to specialize in the genre for two decades to come. The twist is the reduction of success in life to a right combination of numbers representing moods and temperaments.

1959

ZDEZDI / STERNE / Stars. Sc: Angel Wagenstein. Dr: Konrad Wolf. Ph: Werner Bergmann. Set: José Sancha. Mu: Simeon Pironkov. Cast: Sasha Krusharska, Jürgen Frohriep, Erich Klein, Stefan Peychev, Georgi Naumov, Hannjo Hasse. (Coproduction with the German Democratic Republic.) 103 mins. Prem: March 23.

An extraordinary collaborative effort between two former students at the Moscow Film Academy, East Germany's Konrad Wolf and Bulgaria's Angel Wagenstein. This compassionate love story between a German soldier and a Jewish girl during the transportation movements to Auschwitz speaks for humanity. Special Jury Prize at Cannes, 1959.

MALKATA / The Little Girl. Sc: Lyuben Stanev. Dr: Nikola Korabov. Ph: Konstantin Yanakiev. Set: Iskra Licheva. Mu: Parashkev Hadjiev. Cast: Margarita Ilieva, Anani Yavashev, Ivan Dimov, Stefan Gadularov. 94 mins. Prem: May 4.

A love story set in contemporary Bulgaria. The social and political conditions mirror the "changes in the wind" quite accurately.

KOMANDIRAT NA OTRYADA / The Commander of the Detachment. Sc: Velcho Chankov. Dr: Ducho Mundrov. Ph: Dimo Kolarov. Set: Konstantin Russakov. Mu: Lyubomir Pipkov. Cast: Kosta Tsonev, Miroslav Mindov, Irina Aktasheva, Ivan Dimov, Tsvetana Nikolova. 107 mins. Prem: August 31.

A partisan story, made by a director who was to specialize in the "Eastern" genre. One of the stars of the film, Irina Aktasheva, was to form a directorial team with Hristo Piskov. The pair studied at the Moscow Film Academy, Aktasheva as a Soviet actress.

V NAVECHERIETO / On The Eve. Sc: Vladimir Petrov, Orlin Vassilev, based on Ivan Turgenev's story. Dr: Vladimir Petrov. Ph: Vulo Radev. Set: Levan Shengelaya, Simeon Halachev. Mu: Aram Khachaturian. Cast: Lyubomir Kabakchiev, Irina Milopolskaya, Boris Livanov, Olga Androvskaya. (Coproduction with the Soviet Union.) 88 mins. Prem: December 21.

Literary adaptation of Turgenev's story "On the Eve" (1860). The music is by one of the world's skilled film composers, the Armenian Aram Khachaturian. The Bulgarian dramatist, Kamen Zidarov, had adapted the same novel for the stage, and quite successfully.

1960

DOM NA DVE ULITSI / The House on Two Streets. Sc: Buryan Enchev. Dr: Kiril Ilinchev. Ph: Trendafil Zahariev. Set: Konstantin Russakov. Mu: Ivan Marinov. Cast: Anani Yavashev, Ginka Stancheva, Peter Slabakov, Elisaveta Morfova. 96 mins. Prem: January 4.

Antifascist theme developed around a residence of a fugitive after the 1923 uprising.

STUBLENSKITE LIPI / The Lindens of Stublen. Sc: Stoyan Daskalov. Dr: Dako Dakovski. Ph: Emanuil Pangelov. Set: Tsenko Boyadjiev. Mu: Lyubomir Pipkov. Cast: Miroslav Mindov, Graziella Buchvarova, Vladislav Molerov, Ivan Bratanov. 108 mins. Prem: February 1.

The organization of a collective farm by a soldier who has returned home to his village, Stublen, after the Second World War.

OTVAD HORIZONTA / Beyond the Horizon. Sc: Pavel Vezhinov. Dr: Zahari Zhandov. Ph: Vassil Holiolchev. Set: Todor Panayotov. Mu: Konstantin Iliev. Cast: Stefan Petrov, Bogomil Simeonov, Ivan Kondov, Lyubomir Kisselichki. 106 mins. Prem: February 15.

In the days just before the Second World War, the heroes look "beyond the horizon" in their commitment to fight against fascism at home.

PATISHTA / Roads. A feature film in two parts. 100 mins. Prem: March 7.
(1) DRUGOTO SHTASTIE / Another Kind of Happiness. Sc: Vesselin Hanchev. Dr: Anton Marinovich. Ph: Emil Rashev. Set: Naiden Petkov. Mu: Konstantin Iliev. Cast: Bozhidara Zekova, Banko Bankov, Kiril Yanev.

Story of a young girl working in a factory.

(2) PATYAT MINAVA PRES BELOVIR / The Road Passes through Belovir. Sc: Pavel Vezhinov. Dr: Peter Vassilev. Ph: Georgi Georgiev. Set: Simeon Halachev. Mu: Peter Stupel. Cast: Apostol Karamitev, Valentina Borissova, Bozhidar Lechev.

A comedy set in the provinces. The screenplay was written by Pavel Vezhinov, who was to develop into one of the country's leading storytellers and scriptwriters.

V TICHA VETSCHER / On a Quiet Evening. Sc: Emilian Stanev, based on his novel with the same title. Dr: Borislav Sharaliev. Ph: Stoyan Slachkin. Set: Nedelcho Nanev. Mu: Lazar Nikolov. Cast: Lyubomir Dimitrov, Nevena Kokanova, Borislav Ivanov, Nikola Dinev. 89 mins. Prem: March 28.

A chapter in the struggle of the Bulgarian people against fascism at home, it stars the promising Nevena Kokanova in one of the leading roles. The novel, written in 1947, was dedicated to the partisan fighters.

PARVI UROK / First Lesson. Sc: Valeri Petrov. Dr: Rangel Vulchanov. Ph: Dimo Kolarov. Set: Hristo Neykov, Slatka Dabova. Mu: Simeon Pironkov. Cast: Kornelia Bozhanova, Georgi Naumov, Georgi Georgiev-Gets, Georgi Kaloyanchev, Konstantin Kotsev. 98 mins. Prem: April 18.

The revolutionary, antifascist theme raised to a poetic and reflective plane by the outstanding team of Valeri Petrov and Rangel Vulchanov. The tragic love story is set in Sofia in 1942 and has several fine comic touches. The photography and musical score are equally praiseworthy. Bulgarian poetic realism at its best.

HITAR PETER / Sly Peter. Sc: Peter Nesnakomov. Dr: Stefan Surchadjiev. Ph: Boncho Karastoyanov. Set: Bencho Obreshkov. Mu: Filip Kutev. Cast: Rashko Yabandjiev, Leo Konforti, Dimiter Stratev, Konstantin Kissimov. 100 mins. Prem: May 16.

Rangel Vulchanov's *First Lesson* (1960).

Another adaptation of the popular folk tale about Nastradin Hoggia and Sly Peter, brought to the screen by a theater director. The comedy was first filmed in 1939. Sly Peter is a Bulgarian who uses his wits to dumbfound the Turks in Ottoman times.

BEDNATA ULITSA / Poor Man's Street. Sc: Peter Donev. Dr: Hristo Piskov. Ph: Georgi Alurkov, Todor Stoyanov. Mu: Georgi Penkov, Dimiter Genkov. Cast: Kosta Tsonev, Valentin Russetski, Nikolina Genova, Lily Eneva. 95 mins. Prem: November 5.

An antifascist theme, it is particularly remembered for the

work of two cameramen, Georgi Alurkov and Todor Stoyanov, who experimented with a form of expressive poetic realism in the making of the film.

SLUCHAEN KONZERT / Occasional Concert. Sc: Bancho Banov, Kosta Naumov. Dr: Kosta Naumov. Ph: Konstantin Yanakiev. Set: Mony Aladjemov. Mu: opera music. Cast: Vladimir Trandafilov, Emilia Radeva, Ivan Stefanov, Assen Milanov, and opera singers. 86 mins. Prem: unknown.

An impromptu operatic rendition of songs by Bulgarian national artists, within a slightly sketched narrative.

1961

PRIZORI / At The Break of Dawn. Sc: Kiril Voynov. Dr: Dimiter Petrov. Ph: Stoyan Slachkin. Set: Iskra Licheva. Mu: Georgi Ivanov. Cast: Peter Slabakov, Miroslav Mindov, Zheni Bozhinova, Anastasia Bakardjieva. 74 mins. Prem. February 13.

The first attempt at a youth film by a director who was later to excel in films for children. Dimiter Petrov learned his trade at the Prague Film School.

A BYAHME MLADI / We Were Young. Sc: Hristo Ganev. Dr: Binka Zhelyazkova. Ph: Vassil Holiolchev. Set: Simeon Halachev, Mu: Simeon Pironkov. Cast: Rumyana Karabelova, Dimiter Buynozov, Lyudmila Cheshmedjieva, Anani Yavashev, Georgi Georgiev-Gets. 115 mins. Prem: February 13.

One of the pillars of Bulgarian poetic realism, this collaboration between Binka Zhelyazkova and Hristo Ganev concentrated primarily on capturing the atmosphere of the recent war years, and succeeded admirably. It's a tragic love story set in Sofia amid resistance fighters and pursuing police. The final scene, in a prison cell, hasn't lost its effectiveness over the years. Gold Medal at Moscow.

KRAYAT NA PATYA / At the End of the Road. Sc: Pavel Vezhinov. Dr: Peter Vassilev. Ph: Georgi Georgiev. Set: Tsenko Boyadjiev. Mu: Peter Stupel. Cast: Assen Milanov, Nikola Galabov, Andrei Chaprazov, Valentina Borissova. 81 mins. Prem: April 3.

A detective thriller, Bulgarian style. Script by the versatile Pavel Vezhinov. This was the first attempt to make a suspenseful whodunit at the Boyana Studios.

BADI SHTASTLIVA, ANI! / Be Happy, Annie! Sc: Valentin Yeshov, Bancho Banov. Dr: Vladimir Yanchev. Ph: Boncho Karastoyanov. Set: Nedelcho Nanev. Mu: Peter Stupel. Cast: Vassil Merkuriev, Nevena Kokanova, Kosta Tsonev, Assen Kissimov. 84 mins. Prem: May 24.

A comedy with star newcomer Nevena Kokanova in a starring role.

VIATARNATA MELNITSA / The Windmill. Sc: Slavcho Chernishev, Serafim Severniak. Dr: Simeon Zhivachev. Ph: Georgi Alurkov. Set: Lyuben Trapkov. Mu: Ivan Marinov. Cast: Violina Stoychkova, Vera Dragostinova, Grigor Boyadjiev, Rumen Hranov. 80 mins. Prem: May 15.

A children's film groping in the right direction.

NOSHTA SRESHTU TRINADESETI / On the Eve of the 13th. Sc: Alexander Chadjihristov. Dr: Anton Marinovich. Ph: Trendafil Zahariev. Set: Naiden Petkov. Mu: Atanas Boyadjiev. Cast: Apostol Karamitev, Georgi Georgiev-Gets, Ani Tsoneva, Ivan Andonov. 108 mins. Prem: June 5.

Binka Zhelyazkova's *We Were Young* **(1961).**

A detective story along whodunit lines.

POSLEDNIYAT RUND / The Last Round. Sc: Anton Antonov-Tonich. Dr: Lyudmil Kirkov. Ph: Dimo Kolarov. Set: Nikolai Vulkov. Mu: Emil Georgiev. Cast: Anani Yanashev, Adriana Andreyeva, Valentin Russetski, Yakim Michov. 83 mins. Prem: August 21.

The first film by a promising director: the theme is sports and the working class, with a love story on the side.

MARGARITKA, MAMA I AS / Margaritka, Mama and I. Sc: Peter Nesnakomov. Dr: Gencho Genchev. Ph: Todor Stoyanov. Set: Konstantin Djidrov. Mu: Emil Georgiev. Cast: Albena Salabasheva, Sonya Vassileva, Ivan Kondov, Dimiter Handjiev. 85 mins. Prem: October 16.

A family film, about a writer of children's books.

STRAMNATA PATEKA / The Steep Path. Sc: Emil Manov, Kosta Strandjiev. Dr: Yanko Yankov. Ph: Emil Rashev. Set: Konstantin Russakov. Mu: Alexander Raychev. Cast: Lyubomir Kabakchiev, Georgi Georgiev-Gets, Zvetko Nikolov, Ivan Bratanov. 100 mins. Prem: November 16.

A critical film featuring a worker-hero in conflict with the past. The script was by the talented writer Emil Manov.

1962

TSARSKA MILOST / The Tsar's Pardon. Sc: Kamen

Zidarov, based on his play with the same title. Dr: Stefan Surchadjiev. Ph: Georgi Slavchev. Set: Maria Ivanova. Mu: Lyubomir Pipkov. Cast: Ivanka Dimitrova, Ivan Dimov, Tseno Kondov, Milen Kolev. 92 mins. Prem: February 19.

A literary adaptation of Zidarov's first play (written in 1949), directed by a theater director. The setting is just before the First World War, when the country was ruled by Tsar Ferdinand of Coburg after the restoration of the monarchy.

DVAMA POD NEBETO / Two under the Sky. Sc: Angel Wagenstein. Dr: Borislav Sharaliev. Ph: Todor Stoyanov. Set: Georgi Ivanov. Mu: Lazar Nikolov. Cast: Apostol Karamitev, Violetta Doneva, Stefan Gadularov, Stoycho Mazgalov, 86 mins. Prem: March 19.

A contemporary theme dealing with the problems of youth. The new morale in the working classes is clearly felt.

HRONIKA NA CHUVSTVATA / A Chronicle of Sentiments. Sc: Todor Monov. Dr: Lyubomir Sharlandjiev. Ph: Emil Wagenstein. Set: Bogoya Sapundjiev. Mu: Simeon Pironkov. Cast: Vassil Popiliev, Zhorzheta Chakarova, Lyubomir Kisselichki, Yanka Vlahova. 81 mins. Prem: April 9.

A film with a social-conscience message. The setting is a construction site during a moment of crisis when a personal decision has to be made to save the day.

SPETSIALIST PO VSICHKO / Specialist for Everything. Sc: Pavel Vezhinov. Dr: Peter Vassilev. Ph: Georgi Georgiev. Set: Randyo Randev. Mu: Peter Stupel. Cast: Apostol Karamitev, Georgi Kaloyanchev, Ginka Stancheva, Katya Chukova. 89 mins. Prem: May 14.

A comedy penned by Pavel Vezhinov with a flair for contemporary behavior among young people.

PLENENO YATO / Captured Squadron. Sc: Emil Manov. Dr: Ducho Mundrov. Ph: Georgi Alurkov. Set: Angela Danadjieva. Mu: Georgi Genkov. Cast: Peter Slabakov, Kiril Kovachev, Dimiter Buynozov, Stefan Iliev. 90 mins. Prem: September 3.

The best of the Ducho Mundrov "Eastern" series on partisan activities during the Second World War, helped by psychological touches in Emil Manov's screenplay. The prison cell scene, as political prisoners await execution, stands out.

SLANTSETO I SYANKATA / Sun and Shadow. Sc: Valeri Petrov. Dr: Rangel Vulchanov. Ph: Dimo Kolarov. Set: Alexander Djakov. Mu: Simeon Pironkov. Cast: Anna Prucnal, Georgi Naumov. 73 mins. Prem: October 22.

The third in a trilogy of poetic-realist films fashioned by Vulchanov and Petrov. It is, in fact, more of an abstract poem than a narrative feature film, a lyrical avant-garde approach to the dangers of nuclear war. An international prizewinner at Karlovy Vary and San Francisco, Grand Prix at the Los Alamos Peace Festival.

TYUTYUN / Tobacco. Sc: Dimiter Dimov, Nikola Korabov, based on Dimov's novel with the same title. Dr: Nikola Korabov. Ph: Vulo Radev. Set: Konstantin Djidrov. Mu: Vassil Kasandjiev. Cast: Nevena Kokanova, Yordan Matev, Wolfgang Langhoff, Peter Slabakov. 150 mins. Prem: November 5.

Written in 1951 by a physician-turned-novelist, Dimiter Dimov, the epic ranks as one of the high-water marks in Socialist Realism. It covers the years prior to the Second World War, beginning in 1929, and ends with the victory of the Resistance in 1944/45.

SLATNIYAT ZAB / The Golden Tooth. Sc: Konstantin Spassov, Anton Marinovich. Dr: Anton Marinovich. Ph: Kosta Russakov. Mu: Konstantin Iliev. Cast: Georgi Georgiev-Gets, Stefan Peychev, Georgi Kaloyanchev, Nikola Galabov. 103 mins. Prem: December 3.

A detective thriller by the Bulgarian specialist in the genre, Anton Marinovich. It was the best of his mystery films.

1963

KALOYAN. Sc: Dako Dakovski, Anton Donchev, Dimiter Mantov. Dr: Dako Dakovski, Yuri Arnaudov. Ph: Emanuil Pangelov. Set: Borislav Stoev. Mu: Naiden Gerov. Cast: Vassil Stoychev, Bogomil Simeonov, Spas Djonev, Andrei Mihailov, Magdalena Mircheva. 109 mins. Prem: January 21.

Director Dako Dakovski died in the midst of shooting this epic on the medieval Bulgarian tsar, Kaloyan, and the directing chores were completed by documentarist-cameraman Yuri Arnaudov. Crowned in 1204, Kaloyan was a key figure in medieval history: he defeated the Crusaders under Baldwin of Flanders at Adrianople in 1205.

ANKETA / The Investigation. Sc: Kiril Ilinchev, Georgi Markov. Dr: Kiril Ilinchev. Ph: Dimo Kolarov. Set: Petko Bonchev. Mu: Ivan Marinov. Cast: Ivan Andonov, Assen Milanov, Rumyana Karabelova, Violetta Doneva. 72 mins. Prem: February 11.

Rangel Vulchanov's *Sun and Shadow* (1962).

A psychological drama dealing with a problem of conscience: the truth has to be told to save a colleague, but a girl's career is also at stake.

LEGENDA SA PAISIJ / The Legend of Paisy. Sc: Nadeshda Dragova, Parvan Stefanov. Dr: Stefan Surchadjiev. Ph: Vassil Holiolchev. Set: Angela Danadjieva. Mu: Lyubomir Pipkov. Cast: Victor Danchenko, Ivan Kondov, Stoycho Mazgalov, Sava Hashamov. 81 mins. Prem: March 23.

An historical epic, with reservations, on the life and work of Paisy of Hilandar (1723–98), whose *Slav-Bulgarian History* (written 1762 served to awaken the national conscience and thus paved the way for both the National Revival and liberation from the Turks.

NA TICHIYA BRIAG / On a Quiet Bank. Sc: Buryan Enchev. Dr: Gencho Genchev. Ph: Stoyan Slachkin. Set: Todor Hadjinikolov. Mu: Atanas Boyadjier. Cast: Borislava Kusmanova, Ivan Kasabov, Lyubomir Pavlov, Ivan Bratanov. 86 mins. Prem: April 22.

A patriotic counterespionage tale, involving a violinist named Dolly, an impresario called Smiles, and an incident on a river bank.

KAPITANAT / The Captain. Sc: Atanas Pavlov. Dr: Dimiter Petrov. Ph: Trendafil Zahariev. Set: Stefka Mazakova. Mu: Alexander Raychev. Cast: Rayko Bodurov, Yanush Alurkov. 80 mins. Prem: May 13.

The first breakthrough in the genre of the children's film. The theme was friendship, and the view of the world was through the eyes of children—yet the appeal of the film was universal and attracted adult audiences as well. An interna-

tional prizewinner at festivals, the laurels going to Dimiter Petrov.

SREDNOSHTNO SRESHTA / Midnight Meeting. Sc: Pavel Vezhinov. Dr: Nikola Minchev. Ph: Emil Rashev. Set: Konstantin Djidrov. Mu: Ilya Georgiev. Cast: Nevena Kokanova, Ivan Komitov, Lyubomir Dimitrov, Nikola Popov. 68 mins. Prem: October 7.

Psychological plot by one of Bulgaria's popular writers, Pavel Vezhinov.

SMART NYAMA / There Is No Death. Sc: Todor Monov, Hristo Santov, based on Monov's novel with the same title. Dr: Hristo Piskov, Irina Aktasheva. Ph: Todor Stoyanov. Set: Konstantin Djidrov. M: Vassil Kasandjiev. Cast: Peter Slabakov, Grigor Vachkov, Djoko Rossich, Valentin Russetski, Medy Dimitrova. 93 mins. Prem: October 21.

Important film by the directorial pair of Piskov-Aktasheva. It's a tale of love and heroism on a construction site in the Rhodope Mountains. The working conditions and temperaments of the construction team are sharply delineated in flesh-and-blood terms.

INSPEKTORAT I NOSHTA / The Inspector and the Night. Sc: Bogomil Rainov. Dr: Rangel Vulchanov. Ph: Dimo Kolarov. Set: Ivan Kirkov. Mu: Simeon Pironkov. Cast: Georgi Kaloyanchev, Nevena Kokanova, Dimiter Panov, Leo Konforti. 96 mins. Prem: December 16.

A detective thriller with psychological overtones, the script was by a well known writer (Bogomil Rainov) who specialized in the genre. A private detective is murdered, and the

Rangel Vulchanov's *The Inspector and the Night* (1963).

investigation leads to contacts with people from various walks of life. *Ciné noir*, Bulgarian-style.

1964

MEZHDU RELSITE / Between the Rails. Sc: Svoboda Buchvarova. Dr: Venelin Tsankov. Ph: Emil Rashev. Set: Mladen Mladenov. Mu: Kiril Donchev. Cast: Margarita Chudinova, Stoyan Gadev, Radka Sarafova, Stefan Iliev. 98 mins. Prem: January 7.

A resistance tale set during the Second World War. The heroine is the daughter of political emigrants abroad, whose mother dies and father continues the fight in the Belgian Underground. She returns to Bulgaria in hopes of a better future.

NEZAVARSHENI IGRI / Unfinished Games. Sc: Nikola Golanov, Georgi Yanev. Dr: Simeon Zhivachev. Ph: Hristo Vulchanov. Set: Angel Ahrianov. Mu: Lazar Nikolov. Cast: Ivan Enchev, Dolya Popova, Dinko Dinev, Peter Gyurov. 85 mins. Prem: January 27.

An antifascist theme dealing with the sacrifice of youth to fight for a better world against the background of the Second World War.

IVAILO. Sc: Nikola Vulchev, Evgeni Konstantinov. Dr: Nikola Vulchev. Ph: Konstantin Yanakiev. Set: Konstantin Russakov. Mu: Boyan Ikonomov. Cast: Bogomil Simeonov, Ginka Stancheva, Laina Davidova, Tsvyatko Nikolov. 88 mins. Prem: February 17.

Historical epic based on the exploits of the "peasant tsar of Bulgaria," Ivailo Burdokva, a simple swineherd who ruled at Turnovo, 1277–79, after conquering the marauding Mongols and defeating the Byzantines.

CHERNATA REKA / The Black River. Sc: Nikola Tiholov. Dr: Zahari Zhandov. Ph: Emil Wagenstein. Set: Maria Ivanova. Mu: Lazar Nikolov. Cast: Georgi Georgiev-Gets, Zhorzheta Chakarova, Ivan Tonev. 74 mins. Prem: April 6.

A film adaptation of a well known Bulgarian ballad of the hills and country life. It heralds the virtues of family ethics and true love.

NEPRIMIRIMITE / **The Intransigents.** Sc & Dr: Yanko Yankov. Ph: Trendafil Zahariev. Set: Naiden Petkov. Mu: Alexander Raychev. Cast: Ivan Raev, Dušica Žegarac, Banko Bankov, Yordan Matev. 84 mins. Prem: April 27.

A war story, about a truckload of munitions that has to be transported by a group of tough individuals from Yugoslavia to Bulgaria over hazardous roads.

PRIKLYUTSHENIE V POLUNOSHT / Adventure at Midnight. Sc: Kiril Voynov, Anton Marinovich. Dr: Anton Marinovich. Ph: Hristo Vulchanov. Set: Randyo Randev. Mu: Atanas Boyadjiev. Cast: Lyubomir Dimitrov, Vessela Radoyeva, Naicho Petrov, Ivan Andonov, Georgi Popov. 100 mins. Prem: June 1.

A Marinovich detective film, it begins with a mysterious epidemic of fever in an area along the frontier that brings the Secret Service on the scene.

KONNIKAT / The Horseman. Sc: Lyuben Lolov, Georgi Alurkov. Dr: Georgi Alurkov. Ph: Mladen Kolev. Set: Mony Aladjemov. Mu: Peter Stupel. Cast: Stefan Iliev, Sonya Markova, Kliment Denchev, Methodi Tanev. 82 mins. Prem: July 27.

Romance and a renewed sense of dedication as an ex-soldier returns home from the front after the war to begin a new life on a collective farm.

VERIGATA / **The Chain.** Sc: Angel Wagenstein. Dr: Lyubomir Sharlandjiev. Ph: Emil Wagenstein. Set: Alexander Djakov. Mu: Kiril Tsibulka. Cast: Vassil Popiliev, Ivan Bratanov, Leo Konforti, Grigor Vachkov. 91 mins. Prem: August 31.

An antifascist fighter and political prisoner escapes. When he is still a step ahead of his pursuers, he encounters people whom he must come to trust if he is to save his life. This, in turn, awakens doubts in himself and his cause.

TRINAISET DNI / Thirteen Days. Sc: Lozan Strelkov. Dr: Stefan Surchadjiev. Ph: Vassil Holiolchev. Set: Milko Marinov, Bogoya Sapundjiev. Mu: Naiden Gerov. Cast: Emil Stefanov, Lyubomir Kabakchiev, Dimiter Buynozov, Mihail Mihailov, Ani Bakalova. 83 mins. Prem: September 7.

The story focuses on thirteen days before the uprising on 9 September 1944.

KRADETSAT NA PRASKOVI / **The Peach Thief.** Sc: Vulo Radev, based on a story by Emilian Stanev with the same title. Dr: Vulo Radev. Ph: Todor Stoyanov. Set: Nedelcho Nanev. Mu: Simeon Pironkov. Cast: Nevena Kokanova, Rade Marković, Mihail Mihailov, Vassil Vachev, Naum Shopov. 103 mins. Prem: November 9.

One of the finest films to emerge from Bulgaria during the 1960s. The setting is the fortress city of Turnovo during the First World War. A Yugoslav prisoner of war (a Serb) has an affair with the camp commandant's wife, and dies tragically. Memorably acted by Kokanova and Marković as the ill-fated pair—it's the beauty of the images, however, that make it a standout. The novel was published in 1948.

NEVEROYATNA ISTORIYA / An Incredible Story. Sc: Radoi Ralin. Dr: Vladimir Yanchev. Ph: Georgi Slavchev. Set: Nedelcho Nanev. Mu: Peter Stupel. Cast: Rangel Vulchanov, Bistra Guteva, Georgi Cherkelov, Georgi Kaloyanchev. 89 mins. Prem: December 21.

Completed in 1962 but not released until two years later, this comedy stars actor-director Rangel Vulchanov in a rib-tickling satire. A fictitious person is attacked in a loaded newspaper article, which in turn spreads panic among higher-ups who feel the finger just might be pointed at them.

1965

DO GRADA E BLIZO / The City Is Nearby. Sc: Geno Genov, Todor Stoyanov. Dr: Gencho Genchev. Ph: Stoyan Slachkin. Set: Todor Hadjinikolov. Mu: Atanas Boyadjiev. Cast: Lyudmila Cheshmedjieva, Valentin Russetski, Andrei Avramov, Naum Shopov. 81 mins. Prem: January 4.

An "Eastern" about a group of partisans operating clandestinely in the city.

KRAYAT NA EDNA VAKANTSIYA / The End of the Vacation. Sc: Emil Manov. Dr: Lyudmil Kirkov. Ph: Emanuil Pangelov. Set: Violetta Yovcheva. Mu: Simeon Pironkov. Cast: Alexander Karamitsev, Evgeni Statelov, Machet Sakut, Stoyan Peyev. 77 mins. Prem: February 22.

Set in Sofia during the period of the fascist monarchy, the collaboration of Kirkov and Manov raised the story above the ordinary. The theme deals with children and the hope for a better future.

PAROLATA / The Password. Sc: Stanka Gyurova. Dr: Peter Vassilev. Ph: Georgi Georgiev. Set: Georgi Ivanov. Mu: Georgi Ivanov. Cast: Assen Milanov, Ivan Bratanov, Mila Santova, Nikolina Tomanova. 93 mins. Prem: March 15.

An "Eastern" about partisans on a dangerous undertaking.

KASCHE NEBE ZA TRIMA / A Bit of Heaven for Three. Sc: Rangel Ignatov, Kiril Ilinchev. Dr: Kiril Ilinchev. Ph: Trendafil Zahariev. Set: Petko Bonchev. Mu: Ivan Spassov. Cast: Lyubomir Kisselichki, Georgi Nikolov, Radoslav Stoylov, Lyudmila Cheshmedjieva. 91 mins. Prem: May 17.

An action film about three soldiers risking their lives on military maneuvers.

STARINNATA MONETA / The Ancient Coin. Sc: Mormarev Brothers. Dr: Vladimir Yanchev. Ph: Erwin Andres. Mu: Peter Stupel. Cast: Manfred Krug, Liana Antonova, Grigor Vachkov, Georgi Popov. 84 mins. Prem: June 28.

A comedy centering on the search of a German tourist for an ancient Bulgarian coin—it leads to a love affair instead. The tourist is played by Manfred Krug, a popular actor from the German Democratic Republic.

VULA / Permission to Marry. Sc & Dr: Nikola Korabov. Ph & Set: Konstantin Djidrov. Mu: Vassil Kasandjiev. Cast: Nadeshda Randjieva, Ivan Manov, Boris Arabov, Mihail Mihailov. 72 mins. Prem: August 30.

An oddity in that it deals with a certificate for permission to marry, the pair wishing to marry in a prison cell before the spouse's execution in antifascist times.

VALCHITSATA / The She-Wolf. Sc: Chaim Oliver. Dr: Rangel Vulchanov. Ph: Dimo Kolarov. Set: Violetta Yovcheva, Alexander Djakov. Mu: Vassil Kasandjiev. Cast: Ilka Safirova, Georgi Kaloyanchev, Naum Shopov, Krassimira Apostolova. 87 mins. Prem: September 13.

Also known as *The Wolverine.* The focus is on young people and, in particular, a young heroine nicknamed "Wolverine" in a reformatory.

NESPOKOEN DOM / Troubled Home. Sc: Pavel Vezhinov, based on his story with the same title. Dr: Yakim Yakimov. Ph: Emil Wagenstein. Set: Randyo Randev, Belin Belev. Mu: Kiril Tsibulka. Cast: Ivan Kondov, Emilia Radeva, Elena Rainova, Milen Penev. 91 mins. Prem: December 8.

A youth theme, the problems of society and the generation gap are realistically presented in this collaborative effort between Vezhinov and Yakimov.

1966

GORESHTO PLADNE /Torrid Noon. Sc: Yordan Radichkov, based on his story with the same title. Dr: Zako Heskia. Ph: Todor Stoyanov. Set: Georgi Nedjalkov. Mu: Milcho Leviev. Cast: Peter Slabakov, Plamak Nakov, Kamil Kyuchukov, Lachezar Yankov. 88 mins. Prem: January 3.

The first of Yordan Radichkov's stories to be adapted to the screen, this is a fine sketch of human nature, constructed around an incident under a bridge on a hot summer afternoon. A boy playing in water gets his hand wedged between two stones—and the entire population of a sleepy village comes to the rescue!

TSAR I GENERAL / Tsar and General. Sc: Lyuben Stanev. Dr: Vulo Radev. Ph: Borislav Punchev. Set: Konstantin Russakov. Mu: Simeon Pironkov. Cast: Peter Slabakov, Naum Shopov, Stoycho Mazgalov, Georgi Cherkelov. 79 mins. Prem: January 17.

A wide-screen spectacle. The psychological density in this historical account of Tsar Boris and General Zaimov on the eve of World War II is noteworthy for a number of reasons—not only is the figure of the former tsar a complex and human one, but the conflict with his general reaches a philosophical plane.

RITSAR BEZ BRONYA / Knight without Armor. Sc: Valeri Petrov. Dr: Borislav Sharaliev. Ph: Atanas Tassev. Set: Maria Ivanova. Mu: Vassil Kasandjiev. Cast: Oleg Kovachev, Apostol Karamitev, Tsvyatko Nikolov, Maria Russalieva. 85 mins. Prem: February 14.

One of Bulgarian cinema's finest children's films. The script by Valeri Petrov was written during the time of his collaboration with Rangel Vulchanov, then shelved until directed by Borislav Sharaliev. This world of adult discrepancies, as viewed by a small boy, became a domestic and international hit.

PRIZOVANIYAT NE SE YAVI / The Subpoenaed Didn't Come. Sc: Svoboda Buchvarova. Dr: Vladislav Ikonomov. Ph: Emil Wagenstein. Set: Nevena Bultova. Mu: Kiril Tsibulka. Cast: Assen Milanov, Vassil Popiliev, Slavka Slavova, Peter Penkov, Tsvetana Ostrovska. 70 mins. Prem: March 7.

Set in the period after the victory over fascism, a case of possible treason is examined in some detail in a court trial.

MAZHE / Men. Sc: Georgi Markov. Dr: Vassil Mirchev. Ph: Todor Stoyanov. Set: Belin Belinov. Cast: Sava Hashamov, Dobromir Manev, Lyubomir Gulyashki, Rumyana Karabelova, Yoanna Popova. 89 mins. Prem: March 21.

A youth theme about three young friends with their future before them and different goals in life.

VECHEN KALENDAR / Almanach. Sc & Dr: Peter Donev. Ph: Boris Yanakiev. Set: Bogoya Sapundjiev. Mu: Kiril Donchev. Cast: Ivan Bratanov, Margarita Pechlivanova, Ilya Dobrev, Stefan Mavrodiev. 85 mins. Prem: May 2.

A contemporary theme dealing with village life and a girl's decision to dedicate herself to the betterment of society, cost what it may.

NACHALOTO NA EDNA VAKANTSIYA / The Start of the Vacation. Sc: Gercho Atanassov. Dr: Zako Heskia. Ph: Todor Stoyanov. Set: Georgi Nedjalkov. Mu: Boris Karadimchev. Cast: Lily Buchvarova, Maya Dragomanska, Krum Atsev, Rayko Bodurov. 81 mins. Prem: May 23.

It's the start of the summer vacation for a group of teenagers, and a time of maturity as well.

MEZHDU DVAMATA / Between the Two of Them. Sc: Vera Stoymenova. Dr: Dimiter Petrov. Ph: Trendafil Zahariev. Set: Milko Marinov. Mu: Simeon Pironkov. Cast: Georgi Georgiev-Gets, Violetta Minkova, Yanush Alurkov, Dimiter Bonchev. 81 mins. Prem: September 5.

A children's film, about a twelve-year-old boy on his vacation.

KARAMBOL / Crack-Up. Sc: Atanas Tsenev, based on his novel *The White Rose Castle.* Dr: Lyubomir Sharlandjiev. Ph: Emil Wagenstein. Set: Petko Bonchev. Cast: Anani Yavashev, Nevena Kokanova, Evstati Stratev, Elena Rainova, Assen Milanov. 88 mins. Prem: October 17.

A social theme, whose protagonist is a reporter writing a story on contemporary life in the provinces. The crisis comes when the newspaperman has to fake his report.

Vulo Radev's *Tsar and General* **(1966).**

Borislav Sharaliev's *Knight without Armor* **(1966).**

ZAVETAT NA INKITE / DAS VERMACHTNIS DES INKA / The Legacy of the Incas. Sc: Georg Marischka, Franz Marischka, Winfried Groth, based on a novel with the same title by Karl May. Dr: Georg Marischka. Ph: Siegfried Hold. Mu: Riz Ortolani. Cast: Guy Madison, Renato Tamberlani, Francisko Rabal, Walter Gifler. (Coproduction with the Federal Republic of Germany, Italy, and Spain.) 106 mins. Prem: December 30.

A Karl May production with an international cast, filmed in Bulgaria. The official Bulgarian coproduction partner was West Berlin.

PONEDELNIK SUTRIN / Monday Morning. Sc: Nikolai Tiholov. Dr: Hristo Piskov, Irina Aktasheva. Ph: Dimo Kolarov. Mu: Milcho Leviev. Cast: Pepa Nikolova, Assen Kissimov, Peter Slabakov, Kiril Gospodinov, Stefan Danailov, Russi Chanev, Plamen Donchev. 103 mins. Prem: restricted release only.

Controversial film dealing with the problems of youth. A girl from a large provincial city has an unsteady relationship with a boy, then escapes to a youth brigade to find herself and open up to new horizons.

1967

V KRAYA NA LYATOTO / At the End of the Summer. Sc: Emil Manov, based on his story "Meeting at the Seashore." Dr: Ducho Mundrov. Ph: Hristo Vulchanov, Mladen Kolev. Set: Sotir Sotirov, Mu: Georgi Genkov. Cast: Peter Slabakov, Ilka Safirova, Kalina Antonova, Ani Bakalova, Anani Yavashev. 81 mins. Prem: February 1.

A contemporary social theme, it concerns an intellectual in conflict with conservative ideas who renews his spiritual batteries during a meeting with a girl while on vacation at the seashore.

NAY-DALGATA NOSHT / The Longest Night. Sc: Vesselin Branev. Dr: Vulo Radev. Ph: Borislav Punchev. Set: Konstantin Russakov. Mu: Simeon Pironkov. Cast: Georgi Kaloyanchev, Nevena Kokanova, Ivan Bratanov, Georgi Georgiev-Gets, Victor Rebenchuk, Russi Chanev. 100 mins. Prem: February 22.

An "Eastern" that reaches beyond the action genre to become a psychological thriller. It all takes place on a train: a RAF officer is stowed away under the very eyes of Nazi troops, and passengers have to take varying stances on his presence.

PO TROTOARA / On the Pavement. Sc: Milcho Radev. Dr: Anton Marinovich. Ph: Hristo Vulchanov. Set: Randyo Randev. Mu: Kiril Donchev. Cast: Ivan Andonov, Ani Bakalova, Lyubomir Kisselichki, Yordan Spassov. 88 mins. Prem: March 22.

A story about two medical students. The boy can't make the right decision and loses the girl he loves, then finds himself again as a medical doctor in a mountain village.

CHOVEKAT V SYANKA / The Man in the Shadow. Sc: Kiril Voynov, Yakim Yakimov, based on a novel by Pavel Vezhinov. Dr: Yakim Yakimov. Ph: Georgi Georgiev. Mu: Kiril Tsibulka, Alexander Brusitsov. Cast: Stanyo Mihailov, Ivan Kondov, Elena Rainova, Preslav Petrov, Mihail Mihailov, 97 mins. Prem: April 10.

A detective thriller. The caper takes the investigators to Switzerland and the Mediterranean, as well as across Bulgaria.

Hristo Piskov and Irina Aktasheva's *Monday Morning* **(1966).**

MALCHALIVITE PATEKI / Quiet Paths. Sc: Lyubomir Levchev. Dr. Vladislav Ikonomov. Ph: Krum Krumov. Set: Petko Bonchev. Mu: Kiril Tsibulka. Cast: Georgi Cherkelov, Mihail Mihailov, Evstati Stratev. 81 mins. Prem: May 10.

An "Eastern" about partisans in the resistance, with a moral for today.

OTKLONENIE / Sidetrack. Sc: Blaga Dimitrova, based on her short story with the same title. Dr. Grisha Ostrovski, Todor Stoyanov. Ph: Todor Stoyanov. Mu: Milcho Leviev. Cast: Nevena Kokanova, Ivan Andonov, Stefan Iliev, Katya Paskaleva. Prem: May 26.

A successful attempt to review the period of the Personality Cult, directed by a veteran stage personality at Sofia's Satirical Theater (Ostrovski) and an experienced cameraman (Stoyanov). The story begins with a detour off the main highway, whereby an engineer meets an archaeologist and they recall their love affair of twenty years ago. At that time, they sacrificed their love for an ideal that has tarnished, a decision they both regret but can do nothing about in the present—they have both married others in the meantime, and have children. This nostalgic, bittersweet film conveys its message without pretense by simply sustaining a mood. Nevena Kokanova and Ivan Andonov are memorable in their roles as a couple who briefly renew their love.

AKO NE IDE VLAK—MORETO / If the Train Doesn't Arrive—The Sea. A feature film in two parts, 108 mins. Prem: June 23.

(1) **AKO NE IDE VLAK / If the Train Doesn't Arrive.** Sc: Georgi Mischev. Dr: Eduard Zahariev. Ph: Boris Yanakiev. Set: Stefka Masakova. Mu: Kiril Donchev. Cast: Andrei Avramov, Naum Shopov, Kiril Yanev, Ilka Safirova, Georgi Georgiev-Gets. 37 mins.

The first of a string of hilarious satires by the team of Georgi Mishev and Eduard Zahariev. It deals with a wild goose chase in the provinces (the film is also known as *Blinding Lights*).

(2) MORETO / The Sea. Sc: Georgi Branev. Dr: Peter Donev. Ph: Boris Yanakiev. Set: Stefka Masakova. Mu: Kiril Donchev. Cast: Severina Teneva, Stefan Danailov, Itzhak Fintsi. 71 mins.

A psychological drama about a lad who prefers to avoid responsibility and lead an easly life.

SVIRACHAT / The Musician. Sc: Mandy Brown, based on a fairytale by Wilhelm Hauff. Dr: Mandy Brown. Ph: Dimo Kolarov. Set: Nedelcho Nanev. Mu: Tony Velona. Cast: Emmett Kelly, Burt Stratford, Misho Mihailov, Leo Konforti, Bogomil Simeonov, Oleg Kovachev. (Coproduction with the United States.) 89 mins. Prem: June 2.

An adaptation of the Wilhelm Hauff fairy tale, with the famous clown Emmett Kelly in the role of the wandering flutist.

BYAGASHTA PO VALNITE / Hurrying through the Waves. Sc: Alexander Galich, Stefan Tsanev, based on a story by Alexander Grin with the same title. Dr: Pavel Lubimov. Ph: Stoyan Slachkin. Set: Alexander Denkov. Mu: Jan Frenkel. Cast: Sava Hachamov, Natasha Bogunova, Evstati Stratev, Margarita Terehova, Rolan Bykov, Peter Panov, Vassil Popiliev, Yordan Matev, Oleg Yakov. (Coproduction with Soviet Union.) 93 mins. Prem: June 7.

This film adaptation of an Alexander Grin story (published

in 1928) weaves the magic of a fairy tale. A lad finds himself in a strange imaginary country and falls in love with a girl. His hopes are not realized in the end, as dreams and reality are not made to mix in this romantic legendary setting.

S DAH NA BADEMI / The Taste of Almonds. Sc: Pavel Vezhinov. Dr: Lyubomir Sharlandjiev. Ph: Atanas Tassev. Set: Petko Bonchev. Mu: Angel Mihailov. Cast: Nevena Kokanova, Georgi Georgiev-Gets, Iskra Hadjiyeva, Stefan Danailov, Dorothea Toncheva, Antonia Cholcheva. 75 mins. Prem: September 27.

A love triangle in two different unhappy marriages, contrasted with the true love of a younger couple.

PRIVARZANIYAT BALON / The Attached Balloon (The Balloon). Sc: Yordan Radichkov, based on his story "Attempt to Fly." Dr: Binka Zhelyazkova. Ph: Emil Wagenstein. Mu: Simeon Pironkov. Cast: Georgi Kaloyanchev, Ivan Bratanov, Georgi Georgiev-Gets, Georgi Partsalev, Konstantin Kotsev, Lyuben Dimitrov. 98 mins. Prem: December 1.

Finished in 1966, it was not released until a year later—and then only briefly. The high-water mark of the 1960s, this extraordinary story by Yordan Radichkov began as an absurd fantasy in print, then was adapted by the author and Binka Zhelyazkova into an equally imaginative "modern fairy tale" for the screen, and finally into a successful stage production under its original title—a full decade after the film version was shelved, shortly after its release. Its moral: what happens when village peasants are offered the opportunity to fly off in a big balloon in the middle of the Stalinist era.

1968

POSLEDNIYAT VOYVODA / The Last Voyvoda. Sc: Steryo Atanassov, Evgeni Konstantinov. Dr: Nikola Vulchev. Ph: Trendafil Zahariev. Set: Konstantin Russakov. Mu: Boyan Ikonomov. Cast: Vassil Popiliev, Bogomil Simeonov, Emil Grekov. 93 mins. Prem: January 12.

The outlaws, or *haiduks*, under an elected leader known as the *voyvoda*, were at the height of their influence against the Turks in the seventeenth century. Some were still active in the Rhodope Mountains into this century, and this is the story of the last voivoda appearing on the scene during the 1923 uprising.

SCHVEDSKITE KRALE / Swedish Kings. Sc: Nikolai Nikiforov. Dr: Lyudmil Kirkov. Ph: Atanas Tassev. Set: Maria Ivanova. Mu: Boris Karadimchev. Cast: Kiril Gospodinov, Evstati Stratev, Tsvetana Maneva, Assen Georgiev, Radoslav Stoylov, Marianna Almancheva, Nikolai Ouzunov. 100 mins. Prem: February 1.

Also titled *Steel Kings*—the actual title is in the meaning of "to live like a Swedish king"—this is an important critical sketch of working life by a director whose first two films were but formula ventures. A steel worker ventures to the Black Sea to experience how foreign tourists frolic at the new resort hotels.

PARVIYAT KURIER / The First Courier. Sc: Konstantin Issaev. Dr: Vladimir Yanchev. Ph: Anatolia Kusnezov. Mu: Peter Stupel. Cast: Stefan Danailov, Zhanna Bolotova, Vladimir Recepter, Yevgeni Leonov, Valentin Pehlivanov, Valentin Gaft. (Coproduction with the Soviet Union.) 97 mins. Prem: March 1.

The story of a Lenin collaborator on the pre-Revolution

Lyudmil Kirkov's *Swedish Kings* (1968).

journal *Iskra*—the Bulgarian Ivan Zagubanski.

SHIBIL. Sc: Zahari Zhandov, Magda Petkanova, based on a story by Yordan Yovkov with the same title. Dr: Zahari Zhandov. Ph: Ivailo Trenchev. Set: Violetta Yovcheva. Mu: Vassil Kasandjiev. Cast: Peter Slabakov, Dorothea Toncheva, Ivan Bratanov, Dimitrina Savova, Stoycho Mazgalov. 100 mins. Prem: March 22.

A haiduk outlaw-hero in Ottoman times, as portrayed by the versatile Yordan Yovkov.

SLUCHAYAT PENLEVE / The Painlevé Case. Sc: Svoboda Buchvarova, Peter Nesnakomov, Evgeni Konstantinov. Dr: Georgi Stoyanov. Ph: Victor Chichov, Violetta Yovcheva.

Mu: Kiril Donchev. Cast: Naum Shopov, Konstantin Kotsev, Stoyan Gadev, Vassil Vachev, Stefan Mavrodiev, Emilia Radeva, Tatyana Lolova. 83 mins. Prem: April 26.

An omnibus film, all three novellas were directed by newcomer Georgi Stoyanov: "Musicians," "Painlevé," and "Guests." The film's title is taken from the middle episode. Each story focuses on the Second World War, but the gem is "The Painlevé Case": a major in the Bulgarian fascist army takes more care of his pet rooster than of the soldiers directly under his command.

GIBELTA NA ALEKSANDAR VELIKI / The Fall of Alexander the Great. Sc: Lyobomir Levchev. Dr: Vladislav Ikonomov. Ph: Krum Krumov. Set: Konstantin Russakov. Mu: Kiril Tsibulka. Cast: Grigor Vachkov, Dobromir Manev, Zhorzheta Chakarova, Lily Eneva. 89 mins. Prem: September 6.

A contemporary theme, it features a young intellectual working on a construction site, whose brigade leader is nicknamed "Alexander the Great."

BYALATA STAYA / The White Room. Sc: Bogomil Rainov, based on his novel *Roads to Nowhere*. Dr: Metodi Andonov. Ph: Dimo Kolarov. Set: Petko Bonchev. Mu: Dimiter Vulchev. Cast: Apostol Karamitev, Dorothea Toncheva, Elena Rainova, Konstantin Kotsev, Ilka Zafirova, Georgi Cherkelov. 85 mins. Prem: October 18.

A modern parable, with its roots in the period of the Personality Cult. A patient in a clinic suffers from depressions. As he recalls the past in a lengthy monologue and flashbacks, it's revealed that he was a talented scientist waging a losing battle against the dogmatism of the day. The collaboration between director Metodi Andónov and screenplay writer Bogomil Rainov won the Grand Prix at the 1968 Varna Film Festival. The performance of Apostol Karamitev marks a high point in the actor's distinguished career.

OPASSEN POLET / Perilous Flight. Sc: Konstantin Kyulymov. Dr: Dimiter Petrov. Ph: Stoyan Slachkin. Set: Konstantin Russakov. Mu: Milcho Leviev. Cast: Lyubomir Kisselichki, Nevena Kokanova, Preslav Petrov, Peter Slabakov, Bogomil Simeonov. 83 mins. Prem: November 8.

A whodunit, it features a duel of wits between a master spy and his one-time student, now a secret agent on his trail.

PROTSESAT / The Trial. Sc: Pavel Vezhinov. Dr: Yakim Yakimov. Ph: Georgi Georgiev. Set: Iskra Licheva. Mu: Kiril Tsibulka. Cast: Branimira Antonova, Dimo Lolov, Ivan Andonov, Lora Kremen. 90 mins. Prem: December 6.

Youth theme about the generation gap. The psychological plot goes so far as to reveal both father and son infatuated with the same young girl. The high point is a trial scene in a juvenile court.

PROKURORAT / The Prosecutor. Sc: Budimir Metalnikov, based on Georgi Djagarov's drama with the same title. Dr: Lyubomir Sharlandjiev. Ph: Borislav Punchev. Set: Petko Bonchev. Cast: Georgi Georgiev-Gets, Yordan Matev, Olga Kircheva, Stefan Peychev, Dorothea Toncheva. 101 mins. Prem: restricted release only.

Never officially released, this film version of a stage production deals directly with the ills of the Personality Cult. A prosecutor is required to sign a warrant for the arrest of a close friend and fiancé of his sister. But he suspects a frameup and tries to work behind the scenes to save a man he knows to be innocent.

NEBETO NA VELEKA / The Sky over the Veleka. Sc: Diko Fuchedjiev. Dr: Eduard Zahariev. Ph: Ivan Tsonev. Cast: Georgi Georgiev-Gets, Todor Shtonev, Mihail Mihailov, Georgi Kaloyanchev. 101 mins. Prem: restricted release only.

This reflective portrait of the Personality Cult era, set in a village community along the Veleka River, is triggered by a meeting of old friends, who review the past as a painful step to maturity and responsibility. It dealt too with questions of justice and civil duty, virtues that were lacking in the important formative years of a new Socialist society. This is the serious side of director Zahariev, in contrast to his already evident talent for social satire.

1969

SVOBODA ILI SMART / Freedom or Death. Sc: Vassil Popov. Dr. Nikola Korabov. Ph and Set: Konstantin Djidrov. Mu: Krassimir Kyurkchiski. Cast: Milen Penev, Apostol Karamitev, Kosta Tsonev, Stefan Iliev, Vassil Mihailov, Georgi Mihov, Kiril Gospodinov. 91 mins. Prem: January 3.

A patriotic film, it depicts the heroic last days of poet-revolutionary Hristo Botev (1848–76), who led a band of two hundred Bulgarians in 1876 across the Danube to die fighting on Mount Vola. First color feature film production.

IKONOSTASAT / Iconostasis. Sc & Dr: Todor Dinov, Hristo Hristov, based on Dimiter Talev's novel *The Iron Candlestick*. Ph: Atanas Tassev. Mu: Milcho Leviev. Cast: Dimiter Tashev, Emilia Radeva, Violetta Gindeva, Nikolai Ouzunov, Ani Spassova, Stoyan Gudev. 100 mins. Prem: January 3.

A key film in Bulgarian film history, this is a black-and-white tribute to both a historical novel of major literary proportions, Dimiter Talev's *The Iron Candlestick* (published 1952), and the whole of Bulgarian folk art. Set in the nineteenth century during the Bulgarian Renaissance under the Turks, the woodcarver Rafe goes through the same agonies of decision that charged Andrei Tarkovsky's film biography of a Russian icon painter, *Andrei Rublev*. This debut feature by an animation director (Dinov) and a stage director (Hristov) was the high point of the 1969 Varna Film Festival.

GALILEO GALILEI. Sc: Liliana Cavani, Tullio Pinelli. Dr: Liliana Cavani. Ass't Dr: Dora Kovacheva. Ph: Alfio Contini. Mu: Ennio Morricone. Cast: Cyril Cusack, Georgi Kaloyanchev, Giglio Brogi, Miroslav Mindov, Nevana Kokanova, Mila Dimitrova, Maya Dragomanska. (Coproduction with Italy.) 107 mins. Prem: February 14.

Not an adaptation of Bertolt Brecht's play, but a straightforward spectacle on the historical figure, with pomp and circumstance.

TANGO. Sc: Slav. G. Karaslavov, based on a novel with the same title by Georgi Karaslavov. Dr: Vassil Mirchev. Ph: Ivailo Trenchev. Set: Violetta Yovcheva. Mu: Ivan Spassov. Cast: Nevena Kokanova, Peter Penkov, Boris Arabov, Peter Slabakov, Rosizza Danailova, Grigor Vachkov. 78 mins. Prem: February 28.

Set during the Second World War. The title refers to a tango being played in the home of a rich tycoon as an order is given to execute three Communists in a village.

MAZHE V KOMANDIROVKA / Men on a Business Trip. Sc: Lyuben Stanev. Dr: Grisha Ostrovski, Todor Stoyanov.

Ph: Todor Stoyanov. Set: Stefan Savov. Mu: Peter Stupel. Cast: Zhorzheta Chakorova, Ivan Andonov, Neycho Popov, Nevena Kokanova, Georgi Cherkelov. 98 mins. Prem: March 21.

Three novellas—"The Pullover," "The Guest," and "The Episode"—with a theme in common: what really happens when a man tells his wife that he's going on a business trip.

PTITSI I HRATKI / Birds and Greyhounds. Sc: Vassil Akyov. Dr: Georgi Stoyanov. Ph: Victor Chichov. Set: Angel Ahrianov. Mu: Kiril Donchev. Cast: Kiril Gospodinov, Stefan Mavrodiev, Kosta Karageorgiev, Dimiter Kokanov, Peter Slabakov. 82 mins. Prem: April 11.

As the title hints, this is a metaphoric and lyrical statement on youth in a time of trial and oppression. A group of sixteen-year-olds grow to maturity quickly in a small provincial village at the outbreak of the Second World War.

ARMANDO—BELIAT KON / Armando—The White Horse. A feature film in two parts. 75 mins. Prem: April 25.

(1) **ARMANDO.** Sc: Aleksi Naidenov. Dr: Lyudmil Kirkov. Ph: Ivailo Trenchev. Set: Maria Ivanova. Mu: Boris Karadimchev. Cast: Konstantin Kotsev, Assen Georgiev.

(2) **BELIYAT KON / The White Horse.** Sc: Aleksi Naidenov. Dr: Milen Nikolov. Ph: Borislav Punchev. Set: Maria Ivanova. Mu: Boris Karadimchev. Cast: Grigor Vachkov, Ilya Dobrev.

Armando is a melancholic cabaret singer, a comic figure, whose chance meeting with an old friend, now a partisan in the Great War, leads to his tragic end. *The White Horse* features another "outsider"—this time a circus cowboy (Grigor Vachkov in a memorable sketch) whose only possession is his horse, needed by the partisans in an emergency to carry a radio on a mission. Both films take an offbeat approach to the Second World War, somewhat Chaplinesque.

GOSPODIN NIKOY / Mister Nobody. Sc: Bogomil Rainov. Dr: Ivan Terziev. Ph: Dimo Kolarov. Set: Konstantin Djidrov. Mu: Georgi Genlzov. Cast: Kosta Tsonev, Iskra Hadjiyeva, Dorothea Toncheva, Georgi Cherkelov. 111 mins. Prem: May 22.

Spy thriller set along the Greek-Bulgarian border. This was Terziev's first feature and followed the usual formula for the genre.

LYUBOVNITSATA NA GRAMINYA / Gramigna's Lover. Sc: Ugo Pirro, based on the short story by Giovanni Verga. Dr: Carlo Lizzani. Ph: Silvano Ippoliti, Enrico Scisso, Tsanko Tsanchev. Mu: Otello Profazzio. Cast: Gian-Maria Volonté, Stefania Sandrelli, Emilia Radeva, Assen Milanov, Stoyanka Mutafova, Stoycho Mazgalov, Peter Slabakov, Stoyan Stoychev, Gancho Ganchev. (Coproduction with Italy.) 100 mins. Prem: June 26.

The setting is southern Italy at the turn of the century.

MALKI TAYNI / Little Secrets. Sc: Angel Wagenstein. Dr: Wolfgang Staudte. Ph: Wolf Wirth. Set: Iskra Licheva. Mu: Milcho Leviev. Cast: Apostol Karamitev, Karl-Michael Vogler, Konstantin Kotsev, Reinhild Solf, Maya Dragomanska, Ani Bakalova, Andreas Mannkopf, Jürgen Rehmann, Katrin Schaake. (Coproduction via West Berlin with the Federal Republic of Germany.) 90 mins. Prem: July 11.

Despite a talented team of German and Bulgarian filmmakers, this psychological thriller set on the resort beaches of the Black Sea didn't rise above the ordinary.

IVAN SHISHMAN / Tsar Ivan Shishman. Sc & Dr: Yuri Arnaudov, based on Kamen Zidarov's play with same title. Ph: Nedelcho Nanev. Set: Assen Stoychev. Mu: Kiril Tsibulka. Cast: Stefan Getsov, Rusha Delcheva, Vancha Doycheva, Nikola Doychev. 80 mins. Prem: August 29.

The last of the Shishman dynasty, Tsar Ivan (1371–93) ruled during the final days of the Second Bulgarian Empire in Turnovo. This was the second adaptation of a Zidarov drama: *Ivan Shishman* was a popular play on Bulgarian stages.

SKORPION SRESHTU DAGA / "Scorpion" versus "Rainbow." Sc: Pavel Vezhinov. Dr: Vladislav Ikonomov. Ph: Krum Krumov. Set: Violetta Yovcheva. Mu: Kiril Tsibulka. Cast: Vassil Popiliev, Naum Shopov, Dobromir Manev, Rumena Trifonova, Katya Paskaleva. 96 mins. Prem. September 26.

Based on actual events, the action of this "Eastern" is set in the mountains: fascist guerrillas are terrorizing villages in the postwar years.

OSMIYAT / The Eighth. Sc: Peter Hristov, Todor Monov. Dr: Zako Heskia. Ph: Georgi Georgiev. Mu: Milcho Leviev. Cast: Georgi Georgiev-Gets, Nikola Anastassov, Meglena Karalambova, Stoycho Mazgalov, Anton Gorchev, 106 mins. Prem: October 17.

An "Eastern" about eight parachute jumpers, members of a partisan detachment, fighting to the death against fascists during the Second World War. It features Georgi Georgiev-Gets, a popular action actor, as the heroic "eighth."

TRAGNI NA PAT / Set Out Again. Sc & Dr: Peter Donev. Ph: Boris Yanakiev. Set: Bogoya Sapundjiev. Mu: Kiril Donchev. Cast: Nikola Ouzunov, Georgi Georgiev-Gets, Siyka Hristova. 92 mins. Prem: October 31.

About life on cooperative farm. The hero is a young veterinarian who does his job and then sets out again." A diary recalls the events of a bygone day.

PRIZNANIE / Confession. Sc: Dimiter Valev, Yanko Yankov. Dr: Yanko Yankov. Ph: Trendafil Zahariev. Set: Violetta Yovcheva. Cast: Stoycho Mazgalov, Stoyan Gadev, Nina Stamove, Boris Simeonov, Graziella Buchvarova. 89 mins. Prem: November 14.

A compassionate view of the mistakes a former partisan made in the postwar years.

1970

KIT / The Whale. Sc: "Cheremuhin." Dr: Peter Vassilev. Ph: Emil Wagenstein. Set: Iskra Licheva. Mu: Atanas Boyadjiev. Cast: Grigor Vachkov, Stoyanka Mutafova, Tsvyatko Nikolov, Georgi Partsalev, Dimiter Panov, Georgi Kaloyanchev, Georgi Naumov, Lyubomir Kisselichki. 82 mins. Prem: January 26.

A hilarious satire receiving limited release, the "whale" was indeed a modest catch that got stretched by the imagination (and the need to fulfill a quota) into the stuff spectacular news is made out of.

S OSOBENO MNENIE / I Beg To Differ. Sc: Alexander Karasimeonov. Dr: Lada Boyadjieva, Yanush Vazov. Ph: Ivailo Trenchev. Set: Konstantin Russalzov. Mu: Kiril Tsibulka. Cast: Stoycho Mazgalov, Peter Chernev, Rumena Gerogieva. 93 mins. Prem: February 20.

Tale about two ex-partisans now working at a mine who clash over old-fashioned and new ideas in running the

place. The directors come from the documentary field.

PETIMATA OT MOBI DIK / The Five From the Moby Dick. Sc: Boris Aprilov. Dr: Grisha Ostrovski, Todor Stoyanov. Ph: Victor Chichov. Set: Alexander Denkov. Mu: Peter Stupel. Cast: Maya Dragomanska, Sasha Bratanova, Marius Donkin, Irinei Konstantinov. 97 mins. Prem: February 20.

Youth film with an adventure motif. Four young people on a sail boat christened "Moby Dick" have taken little Vasko along for a day on an enchanted island.

EDIN MIG SVOBODA / A Moment of Freedom. A feature film in two parts. 77 mins. Prem: March 27.

(1) STARETSAT / The Old Man. Sc: Ivailo Petrov. Dr: Peter Kaishev. Ph: Dimo Kolarov. Mu: Lazar Nikolov. Cast: Dimiter Panov, Stevfan Iliev, Anton Gorchev, Ivan Manov, Dorothea Toncheva, Nikolai Klissurov.

(2) ISKAM DA ZHIVEYA / I Want To Live. Sc: Lyuben Stanev. Dr: Ivanka Grubcheva. Ph: Georgi Georgiev. Mu: César Franck. Cast: Stoycho Mazgalov, Misho Mihailov, Vassil Mihailov, Todor Kolev, Nadezhda Rancheva, Peter Slabakov.

The Old Man is set in a concentration camp during the time of the partisan resistance, while *I Want to Live* deals with a transfer of prisoners during the same period. In both stories an individual tastes freedom briefly.

SBOGOM, PRIYATELI /Farewell, Friends! Sc: Atanas Tsenev. Dr: Borislav Sharaliev. Ph: Atanas Tassev. Set: Violetta Yovcheva. Mu: Vassil Kasandjiev. Cast: Vladimir Smirnov, Mladen Mladenov, Nikolai Binev, Violetta Pavlova. 100 mins. Prem: May 15.

Youth theme about teachers and students on the verge of adulthood.

KNYASAT / The Prince. Sc: Bancho Banov, Peter Vassilev. Dr: Peter Vassilev. Ph: Tsanko Tsanchev. Set: Naiden Petrov. Mu: Simeon Pironkov. Cast: Stefan Danailov, Georgi Cherkelov, Violetta Gindeva, Dorothea Toncheva. 105 mins. Prem: May 29.

Historical film, the Prince is the 20-year-old Theodore Svetoslav Terter, during whose reign (1300–22) in Turnovo the southern Bulgarian territories were regained in campaigns against the Mongols and the Byzantines.

EZOP / Aesop. Sc: Angel Wagenstein. Dr: Rangel Vulchanov. Ph: Andrei Barla. Set: Boris Moravets. Mu: Zdenek Liška. Cast: Georgi Kaloyanchev, Dorothea Toncheva, Violetta Antonova, Miroslav Mahaček, Radovan Lukavski. (Coproduction with Czechoslovakia.) 96 mins. Prem: June 26.

Shot in 1968 and released a year later, Vulchanov's *Aesop* should be viewed in relation to the ongoing Czechoslovak productions of the time. The Greek fabulist is depicted as a freedom-loving individual in oppressive times. A historical tract.

CHERNITE ANGELI / Black Angels. Sc & Dr: Vulo Radev, based on Mitka Grubcheva's memoirs *In the Name of the People*. Ph: Atanas Tassev. Set: Stefan Savov. Mu: Simeon Pironkov. Cast: Stefan Danilov, Dorothea Toncheva, Violetta Gindeva, Dobrinka Stankova. 137 mins. Prem: Sepetmber 4.

A popular box-office hit, this "Eastern" features six teenagers in the mountains trained for a partisan fighting unit.

TSITADELATA OTGOVORI / The Citadel Replied. Sc: Rangel Ignatov. Dr: Gencho Genchev. Ph: Stoyan Slachkin. Set: Bogoya Sapundjiev. Mu: Atanas Boyadjiev. Cast: Georgi Georgiev-Gets, Peter Slabakov, Evstati Stratev, Ivan Kondov. 100 mins. Prem: September 24.

Spy caper about a Bulgarian intelligence officer winning out over a foreign intelligence agent. Made in color.

1971

TARALEZHITE SE RAZHDAT BEZ BODLI / Porcupines Are Born without Bristles. Sc: Mormarev Brothers. Dr: Dimiter Petrov. Ph: Krum Krumov. Set: Konstantin Russakov. Mu: Peter Stupel. Cast: Sarkis Muhibian, Ivailo Djambazov, Neiko Neikov, Peter Peychev. 82 mins. Prem: January 8.

Delightful children's film, combining the talents of the Mormarev Brothers and Dimiter Petrov, who have natural gifts for the difficult genre. Film is composed of three novellas: "An Alarming Event," "Hooligans," and "The Present."

KRAYAT NA PESANTA / The End of the Song. Sc: Nikolai Haitov. Dr: Milen Nikolov. Ph: Ivailo Trenchev. Set: Boyanka Ahrianova. Mu: Boris Karadimchev. Cast: Vassil Mihailov, Katya Paskaleva, Itzhak Fintsi, Nikola Todev. 93 mins. Prem: January 29.

The Rhodope Mountains with their enchanting beauty and lusty songs and dances, as chronicled in a tale by the area's balladeer, Nikolai Haitov, set at the turn of the century.

NE SE OBRASHTAY NAZAD / Don't Turn Back. Sc: Atanas Tsenev, Mihail Kirkov, Vassil Popov. Dr: Lyudmil Kirkov. Ph: Atanas Tassev. Set: Violetta Yovcheva. Mu: Boris Karadimchev. Cast: Assen Georgiev, Dimiter Buynozov, Anton Gorchev, Yordanka Kuzmanova. 82 mins. Prem: February 19.

An "Eastern" about partisans scrambling to collect a supply of arms dropped by Soviet aircraft in the mountains.

NYAMA NISHTO PO-HUBAVO OT LOSHOTO VREME / There's Nothing Finer than Bad Weather. Sc: Bogomil Rainov. Dr: Metodi Andonov. Ph: Dimo Kolarov. Set: Konstantin Djidrov. Mu: Boris Karadimchev. Cast: Georgi Georgiev-Gets, Elena Rainova, Naum Shopov, Kosta Tsonev. 129 mins. Prem: March 5.

A tale of espionage. The chief character is a counterintelligence officer whose job is to mix with the higher circles of Western agents. His code words form the title.

OTKRADNATIAT VLAK / The Stolen Train. Sc: Anton Antonov-Tonich, Simeon Nazhorny. Dr: Vladimir Yanchev. Ph: Ivan Tsonev. Set: Iskra Licheva. Mu: Peter Stupel. Cast: Georgia Kaloyanchev, Dobrinka Stankova, Stefan Iliev, Peter Slabakov. (Coproduction with the Soviet Union.) 81 mins. Prem: April 16.

Based on a true story, the adventure yarn is about a train stolen by German and fascist officers toward the end of the war in order to cross the southern border with valuable archival information. The partisans and Soviets save the day.

GNEVNO PATUVANE / Wrathful Journey. Sc: Diko Fuchedjiev. Dr: Nikola Korabov. Ph: Borislav Yanakiev. Set: Violetta Yovcheva. Mu: Boris Karadimchev. Cast: Yossif Surchadjiev, Dorothea Toncheva, Severina Teneva. 93 mins. Prem: April 23.

One of the better contemporary themes about a young man, this one a geologist, struggling to find his own identity and meet the challenges about him without compromising his ideals. Made in color.

STRANEN DVUBOY / Strange Duel. Sc: Dino Gochev. Dr: Todor Stoyanov. Ph: Victor Chichov. Set: Stefan Savov. Mu: Atanas Boyadjiev. Cast: Leon Niemczyk, Peter Slabakov, Nevena Kokanova. 102 mins. Prem: May 7.

A spy caper with whodunit motifs thrown in for good measure, set in a foreign land.

MIHAIL STROGOV. Sc: Giannpiero Bina, Eriprando Visconti, based on Jules Verne's novel with the same title. Dr: Eriprando Visconti. Ph: Luigi Cuveiller. Cast: John Philip Law, Mimsy Farmer, Hiram Keller. (Coproduction with Italy.) Prem: May 14.

The Jules Verne tale (published 1867) deals with a royal courier, Mihail Strogov, and his secret mission, set against the background of a revolt in Siberia in 1850.

TRIMATA OT ZAPASA / Three Reserve Officers. Sc: Pavel Vezhinov. Dr: Zako Heskia. Ph: Hristo Vulchanov. Set: Lyuben Trupkov. Mu: Simeon Pironkov. Cast: Georgi Partsalev, Nikola Anastassov, Kiril Gospodinov. 93 mins. Prem: September 3.

Three soldiers on and off the battlefields at the end of the Second World War, made as a comedy with reflective touches.

NEOBHODIMIYAT GRESHNIK / The Indispensable Sinner. Sc: Ivan Ostrikov. Dr: Borislav Sharaliev. Ph: Georgi Russinov. Set: Maria Ivanova. Mu: Boris Karadimchev. Cast: Kosta Tsonev, Maya Dragomanska, Yavor Milushev. 88 mins. Prem: September 24.

A youth theme with a social message: a lawyer is faced with an ethical decision in regard to understanding and helping a youngster on the verge of becoming a criminal and social outcast. Made in color.

GERLOVSKA ISTORIYA / Incident at Gerlovo. Sc: Atanas Slavov. Dr: Grisha Ostrovski. Ph: Borislav Punchev. Set: Mony Aladjemov. Mu: Georgi Genkov. Cast: Vassil Mihailov, Peter Slabakov, Yordanka Kuzmanova, Ivan Nestorov. 93 mins. Prem: October 8.

Set during the first days of Socialist Bulgaria, the story recounts how villagers in the Balkan mountains react to a dilemma—a remnant of the monarchy is still on the scene and has to be coped with.

SHAREN SVYAT / Colorful World. A feature film in two parts. 106 mins. Prem: October 29.

(1) **GOLA SUVEST / Naked Conscience.** Sc: Nikolai Haitov. Dr: Milen Nikolov. Ph: Krum Krumov. Set: Violetta Yovcheva. Mu: Boris Karadimchev. Cast: Konstantin Kotsev, Georgi Georgiev-Gets, Zhelcho Mandadjiev, Naum Shopov, Domna Ganeva, Georgi Cherkelov, Ivan Kondov.

(2) **IZPIT / The Test.** Sc: Nikolai Haitov. Dr: Georgi Djulgerov. Ph: Radoslav Spassov. Set: Violetta Yovcheva. Mu: Simeon Pironkov. Cast: Philip Trifonov, Vulcho Kamarashev, Nikola Todev, Peter Slavov, Stefan Mavrodiev, Evtim Kirilov, Snezhina Balabanova.

A key film in the history of Bulgarian cinema. *Naked Conscience* is set in the 1930s, and is the story of a lad's indignation at the wanton felling of trees in a state forest. *The Test* takes place at the turn of the century, and is about an ancient ritual of testing the strength of a barrel and, with it, the measure of a man. Both are Nikolai Haitov stories, drawn from the legends of the Rhodope Mountains—*The Test* is a gem of a film.

PTITSI DOLITAT PRI NAS / Birds Are Flying Our Way. Sc: Peter Slavinski. Dr: Zahari Zhandov. Ph: Ivan Bossev, Emil Kodov. Set: Nikolai Surchadjiev, Alexander Bruzitsov. Cast: Borislav Ivanov, Victor Danchenko, Nikolina Genova, Yordan Mitov, Nelly Topalova. 82 mins. Prem: November 26.

About children and birds. The chief character is a gypsy boy whose love for nature, particularly birds, sets an example for others. Important experiment in color photography.

1972

KRAGOVE NA OBICHTA / Circles of Love. Sc: Dimiter Gulev. Dr: Kiril Ilinchev. Ph: Stoyan Slachkin. Set: Konstantin Djidrov. Mu: Rumyana Stancheva. Cast: Christian Fokov, Nevena Kokanova, Maya Gacheva. 75 mins. Prem: January 7.

Three novellas on the theme of love in an omnibus film, the stories linked by the tragic fates of three brothers during the resistance movement. Color.

AVTOSTOP / Hitchhiking. Sc: Ivan Radoev. Dr: Nikola Petkov. Ph: Mladen Kolev. Set: Mony Aladjemov. Mu: Boris Karadimchev. Cast: Tsvetana Maneva, Nikolai Ouzunov, Violetta Pavlova. 76 mins. Prem: January 28.

Poet-playwright Ivan Radoev contributed this light comedy in one of his collaborations with the Boyana Studios. The scene is a filling station on a major highway, at which a pretty hitchhiker stops on her way to the seashore. Color.

KOZIYAT ROG / The Goat Horn. Sc: Nikolai Haitov. Dr: Metodi Andonov. Ph: Dimo Kolarov. Set: Konstantin Djidrov. Mu: Maria Neykova. Cast: Anton Gorchev, Katya Paskaleva, Kliment Denchev, Todor Kolev, Milen Penev. 103 mins. Prem: February 18.

The biggest box-office hit in the history of Bulgarian cinema. The popularity abroad of this film might best be understood in the light of history: during the seventeenth century, the *haiduks*, or outlaws in the mountains, practiced a form of resistance under the Turkish yoke with the help of villagers. The film is made in the style of ancient tragedy.

GLUTNITSATA / The Pack of Wolves. Sc: Anton Donchev. Dr: Ivanka Grubcheva. Ph: Georgi Georgiev. Set: Milko Marinov. Mu: Boris Karadimchev. Cast: Kosta Tsonev, Stoycho Mazgalov, Mihail Mihailov, Kiril Gospodinov. 92 mins. Prem: March 3.

An action film about cleaning out a pack of fascist wolves hiding in the mountains after the Second World War. Color.

NA ZAZORYAVANE / At Daybreak. A feature film in two parts. 109 mins. Prem: March 31.

(1) **SURTSE CHOVESHKO / A Human Heart.** Sc: Pavel Vezhinov. Dr: Ivan Nichev. Ph: Atanas Tassev. Set: Iskra Licheva. Mu: Kiril Tsibulka. Cast: Georgi Stoyanov, Nevena Kokanova, Nikolai Binev, Andrei Chaprazov.

(2) **STIHOVE / Verses.** Sc: Pavel Vezhinov. Dr: Margarit Nikolov. Ph: Ivan Sumardjiev. Set: Milko Marinov. Mu: Simeon Pironkov. Cast: Nikolai Buriyaev, Todor Shtopov, Dimo Djikov, Federico Zahariev.

Two novellas from screenplays by the prolific Pavel Vezhinov. *A Human Heart*, set during the fascist period, features a surgeon in a dilemma: he has to perform a heart operation on a partisan leader who is later to be handed over for execution by the fascist government. *Verses* is about a Soviet lad serving in the liberation army who reaches manhood on the Hungarian front in the company of Bulgarian soldiers.

MOMCHETO SI OTIVA / A Boy Becomes a Man. Sc: Georgi Mishev. Dr: Lyudmil Kirkov. Ph: Atanas Tassev. Set: Nedyo Nedev. Mu: Boris Karadimchev. Cast: Filip Trifonov, Sashka Bratanova, Nevena Kokanova, Elena Rainova. 98 mins. Prem: May 19.

Part One of the story of Ran, who comes of age and is about to set his course in life. Part Two, *Don't Go Away*, was produced four years later in 1976. Put both of them together, and the Mishev theme of integrity in an alien society is clearly visible. With this film Lyudmil Kirkov became a major director in Sofia.

TIHIYAT BEGLETS / The Quiet Fugitive. Sc: Emil Manov. Dr: Peter Vassilev. Ph: Tsanko Tsanchev. Set: Donyo Donev. Mu: Dimiter Vulchev. Cast: Konstantin Kotsev, Zhorzheta Chakarova. 77 mins. Prem: June 2.

A bachelor who can't stand the noise of the big city runs off to the seclusion of mountains—only to find that love is just as hectic. Color.

DESET DNI NEPLATENI / Ten Days without Pay. Sc: Todor Monov. Dr: Yanush Vazov. Ph: Radoslav Spassov. Set: Violetta Yovcheva. Cast: Margarita Chudinova, Mladen Mladenov, Elena Stefanova, Todor Kolev. 88 mins. Prem: June 16.

A young engineer has ten days off from his job, but his pockets are empty—then he meets a girl by chance, and one adventure leads to another. This was cameraman Radoslav Spassov's first feature film, and both he and documentarist Yanoush Vazov sought to give the film an atmosphere of natural realism.

NAKOVALNYA ILI CHUK / Hammer or Anvil. Sc: Lyuben Stanev, Ivan Radoev, Wolfgang Ebeling. Dr: Hristo Hristov. Ph: Atanas Tassev. Set: Hristo Stefanov. Mu: Simeon Pironkov. Cast: Stefan Getsov, Hannjo Hasse, Martin Flörchinger, Frank Oberman, Michaela Kreisler. (Co-production with the German Democratic Republic and the Soviet Union.) 160 mins. Prem: September 8.

Large-scale spectacle on the Leipzig Trial in 1933, during which Georgi Dimitrov defended himself against accusations that he conspired in the Reichstag Fire, fifty years ago. The anniversary was celebrated with this Soviet-German-Bulgarian epic.

TATUL / Thorn-Apple. Sc.: Slav G. Karaslavov, based on Georgi Karaslavov's novel with the same title. Dr: Atanas Traikov. Ph: Krum Krumov. Set: Kiril Nedelchev. Mu: Vassil Kasandjiev. Cast: Elena Stefanova, Meglena Karalambova, Ivan Nalbantov. 98 mins. Prem: October 6.

A straight forward literary adaptation of a popular novel by one of Bulgaria's masterful storytellers, Georgi Karaslavov. It's a tale of family greed, set in a provincial village of the 1930s.

TRETA SLED SLANTSETO / The Third Planet in the Solar System. Sc: Pavel Vezhinov. Dr: Georgi Stoyanov. Ph: Ivan Trenchev. Set: Galin Malakchiev. Mu: Kiril Donchev. Cast: Kiril Gospodinov, Naum Shopov, Nikolai Nikolov. 124 mins. Prem: October 20.

Lyudmil Kirkov's *A Boy Becomes a Man* (1972).

The first attempt at a science-fiction film, comprised of four novellas originally: "The Birth of Man," "Bayan," The Stranger," and "My First Day." "Bayan" was then dropped from the project during the production shooting. Color.

HLYAB—CHERTICHKATA / Bread—The Dash. A feature film in two parts. 89 mins. Prem: November 3.

(1) HLYAB / BREAD. Sc & Dr: Naum Shopov, based on Yordan Radichkov's story with the same title. Ph: Ivailo Trenchev. Set: Iskra Licheva. Mu: Kiril Donchev. Cast: Nikola Hadjiyski, Rumyana Bocheva. 44 mins.

Based on a short story by Bulgaria's leading literary figure, Yordan Radichkov. The period setting of the antifascist struggle sets the stage for a baker's heroism.

(2) CHERTICHKATA / The Dash. Sc: Zhanna Avishai. Dr: Rashko Ouzunov. Ph: Tsvetan Chobanski. Set: Mony Aladjemov. Mu: Alexander Yossifov. Cast: Violetta Gindeva, Plamen Petkov, Adriana Andreyeva. 45 mins.

A love story set in the antifascist period, the title refers to a code name for the two young people in the resistance movement.

VYATARAT NA PATESHESTVIYATA / The Trip with the Wind. Sc: Kolyo Nikolov. Dr: Lada Boyadjieva. Ph: Krassimir Kostov. Set: Stefka Mazakova, Konstantin Djidrov, Cast: Yossif Surchadjiev, Ivan Arshinkov, Violetta Nikolova. 93 mins. Prem: November 3.

A youth film, about a village boy who leaves his cow on a summer day to discover the world of grown-ups.

S DETSA NA MORE / With Children at the Seaside. Sc: Mormarev Brothers. Dr: Dimiter Petrov. Ph: Krum SKrumov. Set: Konstantin Russakov. Mu: Peter Stupel. Cast: Georgi Partsalev, Mihail Mutafov, Kiril Petrov. 81 mins. Prem: November 17.

Children's film. It's the sequel to *Porcupines Are Born without Bristles* (1971). The same kids are now at the seashore on their summer vacation. Color.

OBICH / Affection. Sc: Alexander Karasimeonov. Dr: Lyudmil Staikov. Ph: Boris Yanakiev. Set: Maria Ivanova. Mu: Simeon Pironkov. Cast: Violetta Doneva, Nevena Kokanova, Ivan Kondov, Nikolai Binev. 91 mins. Prem: December 8.

Prizewinner at the 1973 Moscow Film Festival. This is a youth theme and deals with the generation gap, but in the deft directorial hands of newcomer Lyudmil Staikov it rises about the ordinary. A young nurse awakens to the human sacrifice of her aunt, a doctor abroad. Color.

1973

IGREK 17 / Y-17. Sc: Ivan Ohridski, Assen Georgiev. Dr: Willy Tsankov. Ph: Venets Dimitrov. Set: Irina Marichkova. Mu: Angel Mihailov. Cast: Ivan Kondov, Joseph Blacha,

Dorothea Toncheva, Georgi Georgiev-Gets. 104 mins. Prem: January 5.

Spy caper—the secret agent goes by the code word "Y-17."

GOLYAMATA POBEDA / The Great Victory. Sc: Doncho Tsonchev. Dr: Vassil Mirchev. Ph: Georgi Mateyev, Krassimir Kostov, Angel Ivanov, Emil Dimitrov, Konstantin-Gossev. Set: Russi Doychinov. Mu: Boris Karadimchev. Cast: Kosta Tsonev, Yossif Surchadjiev, Dobromir Manev, Itzhak Fintsi, Dossyo Dossev, Pepa Nikolova, Zhivka Peneva. 104 mins. Prem: February 9.

Action film about an international car rally across Bulgaria.

MAZHE BEZ RABOTA / Men without Work. Sc: Nikolai Nikiforov. Dr: Ivan Terziev. Ph: Rumen Georgiev. Set: Donyo Donev. Mu: Emil Pavlov. Cast: Stefan Peychev, Anton Karastoyanov, Katya Paskaleva. 74 mins. Prem: February 23.

The first of Ivan Terziev's deliberations on men and work—or their disinclination to work. The scene is the hapless construction of a road, the drama lies in the social outlook of each of the workers. Black-and-white.

KATO PESEN / Like a Song. Sc: Slavcho Dudov. Dr: Irina Aktasheva, Hristo Piskov. Ph: Yatsek Todorov. Set: Boyanka Ahryanova. Mu: Boris Karadimchev. Cast: Filip Trifonov, Irina Rossich, Vassil Mihailov. 97 mins. Prem: March 9.

The story of the socialist revolution in Bulgaria in 1944, viewed through the eyes of the younger generation.

BYALATA ODISEYA / White Odyssey. Sc: Rangel Ignatov. Dr: Vassil Mirchev. Ph: Ivan Sumardjiev. Set: Mladen Mladenov. Mu: Kiril Tsibulka. Cast: Katya Paskaleva, Anton Gorchev, Russi Chanev, Naum Shopov. 97 mins. Prem: March 24.

An "Eastern" with four partisans surrounded by fascists amid snow-capped mountains.

TIGARCHETO / The Little Tiger. Sc: Vassil Akyov. Dr: Marianna Evstatieva. Ph: Petko Petkov. Set: Violetta Yovcheva. Mu: Vassil Kasandjiev. Cast: Nevena Kokanova, Emilia Radeva, Vassil Mihailov. 84 mins. Prem: April 6.

Children's film, about the difficulties of getting used to attending kindergarten. Black-and-white.

MANDOLINATA / The Mandolin. Sc & Dr: Ilya Velchev. Ph & Set: Konstantin Djidrov. Mu: Ivan Halachev. Cast: Peter Slabakov, Yuri Angelov, Sashka Bratanova, Dossyo Dossev, Ivan Grigorov, Nadeshda Kasassyan. 66 mins. Prem: May 11.

A story about the Resistance, pitting a prison doctor against a poet in his grasp. Black-and-white.

OCHAKVANE / Expectation. Sc: Atanas Tsenev. Dr: Borislav Sharaliev. Ph: Venets Dimitrov. Set: Angel Ahryanov. Mu: Georgi Genkov. Cast: Georgi Cherkelov, Ivan Andonov, Georgi Dyubrilov, Albena Kasakova. 77 mins. Prem: May 25.

A TV unit prepares to film the arrival of an ocean-sailing trawler, only to stumble upon a human drama on board of greater meaning.

SIROMASHKO LYATO / Indian Summer. Sc: Mormarev Brothers. Dr: Milen Nikolov. Ph: Rumen Georgiev. Set: Petko Bonchev. Mu: Boris Karadimchev. Cast: Georgi Partsalev, Tatyana Lolova, Ivan Kondov, Leda Tasseva. 79 mins. Prem: June 22.

A comedy about a man looking forward to his day of retirement—only to discover that his own family badly needs a housemaid to take care of the daily domestic chores.

BYAGSTVO V ROPOTAMO / Escape to Ropotamo. Sc: Boris Aprilov, Rangel Vulchanov. Dr: Rangel Vulchanov. Ph: Atanas Tassev. Set: Bogomil Yanchulev. Mu: Ivan Staikov. Cast: Natalia Markova, Georgi Kaloyanchev, Konstantin Kotsev, Dimiter Tashev. 101 mins. Prem: July 13.

The first attempt at the Boyana Studios at a musical, set at a Black Sea resort at the mouth of the Ropotamo River. Rangel Vulchanov had worked for a while at the Barrandov Studios in Prague, where Czech musicals featuring pop stars are common.

POSLEDNATA DUMA / The Last Word. Sc & Dr: Binka Zhelyazkova. Ph: Boris Yanakiev. Set: Iskra Licheva. Mu: Boris Karadimchev. Cast: Emilia Radeva, Tsvetana Maneva, Bela Tsoneva, Dorothea Toncheva, Aneta Petrovska. 118 mins. Prem: September 7.

The story of six women sharing a "condemned cell." The depth of the film is in the character sketches. Zhelyazkova drew upon her own experiences in the Resistance, much as she did in *We Were Young* (1961).

GOLIAMATA SKUKA / The Great Boredom, Sc: Bogomil Rainov. Dr: Metodi Andonov. Ph: Dimo Kolarov. Set: Konstantin Djidrov. Mu: Dimiter Vulchev. Cast: Anton Gorchev, Kosta Tsonev, Tsvetana Maneva, Elena Rainova, Nikolai Binev. 70 mins. Prem: October 5.

A variation on the Western secret service theme, it's the story of an ace Bulgarian agent on an assignment in Copenhagen.

NAY-DOBRIYAT CHOVEK KOGOTO POSNAVAM / The Kindest Man I Know. Sc: Liliana Mihailova. Dr: Lyubomir Sharlandjiev. Ph: Borislav Punchev. Set: Bogoya Sapundjiev. Mu: Dimiter Vulchev. Cast: Nevena Kokanova, Vladimir Smirnov, Peter Slabakov, Grigor Vachkov, Vassil Popiliev. 91 mins. Prem: October 19.

A social comedy about a language teacher whose students are workers attending night school. Both sides benefit from the unusual circumstances.

NONA. Sc: Stefan Tsanev, based on Yordan Yovkov's novel "The Farm near the Frontier." Dr: Grisha Ostrovski. Ph: Krassimir Kostov. Mu: Georgi Genkov. Set: Mony Aladjemov. Cast: Dorothea Toncheva, Stefan Danailov, Todor Todorov, Nikola Todev. 84 mins. Prem: November 16.

Yordan Yovkov's Nona, in his novel *The Farm near the Frontier* (published 1934), is one of the great figures in Bulgarian literature. The setting is the Dobruja region of the Danube delta, on the estate of a rich landowner in 1923. the year of the historic September Uprising. This was a fiftieth anniversary production.

PREBROYAVANE NA DIVITE ZAYTSI / The Hare Census. Sc: Georgi Mishev. Dr: Eduard Zahariev. Ph: Venets Dimitrov. Set: Mihalis Garudis, Kolyo Getsov. Mu: Kiril Donchev. Cost: Itzhak Fintsi, Nikola Todev, Filip Trifonov. 69 mins. Prem: November 30.

A milestone in Bulgarian cinema. The satirical talents of screenplay writer Mishev and director Zahariev were augmented by the comic mugging of actor Fintsi and a troupe of unforgettable bit players. The title itself is a tickler.

Binka Zhelyazkova's *The Last Word* (1973).

Eduard Zahariev's *The Hare Census* (1973).

I DOYDE DENYAT / And the Day Came. Sc: Vassil Akyov. Dr: Georgi Djulgerov. Ph: Radoslav Spassov. Set: Ivan Koshucharov. Mu: Selected music by Mozart, Pipkov, and Penderecki. Cast: Plamen Mazlarov, Elena Mirchovska, Panteley Panteleyev, Kliment Mihailov. 86 mins. Prem: December 21.

One of the best war films made in Bulgaria. The realism and psychological depth owe much to Vassil Aykov's autobiographical script; the rest is Djulgerov.

1974

IVAN KONDAREV. Sc: Nikola Ticholov, Nikola Korabov, based on Emilian Stanev's novel with the same title. Dr: Nikola Korabov. Ph: Emil Wagenstein. Set: Maria Ivanova. Cast: Anton Gorchev, Katya Paskaleva, Ivan Andonov, Todor Kolev, Stefan Danailov, Vassil Popiliev. 169 mins. Prem: January 11.

An epic chronicle of the turbulent years between the First World War and the September 1923 Uprising as set down in Emilian Stanev's historical novel (published 1958).

KASHTI BEZ OGRADI / Houses without Fences. Sc: Nikola Russev. Dr: Georgi Stoyanov. Ph: Ivailo Trenchev. Set: Boyanka Ahryanova. Mu: Kiril Donchev. Cast: Kiril Petrov, Konstantin Kotsev, Stefan Danailov, Leda Tasseva. 86 mins. Prem: February 8.

Children's film about a lad committed to a children's home, with observations on contemporary social conditions.

ZAREVO NAD DRAVA / Dawn over the Drava. Sc: Pavel Vezhinov, Rangel Ignatov. Dr: Zako Heskia. Ph: Krum Krumov. Set: Konstantin Russakov. Mu: Simeon Pironkov. Cast: Georgi Georgiev-Gets, Andrei Chaprazov, Georgi Kaloyanchev, Georgi Cherkelov, Dobrinka Stankova. 165 mins. Prem: March 15.

Quite respectable "Eastern" in the "super" category by the Bulgarian specialist in the field, Zako Heskia, and starring the actor primarily associated with the genre, Georgi Georgiev-Gets. The time is March 1945: the newly formed first Bulgarian Army engages the Nazis in battle on the Drava River.

IZPITI PO NIKOE VREME / Exams at Any Odd Time. Sc: Mormarev Brothers. Dr: Ivanka Grubcheva. Ph: Yatsek Todorov. Set: Konstantin Russakov. Mu: Peter Stupel. Cast: Dimiter Ganev, Ognyan Zhelyazkov, Ani Bakalova, Georgi Russev, Yanko Yankov. 80 mins. Prem: April 5.

Fine children's film and winner of several international prizes in the genre. Ivanka Grubcheva and the Mormarev Brothers became household words with this film.

SPOMEN / Memory. Sc: Svoboda Buchvarova. Dr: Ivan Nichev. Ph: Victor Chichov. Set: Irina Marichkova. Mu: Kiril Tsibulka, Kiril Donchev. Cast: Ivan Arshinkov,

Georgi Djulgerov's *And the Day Came* **(1973).**

Zako Heskia's *Dawn over the Drava* (1974).

Ivanka Grubcheva's *Exams at Any Odd Time* (1974).

Tadeusz Fijewski, Leda Tasseva, Vladimir Smirnov. 87 mins. Prem: April 19.

A youth theme set in the immediate postwar years. A boy remembers the tragic past vividly, but the scars are healed via a contact with a warm-hearted musician.

PAZACHAT NA KREPOSTA / The Fortress Guard. Sc: Stanislav Stratiev. Dr: Milen Nikolov. Ph: Tsvetan Chobanski. Set: Violetta Yovcheva. Mu: Alexander Bruzitsov. Cast: Yordan Kovachev, Pavel Poppandov, Silvia Rangelova, Georgi Mamalev. 74 mins. Prem: May 3.

First screenplay by a young satirist, Stanislav Stratiev, who was later to excel as a dramatist at Sofia's Satirical Theater. The setting is one of the country's archaeological treasures, a medieval fortress now a tourist attraction.

IZKUSTVENATA PATITSA / The Decoy. Sc: Lyuben Stanev. Dr: Yanush Vazov. Ph: Krassimir Kostov. Set: Nikolai Surchadjiev. Mu: Kiril Tsiboulka. Cast: Evgenia Barakova, Ivan Kutevski. 85 mins. Prem: May 17.

A spy thriller set in a foreign country. The feminine side of a secret mission serves as a decoy to entice a crooked foreign businessman out into the open.

POSLEDNO LYATO / The Last Summer. Sc: Yordan Radichkov, based on his story with the same title. Dr: Hristo Hristov. Ph: Tsvetan Chobanski. Set: Hristo Hristov. Mu: Krassimir Kyurkchiski. Cast: Grigor Vachkov, Bogdan Spassov, Dimiter Ikonomov, Vesko Sehirov. 86 mins. Prem: May 10.

Released approximately a year after completion, this is a key film in the development of contemporary Bulgarian cinema and a director's major contribution to a maturing national cinematography. Yordan Radichkov's novel mourns the passing of village life and peasant traditions in a surrealistic style.

POSLEDNIYAT ERGEN / The Last Bachelor. Sc & Dr: Vladimir Yanchev. Ph: Krum Krumov. Set: Petko Bonchev. Mu: Naiden Andreyev. Cast: Todor Kolev, Georgi Georgiev-Gets, Andrei Chaprazov, Tatyana Lolova, Tsvetana Maneva. 82 mins. Prem: July 16.

A comedy about an eligible bachelor still romping around free in a district where everyone else in his category is already married.

DARVO BEZ KOREN / A Tree without Roots. Sc: Hristo Hristov, Panteley Panteleyev, based on Nikolai Haitov's stories "A Tree without Roots" and "Toward the Peak." Dr: Hristo Hristov, Ph: Atanas Tassev. Set: Hristo Hristov. Mu: Krassimir Kyurkchiski. Cast: Nikola Dadov, Nevena Kokanova, Marin Yanev. 83 mins. Prem: September 6.

An oldtimer from the mountains loses his wife and comes to live with his son in the city, but the pace and alienation of the urban community leave him an outsider.

DNEVNA SVETLINA / Daylight. Sc: Nedyalko Yordanov. Dr: Margarit Nikolov. Ph: Ivan Sumardjiev. Set: Milko Marinov. Mu: Simeon Pironkov. Cast: Mladen Kisselov, Vesselin Tanev, Ivan Kondov, Evgenia Barakova. 86 mins. Prem: September 27.

A psychological drama dealing with the intelligentsia and the problems of communicating with both the older and the younger generations.

NA CHISTO / Squared Accounts. Sc: Vesselin Panayotov. Dr: Leon Daniel. Ph: Ivailo Trenchev. Set: Angel Ahryanov.

Hristo Hristov's *The Last Summer* (1974).

Lyudmil Kirkov's *Peasant on a Bicycle* (1974).

Mu: Kiril Donchev. Cast: Itzhak Fintsi, Ivan Andonov, Peter Slabakov, Filip Trifonov, Rashko Mladenov, Vladimir Parushev, Iva Ivanova, Petya Vangelova. 91 mins. Prem: September 30.

A social drama, the theme is rape and the innocence of a young worker, who is helped by relatives and acquaintances when the chips are down.

TRUDNA LYUBOV / A Difficult Love. Sc: Assen Georgiev. Dr: Ivan Andonov. Ph: Emil Wagenstein. Set: Maria Ivanova. Mu: Georgi Genkov. Cast: Tsvetana Maneva, Ivan Andonov, Georgi Cherkelov, Stefan Iliev. 85 mins. Prem: October 4.

Two individuals in love at a construction site. Their love is tested by having to make a difficult choice between their feelings and reason.

DUBLYORAT / The Stunt Man. Sc: Raina Tomova. Dr: Ilya Velchev. Ph: Krassimir Kostov. Set: Konstantin Djidrov, Emilia Gemedjiska. Mu: Mitko Shterev. Casts: Madeleine Cholakova, Irinei Konstantinov, Naum Shopov, Dossyo Dossev. 104 mins. Prem: October 18.

A psychological drama, about two professional people (an actress and an engineer) in love with each other. He is not about to play a role or perform "stunts" to improve his social status.

SELKOR / The Provincial Correspondent. Sc: Slav G. Karaslavov, based on Georgi Karaslavov's novel with same title. Dr: Atanas Traikov. Ph: Hristo Vulchanov, Emil Kodov. Set: Iskra Licheva. Mu: Krassimir Kyurkchiski. Cast: Anton Gorchev, Grigor Vachkov, Stoycho Mazgalov. 87 mins. Prem: November 1.

Literary adaptation of Georgi Karaslavov's 1933 novella on building a social conscience among the peasants at that time. Karaslavov was the "Bulgarian Gorky," whose *Provincial Correspondent* set standards in Socialist Realism.

SELYANINAT S KOLELOTO / Peasant on a Bicycle. Sc: Georgi Mishev. Dr: Lyudmil Kirkov. Ph: Georgi Russinov. Set: Bogoya Sapundjiev. Mu: Boris Karadimchev. Cast: Georgi Georgiev-Gets, Diana Chelebieva, Georgi Russev. 102 mins. Prem: November 22.

The best of the fruitful collaborations between scriptwriter Mishev and director Kirkov, this is a human and comic sketch of a born-and-bred peasant who can't get used to life in town—so he's off on a bicycle to the abandoned village in his free time, and falls fatally in love.

LAMYATA / The Dragon. Sc: Nikolai Haitov. Dr: Todor Dinov. Ph: Boris Yanakiev. Set: Mony Aladjemov. Mu: Alexander Bruzitsov. Cast: Nikola Todev, Georgi Partsalev, Peter Slabakov, Vassil Mihailov. 78 mins. Prem: December 6.

A fairytale set in medieval Bulgaria, directed by a renowned animation filmmaker, Todor Dinov.

1975

SVATBITE NA IOAN ASSEN / The Weddings of Ivan Assen. Sc: Evgeni Konstantinov. Dr: Willy Tsankov. Ph: Venets Dimitrov. Set: Assen Matev. Mu: Boris Karadimchev. Cast: Apostol Karamitev, Ivan Kondov, Kosta Tsonev, Nevena Kokanova, Violetta Gindeva, Anton Gorchev, Annetta Sotirova. 158 mins. Prem: January 3.

A historical spectacle that takes up in medieval Bulgaria where *Kaloyan* (1963) left off: Ivan Assen II, son of Tsar Assen I, ruled the Second Bulgarian Empire from 1218 to 1241 (considered by historians to have been a brilliant reign, marked by a string of victories over the conspiring boyars and the Byzantine emperor). As the title indicates, this is the story of the enlightened Bulgarian ruler forced to send his legitimate wife to a monastery in order to wed the daughter of the King of Hungary for reasons of state.

MAGISTRALA / The Highway. Sc: Atanas Tsenev, Kolyo Sevov, Mihail Kirkov. Dr: Stefan Dimitrov. Ph: Tsancho Tsanchev. Set: Maria Deyenichina. Mu: Peter Stupel. Cast: Ivan Kondov, Kosta Tsonev, Anton Gorchev. 90 mins. Prem: January 24.

The scene is a construction site, the hero is an engineer, and the theme is self-sacrifice for the betterment of the people.

VECHNI VREMENA / Eternal Times. Sc: Vassil Popov. Dr: Assen Shopov. Ph: Ivailo Trenchev. Set: Angel Ahryanov. Mu: Kiril Donchev. Cast: Peter Slabakov, Grigor Vachkov, Konstantin Kotsev, Nikola Todev. 93 mins. Prem: February 7.

Strong film about abandoned villages in the mountains. One by one, the last inhabitants leave a village community—until only an adamant forester is left.

TOZI HUBAV ZHIVOT / This Wonderful Life. Sc: Vladimir Tsarev. Dr: Maria Russeva. Ph: Venets Dimitrov. Set: Boyanka Ahryanova. Mu: Alexander Yossifov. Cast: Vassil Popiliev, Georgi Stoyanov, Svetla Dobrinovich. 74 mins. Prem: February 28.

A social comedy, about a factory manager (the enterprise is shirt making) adjusting to his destiny by examining three levels of conscience: past, present, future.

TOZI ISTINSKI MAZH / A Real Man. Sc: Ivan Ostrikov. Dr: Alexander Obreshkov, Ph: Rumen Georgiev. Set: Mony Aladjemov. Mu: Alexander Bruzitsov. Cast: Stefan Danailov, Elena Dimitrova, Rosizza Danailova, Dobromir Manev. 74 mins. Prem: March 21.

A social theme, about a young man who can't cope with the responsibilities of life.

VIZA ZA OKEANA / Visa for the Ocean. Sc: Emil Markov. Dr: Lada Boyadjieva. Ph: Victor Chichov. Set: Irina Marichkova. Mu: Georgi Genkov. Cast: Anton Gorchev, Silvia Rangelova, Georgi Stoyanov. 77 mins. Prem: April 11.

A Bulgarian deep-freeze freighter, *Sunny Beach*, is docked in Las Palmas, but instead of heading for home after a long cruise, it's off to Lagos for a stretch.

PRI NIKOGO / With Nobody. Sc: Georgi Danailov. Dr: Ivanka Grubcheva. Ph: Yatsek Todorov. Set: Konstantin Russakov. Mu: Simeon Pironkov. Cast: Aleko Kochev, Ani Bakalova, Stoycho Mazgalov. 75 mins. Prem: May 9.

Very fine children's film, and the second international success—after *Exams at Any Odd Time* (1974)—for Ivanka Grubsheva. A boy of fourteen has to cope with divorced parents and a messy courtroom scene.

PRISASTVIE / Presence. Sc: Dimiter Velchev. Dr: Todor Stoyanov. Ph: Venets Dimitrov. Set: Konstantin Kussakov. Mu: Ivan Iliev. Cast: Kolyo Donchev, Georgi Cherkelov, Alexander Pritup, Marianna Dimitrova. 93 mins. Prem: May 16.

A talented engineer returns to his job after two years in prison for the sake of others more responsible than himself for the wasteful destruction of a new catalyzer in a chemical plant—but his presence stirs unrest among the guilty.

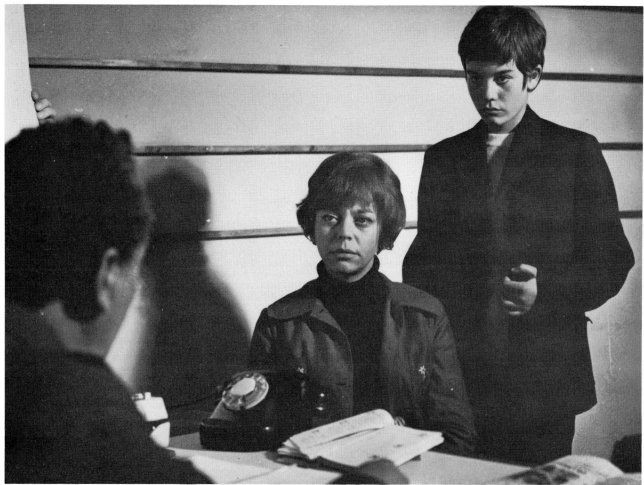

Ivanka Grubcheva's *With Nobody* (1975).

VILNA ZONA / Villa Zone. Sc: Georgi Mishev. Dr: Eduard Zahariev. Ph: Radoslav Spassov. Set: Nikolai Surchadjiev Mu: Kiril Donchev. Cast: Katya Paskaleva, Itzhak Fintsi, Naum Shopov, Evstati Stratev. 79 mins. Prem: May 30.

The domestic and international success of this satire by the team of Zahariev-Mishev-Spassov-Fintsi inspired Georgi Mishev to pen a novella afterward: it's about a garden party that goes downhill from the first moment of planning.

NEDELNITE MACHOVE / Sunday Matches. Sc: Anton Kafeschiev, Todor Andreikov. Dr: Todor Andreikov. Ph: Ivan Tsonev, Stoyan Slachkin. Set: Dora Nikolova. Cast: Konstaintin Kiriyakov, Kornelia Petkova, Ivo Russev. 91 mins. Prem: July 4.

Fine debut film by critic-filmmaker Todor Andreikov. The scene is a mining town in the mountains where the Sunday soccer matches form a way of life. Black-and-white.

NACHALOTO NA DENYA / Daybreak. Sc: Alexander Karasimeonov. Dr: Dimiter Petrov. Ph: Boris Yanakiev. Mu: Alexander Yossifov. Cast: Tsvetana Maneva, Stefan Danailov, Dorothea Toncheva, Vladimir Smirnov. 88 mins. Prem: September 5.

A social drama about a professional woman, an engineer, whose husband, also an engineer, is stationed miles away on another project. They find a way to see each other at last, but separation comes again at breakfast.

SILNA VODA / Strong Water. Sc: Boyan Papazov. Dr: Ivan Terziev. Ph: Plamen Wagenstein. Mu: Kiril Tsibulka. Cast: Ivan Grigorov, Kiril Kavadarkov, Meglena Terzieva. 84 mins. Prem: September 19.

Terziev's best film, on workers and a lack of work at a construction site. The crew here is drilling for water in an area where "strong water" from a spring is but an excuse to pass the time of day—then boredom leads to pranks, and worse.

BUNA / The Uprising. Sc & Dr: Willy Tsankov. Ph: Dimo Kolarov. Set: Irina Marichkova. Mu: Boris Karadimchev. Cast: Ivan Kondov, Tsvetana Maneva, Ilka Zafirnova, Peter Slabakov. 90 mins. Prem: October 3.

Action film set in a mountain village during the 1910s as ideologies clash.

OSADENI DUSHI / Doomed Souls. Sc & Dr: Vulo Radev, based on a novel with the same title by Dimiter Dimov. Ph: Hristo Totev. Set: Konstantin Djidrov. Mu: Mitko Sheterev. Cast: Edith Szalai, Jan Englert, Russi Chanev, Marianna Dimitrova. 137 mins. Prem: October 17.

Large-scale literary adaptation in Eastmancolor and wide screen. It's the tale of a doomed love between an American nurse, Fanny Horn, and a Spanish priest, against the backdrop of the Spanish Civil War.

Eduard Zahariev's *Villa Zone* **(1975).**

Todor Andreikov's *Sunday Matches* **(1975).**

Vulo Radev's *Doomed Souls* **(1975).**

NEZABRAVIMIYAT DEN / The Memorable Day. Sc: Peter Donev, Nikola Tiholov. Dr: Peter Donev. Ph: Krassimir Kostov. Set: Petko Bonchev. Mu: Toncho Russev. Cast: Stoycho Mazgalov, Ognyan Zhelyazkov, Natalia Markova, Bozhidar Grigorov. 94 mins. Prem: November 14.

A soccer team and its self-sacrificing trainer go through a difficult phase when an important match is lost and the coach temporarily fired.

SLADKO I GORCHIVO / Bittersweet. Sc: Lyubomir Levchev. Dr: Ilya Velchev. Ph: Krassimir Kostov. Set: Konstantin Djidrov. Mu: Mitko Shterev. Cast: Peter Slabakov, Yuri Angelov, Nikola Dadov, Galina Koteva, Adriana Banova. 93 mins. Prem: November 27.

A social drama with thriller aspects. The hero is a boy about to enter manhood the hard way: his father has been involved in criminal activities and is killed, whereby the lad learns courage and endurance from a retired general of Resistance fame.

SLEDOVATELYAT I GORATA / The Inspector and the Forest. Sc & Dr: Rangel Vulchanov. Ph: Victor Chichov. Set: Boyanka Ahryanova. Mu: Kiril Donchev. Cast: Sonya Boshkova, Lyudomir Buchvarov, Alexander Pritup. 100 mins. Prem: December 12.

Based on actual criminal records, the case of murder takes the investigating inspector behind the scenes to uncover more than first meets the eye: the girl who committed the deed was, in turn, a victim of a pimp and blackmailer. This is a remarkable examination of the mores of the day.

1976

DA IZYADESH YABALKATA / To Eat the Apple. Sc: Svodoba Buchvarova. Dr: Nikola Rudarov. Ph: Plamen Wagenstein. Set: Irina Marichkova. Mu: Kiril Tsibulka. Cast: Assen Angelov, Tsvetana Maneva, Stefan Iliev, Stoyan Gadev. 92 mins. Prem: January 9.

A whodunit with a political twist. A former member of the Resistance has been killed, it turned out, by a former member of the royal army—out of a sense of honor.

NE SI OTIVAY / Don't Go Away. Sc: Georgi Mishev. Dr: Lyudmil Kirkov. Ph: Georgi Russinov. Set: Bogoya Sapundjiev. Mu: Boris Karadimschev. Cast: Filip Trifonov, Sashka Bratanova, Elena Mirchovska, Nevena Kokanova, Georgi Russev. 96 mins. Prem: January 30.

The sequel to Kirkov and Mischev's *A Boy Becomes a Man* (1972). The young protagonist is now an elementary schoolteacher in a provincial town—his ideals put him on the opposite side of the authorities and, disappointed, he leaves the school.

Rangel Vulchanov's *The Inspector and the Forest* (1975).

DVA DIOPTARA DALEKOGLEDSTVO / Farsighted by Two Diopters. Sc: Mormarev Brothers. Dr: Peter Vassilev. Ph: Yatsek Todorov. Mu: Peter Stupel. Cast: Georgi Partsalev, Sashka Bratanova, Valentin Gadshokov. 89 mins. Prem: February 20.

A social comedy about a young couple wanting to marry but hindered by family considerations.

NAD SANTIAGO VALI / Rain over Santiago. Sc: Helvio Soto, Georges Conchon. Dr: Helvio Soto. Ph: Georges Barsky. Set: Konstantin Djidrov, Milko Marinov. Mu: Astor Piazzola. Cast: Riccardo Cucciolla, Annie Girardot, Bibi Andersson. (Coproduction with France.) 112 mins. Prem: March 12.

This international production was possible owing in some part to a similarity between the geographical terrain surrounding Santiago and Sofia. It follows recorded accounts of the military coup, and features Allende, Victor Jara, and the generals.

VOINIKUT OT OBOZA / The Soldier from the Supply Column. Sc: Slavcho Dudov, Atanas Tsenev, Aleksei Leontiev. Dr: Igo Dobrolyubov. Ph: Grigori Massalski, Tsancho Tsanchev. Set: Vladimir Dementiev, Lyuben Trupkov. Mu: Jan Frenkel. Cast: Vladimir Bassov, Stefan Danailov, Svetlana Toma, Nikola Todev. (Coproduction with the Soviet Union.) 79 mins. Prem: March 26.

A human aspect of the war years, about a kindly Soviet soldier with a horse-drawn cart in a supply column, 1944. The coproduction partner was Belarussfilm.

APOSTOLITE / The Apostles. Sc: Vesselin & Georgi Branev, Borislav Sharaliev, based on Zahari Stoyanov's book of memoirs. Dr: Borislav Sharaliev. Ph: Atanas Tassev. Set: Violetta Yovcheva, Angel Ahryanov. Mu: Krassimir Kyurkchiski. Cast: Radko Dishliev, Antoni Genov, Stoyan Stoev. 130 mins. Prem: April 9.

Patriotic spectacle commemorating—in a reedited TV version—the "Apostles", revolutionaries who led the April Rising in 1876 against the Turks.

SHTURETS V UHOTO / A Cricket in the Ear. Sc: Nikola Russev. Dr: Georgi Stoyanov. Ph: Ivailo Trenchev. Set: Elena Dimyakova. Cast: Stefan Mavrodiev, Pavel Poppandov, Tatyana Lolova. 92 mins. Prem: April 30.

A Beckettian scene: a pair of hitchhikers at a crossroads meet assorted social types. The satire contains some inspired moments.

KATINA. Sc: Tsilia Lacheva. Dr: Yanush Vazov. Ph: Tsvetan Chobanski. Set: Yuliana Bozhkova. Cast: Katya Paskaleva, Dimiter Ignatov, Nevena Mandadjieva, Dimiter Hadjiyski. 95 mins. Prem: May 28.

The tale of a girl always in trouble because she's outspoken and daring.

SAMODIVSKO HORO / Fairy Dance. Sc: Georgi Mishev. Dr: Ivan Andonov. Ph: Radoslav Spassov. Set: Ivan Andonov. Mu: Simeon Pironkov. Cast: Pavel Poppandov, Marianna Dimitrova, Peter Slabakov, Katya Chukova. 85 mins. Prem: July 20.

Actor-cartoonist Ivan Andonov's first feature, a collaboration with satirist Georgi Mishev. The spoof of the art world is all the more delightful in view of the director's own reputation as a Sunday painter.

SPOMEN ZA BLIZNACHKATA / Memory of the Twin Sister. Sc: Konstantin Pavlov. Dr: Lyubomir Sharlandjiev. Ph: Tsancho Tsanchev. Set: Alexander Djakov. Mu: Dimiter Vulchev. Cast: Nevena Kokanova, Nikola Todev, Grigor Vachkov, Emilia Radeva. 137 mins. Prem: September 3.

A film of recollections, dealing with life in a village thirty years ago and the Great War as the historical moment in the past.

VINATA / Guilt. Sc: Lyuben Stanev. Dr: Vesselina Gerinska. Ph: Plamen Wagenstein. Set: Boyanka Ahryanova. Mu: Dimiter Griva. Cast: Tsvetana Maneva, Katya Paskaleva, Stefan Danailov, Bela Tsoneva. 84 mins. Prem: September 24.

A film about rape and the moral question of guilt confronted by all the participants in a trial set in an otherwise calm provincial town.

SNAHA / The Daughter-in-Law. Sc: Slav G. Karaslavov, based on a novel by Georgi Karaslavov. Dr: Vassil Mirchev. Ph: Tsvetan Chobanski. Set: Milko Marinov. Mu: Kiril Tsibulka. Cast: Stefan Getsov, Emilia Radeva, Dobromir Manev, Violetta Gindeva. 114 mins. Prem: October 8.

Georgi Karaslavov wrote the novel in 1942. Set in a village in the 1930s, this is a faithful literary adaptation.

DOPALNENIE KAM ZAKONA ZA ZASHTITO NA DARZHAVATA / Amendment to the Defense-of-State Act. Sc: Angel Wagenstein. Dr: Lyudmil Staikov. Ph: Boris Yanakiev. Set: Petko Bonchev. Mu: Simeon Pironkov. Cast: Stefan Getsov, Violetta Doneva, Ivan Kondov, Stefan Danailov, Georgi Cherkelov, Naum Shopov. 157 mins. Prem: October 22.

A reconstruction of events surrounding the bombing of the Saint Nedelya Cathedral in the heart of Sofia in 1925 during a state funeral, leading to a suppression of rights and the advent of a harsh dictatorship.

TSIKLOPAT / Cyclops. Sc, Dr & Set: Hristo Hristov. Ph: Venets Dimitrov. Mu: Kiril Tsibulka. Cast: Mihail Mutaffov, Nevena Kokanova, Penka Tsizelkova. 95 mins. Prem: November 26.

A science-fiction film, the action may be taking place entirely in the mind: it's a fragmented story of flashbacks and fantasies the protagonist being a U-boat commander on a mysterious cruise.

Lyubomir Sharlandjiev's *Memory of the Twin Sister* **(1976).**

Vassil Mirchev's *The Daughter-in-Law* (1976).

Hristo Hristov's *Cyclops* (1976).

MALKATA ROUSSALKA / The Mermaid. Sc: Victor Victovich, Gregori Jagdfeld, based on Hans Christian Andersen's fairy tale. Dr: Vladimir Bichkov. Ph: Emil Wagenstein. Set: K. Zagorski, Bogoya Sapundjiev. Mu: E. Krilatov. Cast: Vika Novikova, Yui Senkevich, Galina Artemova, Valentin Nikulin. (Coproduction with the Soviet Union.) 81 mins. Prem: December 17.

An adaptation of Andersen's fairy tale "The Little Mermaid."

1977

GODENITSATA S NAY-KRASIVITE OTCHI / The Fiancée with the Loveliest Eyes. Sc: Jiří Cirkl & Vladislav Dvorski, based on motifs supplied by M. Bořishkova. Dr: Jan Schmidt. Ph: Jiří Macak. Set: Jindřich Gec. Mu: Zdenek Liška. Cast: Milan Knjažko, Elena Dimitrova, Bohumil Vavra, Suzanna Kocurikova. (Coproduction with Czechoslovakia.) 82 mins. Prem: January 7.

A fairy tale aobut a peasant winning the hand of "the loveliest girl in the world."

BOY POSLEDEN / The Last Battle. Sc: Svoboda Buchvarova, Nikola Russev, based on Vesselin Andreyev's memoirs, *They Died Immortal.* Zako Heskia. Dr: Zako Heskia. Ph: Victor Chichov. Set: Stefan Savov. Mu: Kiril Donchev. Cast: Ivan Burdjiev, Ilya Karaivanov, Dimiter Hadjiyski. 150 mins. Prem: January 21.

Large-scale "Eastern," half epic, half documentary, by the genre's Bulgarian specialist. The year is 1943, when the resistance was growing against a reign of fascist terror.

HIRURZI / Surgeons. Sc: Georgi Danailov. Dr: Ivanka Grubcheva. Ph: Yatsek Todorov. Set: Konstantin Russakov. Mu: Kiril Tsibulka. Cast: Vassil Mihailov, Mihail Mihailov, Anton Radichev, Angel Lambev, Iskra Radeva, Tsvetana

Zako Heskia's *The Last Battle* **(1977).**

Maneva, Stoycho Mazgalov, Lyudmila Cheshmedjieva. 72 mins. Prem: February 11.

First try by a well-known children's film director at a psychological drama. Set in a hospital ward.

MATRIARHAT / Matriarchate. Sc: Georgi Mishev. Dr: Lyudmil Kirkov. Ph: Georgi Russinov. Set: Bogoya Sapundjiev, Assya Popova. Mu: Boris Karadimchev. Cast: Katya Paskaleva, Nevena Kokanova, Emilia Radeva, Katya Chukova, Georgi Georgiev-Gets, Georgi Russev. 103 mins. Prem: March 25.

Another fine Mishev-Kirkov collaboration. This bittersweet social satire deals with the increasing number of abandoned villages as the men go to work in nearby and distant factories and the women are left to tend the collective farm.

HORA OT DALECHE / People from Afar. Sc: Atanas Tsenev. Dr: Nikola Rudarov. Ph: Georgi Georgiev. Set: Anastas Yanakiev. Mu: Kiril Tsibulka. Cast: Vassil Mihailov, Milanka Petrova, Assen Angelov, Konstantin Kotsev, Kiril Gospodinov, Penko Penkov. 91 mins. Prem: April 15.

The story of a working brigade on a construction site.

MUZHKI VREMENA / Manly Times. Sc: Nikolai Haitov. Dr: Eduard Zahariev. Ph: Radoslav Spassov. Set: Angel Ahryanov. Mu: Kiril Donchev. Cast: Grigor Vachkov, Marianna Dimitrova, Nikola Todev, Trayan Yankov, Georgi Georgiev-Gets, Velko Kunev, Teofil Badelov. 125 mins. Prem: April 29.

Although this is a distinct folkloric legend woven into an original tale by master storyteller Nikolai Haitov, its roots are probably in Greek tragedy. An outlaw is hired to kidnap a peasant girl for a rich suitor, but this Helen enchants her Paris—and the rest is tragedy of the heart. A key film in Bulgarian cinema, directed with a light hand and sharply photographed by Radoslav Spassov.

GODINA OT PONEDELNITSI / A Year of Mondays. Sc: Nikolai Nikiforov. Dr & Ph: Borislav Punchev. Set: Petko Bonchev. Mu: Simeon Pironkov. Cast: Kosta Tsonev, Luchezar Tsonchev, Yordanka Kuzmanova. 114 mins. Prem: May 13.

The day-by-day duties and trials of a Party Secretary in a provincial town.

LUZHOVNI ISTORII / Illusive Stories. A feature film in two parts. 72 mins. Prem: June 10.

(1) **PET PLYUS EDNO / Five Plus One (5 + 1).** Sc: Georgi Mishev. Dr: Maya Vaptsarova. Ph: Dimko Minov. Set: Belin Belinov. Mu: Kiril Tsibulka. Cast: Katya Paskaleva, Peter Petrov, Ivan Grigorov, Anton Karastoyanov, Dimiter Bochev. 37 mins.

When Grandpa Doncho wins big on a lottery ticket, the vultures among relatives and acquaintances are there with their hands out.

(2) **DVUBOY '77 / Duel '77.** Sc: Georgi Misher. Dr: Maya Vaptsarova. Ph: Dimko Minov. Set: Iskra Licheva. Mu: Al-

178

Lyudmil Kirkov's *Matriarchate* **(1977).**

Eduard Zahariev's *Manly Times* **(1977).**

exander Bruzitsov. Cast: Anton Gorchev, Veliko Stoyanov, Liliana Kovacheva. 37 mins.

About triangle. The performance of an amateur theater group parallels a drama in real life.

BASSEYNAT / The Swimming Pool. Sc: Hristo Ganev. Dr: Binka Zhelyazkova. Ph: Ivailo Trenchev. Set: Marie-Thérèse Gospodinova. Mu: Simeon Pironkov. Cast: Yanina Kasheva, Kosta Tsonev, Kliment Denchev, Tsvetana Maneva, Peter Slabakov, 145 mins. Prem: July 29.

In this review of the past, the swimming pool is used as a motif to trigger the memory of a revolutionary type who challenged those about him with the integrity of his moral vision, back in the period of the Personality Cult.

BAROUTEN BOUKVAR / Gunpowder. Sc & Dr: Todor Dinov, based on Yordan Radichkov's story with the same title. Ph: Boris Yanakiev. Set: Stefan Savov. Mu: Kiril Tsibulka. Cast: Assen Angelov, Marin Yanev, Ivan Grigorov, Anton Karastoyanov, Vassil Popiliev. 77 mins. Prem: September 5.

This adaptation of a Yordan Radichkov story is set in a village on the eve of the September 1944 revolution, an outside event that draws common people into a situation requiring a moral decision.

ZVEZDI V KOSSITE, SALZI V OCHITE / Stars in Her Hair, Tears in Her Eyes. Sc: Angel Wagenstein. Dr: Ivan Nichev. Ph: Tsvetan Chobanski. Set: Angel Ahryanov. Mu:

Kiril Tsibulka. Cast: Katya Paskaleva, Peter Slabakov, Tatyana Lolova, Nikolai Binev, Ivan Dervishev, Leda Tasseva, Antoni Genov, Ivan Tsvetarski, Nikolai Nachkov. 110 mins. Prem: September 19.

A nostalgic piece, about a traveling theater group at the turn of the century. It's a quite accurate portrait of the founding of a new Bulgarian theater after centuries of oppression under the Turks. The company's name is, appropriately, "Renewal."

AVANTAZH / Advantage. Sc: Georgi Djulgerov, Russi Chanev. Dr: Georgi Djulgerov. Ph: Radoslav Spassov. Set: Russi Dundakov, Georgi Todorov. Mu: Bozhidar Petkov. Cast: Russi Chanev, Maria Statulova, Plamena Getova, Radosveta Vasisleva, Plamen Donchev, Velyo Goranov. 137 mins. Prem: October 10.

Winner of the Best Director Prize at the Berlin Film Festival, it marked the second breakthrough for New Bulgarian Cinema on the international festival scene. It's the story of a con man in Stalinist times. A major collaborative effort on all sides.

STO TONA SHTASTIE / One Hundred Tons of Happiness. Sc: Myron Ivanov. Dr: Peter Vassilev-Milevin. Ph: Yatsek Todorov. Set: Ivan Apostolov. Mu: Atanas Kossev. Cast: Ivan Yanchev, Kiril Gospodinov, Todor Kolev, Diana Hristova. 70 mins. Prem: October 24.

A social comedy: a public official gets the bright idea of marrying one hundred couples on a single day, and everyone shows up for the televised occasion—save for the clerk in charge of marrying them.

Binka Zhelyazkova's *The Swimming Pool* (1977).

Georgi Djulgerov's *Advantage* (1977).

SLANTCHEV UDAR / SUNSTROKE. Sc & Dr: Irina Ak-tasheva, Hristo Piskov, based on a story by Georgi Djagarov. Ph: Leonid Kalashnikov. Set: Assen Mitev, Borislav Borizov. Mu: Kiril Donchev. Cast: Armen Djigarhanian, Itzhak Fintsi, Nikolai Binev, Rashko Mladenov, Katya Paskaleva, Bela Tsoneva, Ivan Kondov, Nevena Kokanova, Konstantin Kotsev. 131 mins. Prem: September 14.

Contemporary theme presenting an ecological problem: an industrial plant may ruin the landscape about it, thus pitting truthseeker against opportunist.

OT DRUGATA STRANA NA OGLEDALOTO / From the Other Side of the Mirror. Sc: Anton Donchev. Dr: Ilya Velchev. Ph: Konstantin Djidrov. Set: Zahari Savov. Mu: Mitko Shterev. Cast: Renata Draicheva, Yuri Angelov, Raina Vassileva. 93 mins. Prem: December 5.

Spy caper set in Germany in 1943. The heroine is a young Bulgarian sent to contact Communists in the underground resistance movement in Berlin.

1978

ADIOS, MUCHACHOS! Sc: Vassil Tsonev. Dr: Yanko Yankov. Ph: Victor Chichov. Set: Marie-Thérèse Gospodinova. Mu: Georgi Genkov. Cast: Peter Stoyanov, Luchezar Tsonchev, Kosta Tsonev. 78 mins. Prem: January 9.

Youth-oriented theme. A father and son compare the re-wards of dreamers and creators with careerists and social climbers.

JULIA VREVSKAYA. Sc: Stefan Tsanev, Simeon Lungin. Dr: Nikola Korabov. Ph: Vadim Yusov. Set: Maria Ivanova, Valeri Filipov. Cast: Lyudmilla Savelieva, Stefan Danailov, Regimantas Adomaitis, Kosta Tsonev, Anatoli Solonitsyn, Yuri Yakovlev, Lydia Terletska. (Coproduction with the Soviet Union.) 131 mins. Prem: January 23.

Andrei Tarkovsky's cameraman (Yusov) and actor (Solonitsyn) honor the credits. Produced on the occasion of the one hundredth anniversary of Bulgaria's liberation from the Turks. The superspectacle features a Russian countess who joins the Russo-Turkish war as a nurse on the battlefront, then dies a martyr's death from typhus.

BADI BLAGOSLOVENA! / Be Blessed! Sc: Kiril Topalov. Dr: Alexander Obreshkov. Ph: Krum Krumov. Set: Konstantin Russakov. Mu: Dimiter Griva. Cast: Marianna Dimtrova, Dorothea Toncheva, Evgenia Barakova, Maria Statulova. 87 mins. Prem: February 5.

A socially engaged film, the theme is unwed mothers in a state institution.

OUTROTO E NEPOVTORIMO / A Unique Morning. Sc: Kamen Kalchev, based on his book *Sofia Short Stories*. Dr: Nikola Lyubomirov. Ph: Krassimir Kostov. Set: Lyuben Trupkov. Mu: Simeon Pironkov. Cast: Bogdan Glishev, Grigor Vachkov, Gavril Gavrilov, Ilka Zafirova. 95 mins. Prem: February 27.

The unique morning is the ninth of September 1944. When the first train arrives at the Sofia station with this inscription on a Communist banner, a little man in the group celebrates the occasion in his own way.

TALISMAN. Sc: Pravda Kirova. Dr: Rashko Ouzunov. Ph: Tsvetan Chobanski. Set: Milko Marinov. Mu: Alexander Yossifov. Cast: Daniela Boyanova, Lilyana Yovanovich, Emilia Radeva, Lyubomir Kirilov. 76 mins. Prem: March 13.

Fine children's film set in a fifth-grade classroom. The in-depth character study makes this one a standout. It's the story of a young girl who feels all alone.

PANTELEY. Sc: Vassil Akyov. Dr: Georgi Stoyanov. Ph: Radoslav Spassov. Set: Georgi Todorov. Mu: Bozhidar Petkov. Cast: Pavel Poppandov, Dobrinka Stankova, Velko Kunev, Nikola Anastassov, Nikolai Nikolaev. 101 mins. Prem. March 27.

A witty, absurd satire on events surrounding the 1944 revolution in Bulgaria. An apolitical innocent gentleman with a Beckettian bowler hat stumbles into the middle of the Resistance movement and is pursued by both sides for different reasons.

COMPARSITA. Sc: Todor Monov. Dr: Nikola Petkov. Ph: Dimo Kolarov. Set: Boyanka Ahryanova. Mu: Georgi Minchev. Cast: Stefan Iliev, Bistra Marcheva, Ivan Kondov, Yuri Yakovlev, Svetoslav Nedelchev, Ruth Rafailova. 76 mins. Prem: April 10.

Contemporary tale about a chief on a construction site who has fallen from favor and has to face the future with new courage and conviction.

S LYUBOV I NEZHNOST / With Love and Tenderness.
Sc: Valeri Petrov. Dr: Rangel Vulchanov. Ph: Dimko Minov. Set: Maria Ivanova. Mu: Kiril Donchev. Cast: Alexander Djakov, Tsvetana Eneva, Gergana Gerassimova, Yossif Surchadjiev, Teodor Yurukov. 85 mins. Prem: May 8.

The long-awaited return of Petrov and Vulchanov to Bulgarian cinema after the pair's international success two decades earlier. This "human comedy" features a sculptor and his acquaintances at a Black Sea exile.

POKRIV / The Roof. Sc: Kuncho Atanassov. Dr: Ivan Andonov. Ph: Victor Chichov. Set: Yuliana Bozhkova. Mu: Georgi Genkov. Cast: Peter Slabakov, Pepa Nikolova, Katya Paskaleva, Velko Kunev, Maria Statulova, Nadya Todorova. 98 mins. Prem: May 22.

A tragicomedy that marked director Ivan Andonov as a talent to keep an eye on in Bulgarian cinema. It's about a wheeler-dealer, his dream-house, and a spitfire he falls in love with on his rounds to collect materials for the roof over his head.

RALI. Sc: Stefan Dichev, Ivailo Dichev, based on a novel by Stefan Dichev. Dr: Willy Tsankov. Ph: Krassimir Kostov. Set: Irina Marichkova. Mu: Kiril Donchev. Cast: Ivo Hristov, Mihail Mutafov, Shakur Burhanov, Dilarom Kombarova, Djoko Rossich. 163 mins. Prem: June 26.

Patriotic film to celebrate the one hundredth anniversary of liberation from the Ottoman Turks. The hero is a lad of fifteen who sets off to Asia Minor to find and rescue his brother, a political prisoner sentenced to lifelong exile.

Rashko Ouzunov's *Talisman* **(1978).**

VSICHKI I NIKOY / Everybody and Nobody. Sc: Yordan Radichkov, based on his story with the same title. Dr: Krikor Azarian. Ph: Plamen Wagenstein. Set: Nikolai Surchadjiev, Stoyan Chiflichki. Mu: Kiril Donchev. Cast: Velko Kunev, Georgi Novakov, Nikola Dadov, Konstantin Kotsev, Vassil Mihailov, Grigor Vachkov, Emilia Radeva, Katya Paskaleva. 103 mins. Prem: September 4.

Curious adaptation of a Yordan Radichkov story, about a murder case with a twist at the end. The story allows for a range of characters in a village setting: an archaeologist, a monk, a camp of gypsies.

VSEKI DEN, VSYAKA NOSHT / Every Day, Every Night. Sc. Kiril Voynov. Dr: Vladislav Ikonomov. Ph: Emil Wagenstein. Set: Assya Popova. Mu: Kiril Tsibulka. Cast: Velyo Goranov, Georgi Vassilev, Emil Djurov. 81 mins.

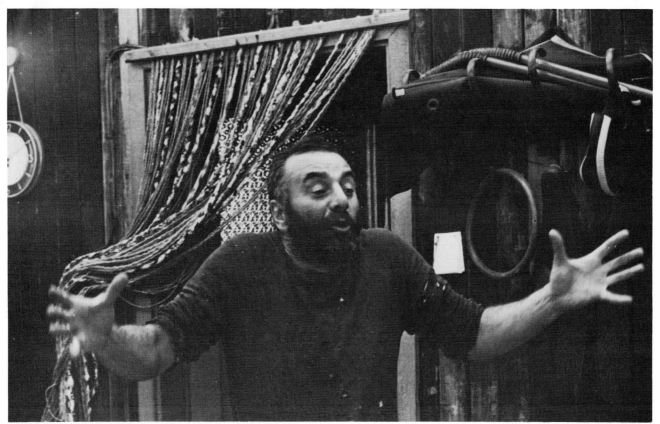

Rangel Vulchanov's *With Love and Tenderness* (1978).

Ivan Andonov's *The Roof* (1978).

A thriller, about a policeman tracking down an armed murderer in a district of Sofia.

CHUI PETELA! / Hark to the Cock! Sc: Konstantin Pavlov. Dr: Stefan Dimitrov. Ph: Emil Wagenstein. Set: Nikolai Surchadjiev. Mu: Georgi Genkov. Cast: Nikolai Binev, Nevena Kokanova, Ivan Tsvetarski, Elena Kuneva. 80 mins. Prem: October 16.

Human sketch of old people in an abandoned village fetchingly named "Hark to the Cock." A superbly acted Senior Citizen theme.

INSTRUMENT LI E GAYDATA? / Is the Bagpipe an Instrument? Sc: Kiran Kolarov. Dr: Assen Shopov. Ph: Ivailo Trenchev. Set: Boyanka Ahryanova. Mu: Kiril Donchev. Cast: Filip Trifonov, Peter Slabakov, Grigor Vachkov, Nikola Todev. 90 mins. Prem: November 6.

Nostalgic tale. Again, the scene is a forgotten village—an army recruit returns home to look for a bagpipe for the army band, but the native instrument has seen its day.

TOPLO / Warmth. Sc & Dr: Vladimir Yanchev. Ph: Tsancho Tsanchev. Set: Bogoya Sapundjiev. Mu: Simeon Shterev. Cast: Naum Shopov, Georgi Cherkelov, Konstantin Kotsev, Stoyan Stoychev, Tatyana Lolova, Luchezar Stoyanov, Valentin Russetski, Georgi Popov, Grigor Vachkov, Stefan Danailov, Todor Kolev. 94 mins. Prem: November 20.

Comedy, about housing projects and the problems of getting them properly heated.

TRAMPA / Swap. Sc: Vladimir Ganev, Georgi Djulgerov, based on Ivailo Petrov's "Three Meetings and Confused Notes." Dr: Georgi Djulgerov. Ph: Radoslav Spassov. Set: Georgi Todorov. Mu: Bozhidar Petkov. Cast: Ilya Dobrev, Tanya Shahova, Margarita Pehliyanova, Zhanna Mircheva. 89 mins. Prem: December 11.

Complex psychological drama about an eminent writer returning to a provincial town to judge a creative writing course. The event triggers memories of the past—back in the period of the Personality Cult, he covered turbulent co-op meetings here for Radio Sofia.

SLOUZHEBNO POLOZHENIYE—ORDINARETS / Status—Orderly. Sc & Dr: Kiran Kolarov, based on Georgi Stamatov's short story "Orderly Dimo." Ph: Radoslav Spassov. Set: Ivan Apostolov. Mu: Kiril Donchev. Cast: Elefteri Elefterov, Tsvetana Maneva, Peter Despotov, Vulcho Kamarashev. 80 mins. Prem: unknown.

Very fine debut film by one of the first graduates of VITIS, the Sofia Film Academy. Made originally for television, this classic in Bulgarian literature depicts the decaying moral environment in a royal barracks at the turn of the century.

1979

ROYALUT / The Grand Piano. Sc: Nikola Roussev. Dr: Borislav Punchev. Ph: Georgi Mateyev. Set: Peter Goranov. Mu: Simeon Pironkov. Cast: Georgi Kaloyanchev, Ivan Grigorov, Georgi Partsalev, Naum Shopov, Konstantin Kotsev, Velko Kunev, Madeleine Cholakova. 99 mins. Prem: January 15.

Georgi Djulgerov's *Swap* **(1978).**

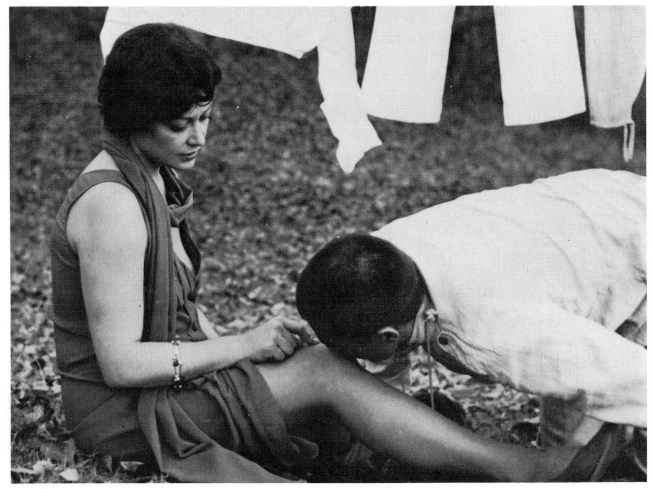

Kiran Kolarov's *Status—Orderly* (1978).

A social comedy: workers at a construction site wish to celebrate the completion of work with a concert—but where to find a grand piano for the gala?

MIGOVE V KIBRITENA KOUTIYKA / Moments in a Matchbox. Sc: Olga Krusteva. Dr: Marianna Evstatieva. Ph: Emil Wagenstein. Set: Eva Yordanova. Mu: Simeon Pironkov. Cast: Dilyana Simeonova, Vladimir Vassilev, Violetta Doneva, Dossyo Dossev, Stefan Danailov. 86 mins. Prem: February 5.

Children's film. Two classmates, aged twelve, are introduced to life and its adventures on a trip to the country to meet their relatives.

KRATKO SLUNTSE / Short Sun. Sc: Stanislav Stratiev. Dr. Lyudmil Kirkov. Ph: Georgi Russinov. Set: Assya Popova. Mu: Boris Karadimchev. Cast: Vihur Stoychev, Nikola Todev, Anton Gorchev, Rosizza Petrova, Georgi Kishkilov, Kiril Gospodinov, Pavel Poppandov. 106 mins. Prem: February 19.

Strong critical film of social conscience, whose title is perhaps better translated *A Ray of Sunlight*. A university student has a summer job working with a well-digging crew in the so-called villa zone of Sofia. Bones are discovered—but the villa owner wants his well completed without delays. It leads to a tragedy.

Marianna Evstatieva's *Moments in a Matchbox* (1979).

Liliana Pencheva's *The Fatal Comma* **(1979).**

BUMERANG / Boomerang. Sc: Svoboda Buchvarova, Ivan Nichev, Jenny Radeva. Dr: Ivan Nichev. Ph: Victor Chichov. Set: Angel Ahryanov. Mu: Kiril Tsibulka. Cast: Lyuben Chatalov, Yavor Spassov, Nikolai Binev, Katya Paskaleva, Krassimira Damyanova. 110 mins. Prem: March 5.

A film of social criticism. Two graduates of the university's school of journalism confront their future, and one decides to scale the heights the fast way—through connections. The venture boomerangs.

FATALNATA ZAPETAYA / The Fatal Comma. Sc: Maxim Assenov. Dr: Liliana Pencheva. Ph: Dimko Minev. Set: Juliana Bozhkova. Mu: Bozhidar Petkov. Cast: Tatyana Tsvetkova. Georgi Kadourin, Dimiter Marin, Nikolai Kolev, Katya Dineva, Yakim Mihov. 81 mins. Prem: March 19.

Youth film about teenagers in the classroom and one student's unseemly conduct.

PO DIRYATA NA BEZSLEDNO IZCHEZNALITE / On the Tracks of the Missing. Sc: Nikolai Hristozov. Dr: Margarit Nikolov. Ph:Ivan Sumardjiev. Set: Zahari Savov. Mu: Kiril Donchev. Cast: Naum Shopov, Boris Lukanov, Assen Milanov, Lyubomir Mladenov, Itzhak Fintsi, Lyubomir Buchvarov. 195 mins. Prem: April 2.

TV serial cut down to scale of a two-part feature film. It's the historical account of the White Terror of 1923–25 under the fascist government headed by Alexander Tsankov and supported by Tsar Boris.

BYAGAY . . . OBICHAM TE / Run Away . . . I Love You. Sc: Kiril Topalov. Dr: Rashko Ouzunov. Ph: Tsvetan Chobanski. Set: Mony Aladjemov. Mu: Peter Yossifov. Cast: Stanimir Stoilov, Ventsislav Kulev, Zoya Kircheva. 83 mins. Prem: April 16.

Margarit Nikolov's *On the Tracks of the Missing* **(1979).**

A youth film centering on sixteen-year-old boys in the classroom and on the sports field. Two friends are pitted against each other in a boxing ring, thus posing a problem for both of them and their fellow students.

LACHENITE OBOUVKI NA NEZNAINIYA VOIN / The Unknown Soldier's Patent Leather Shoes.
Sc & Dr: Rangel Vulchanov. Ph: Radoslav Spassov. Set: Georgi Todorov. Mu: Kiril Donchev. Cast: Borislav Tsankov, Slavka Ankova, Ivan Stoychkov, Emilia Marinska, Nikolai Velichkov. 109 mins. Prem: May 7.

After waiting some fifteen years to film his own screenplay, Rangel Vulchanov made one of the endearing productions in Bulgarian cinema. This lyrical poem on a fading peasant culture and the irretrievable past—back to the turn of the century—features nonprofessionals in all the leading roles.

CHERESHOVA GRADINA / The Cherry Orchard.
Sc: Nikolai Haitov. Dr: Ivan Andonov. Ph: Plamen Wagenstein. Set: Angel Ahryanov. Mu: Simeon Pironkov. Cast: Peter Slabakov, Nikola Todev, Maria Statulova, Stoyan Gudev, Ani Petrova. 86 mins. Prem: May 21.

Human interest story about an honest forester of partisan ilk and a crooked director of a cooperative farm. The conflict arises over a cherry orchard and leads to the good man's tragic death. This arouses the villagers to take a stand.

BEDNIYAT LOUKA / Poor Lucas.
Sc: Ivan Stanev, based on a novella with the same title by Dobri Nemirov. Dr: Yakim Yakimov. Ph: Ivan Velchev. Set: Bogoya Sapundjiev. Mu: Kiril Tsibulka. Cast: Naum Shopov, Katya Paskaleva. 89 mins. Prem: June 4.

Set in the interregnum period, this psychological tale features a poor photographer who suddenly comes into possession of a suitcase stuffed with money meant for the resistance movement.

OT NISHTO NESHTO / Something out of Nothing.
Sc: Nikolai Nikiforov. Dr: Nikola Rudarov. Ph: Georgi Georgiev. Set: Vladimir Lekarski. Mu: Boris Karadimchev. Cast: Annetta Sotirova, Stefan Danailov, Assen Angelov. 91 mins. Prem: July 9.

Light comedy—the story of a popular television personality visiting a provincial town to look for a boyhood friend. He's not at home, but his lovely wife is—which leads to a number of embarrassingly innocent situations.

TAIFOUNI S NEZHNI IMENA / Typhoons with Gentle Names.
Sc: Bogomil Rainov, based on motifs in his detective stories. Dr: Milen Getov. Ph: Hristo Vulev. Set: Peter Bonchev. Mu: Toncho Russev. Cast: Kosta Tsonev, Ani

Rangel Vulchanov's *The Unknown Soldier's Patent Leather Shoes* **(1979).**

Pencheva, Lilyana Kovacheva, Stoycho Mazgalov, Kliment Denchev. 162 mins. Prem: July 23.

Writer Bogomil Rainov specializes in spy and detective stories—this is a thriller and describes the adventures of his favorite character, Emil Boyev of the Secret Service. The setting is Bern, Switzerland.

SNIMKI ZA SPOMEN / Snapshots as Souvenirs. Sc: Atanas Tsenev, Dimiter Dimitrov. Dr: Rumen Surdjiyski. Ph: Vyacheslav Anev. Set: Ivan Apostolov. Mu: Bozhidar Petkov. Cost: Elena Dimitrova, Svetlana Atanassova, Iskra Genkova, Mihail Mihailov, Alexander Ilindenov, Svilen Stoyanov, Slavka Slavova, Stefan Iliev. 85 mins. Prem: August 13.

A youth theme with a harsh social message. On the eve of graduation from secondary school, two students stand up to an injustice which reaches to the school's administration. The students are the losers, save for their moral example.

BELYAZANI ATOMI / Tagged Atoms. Sc: Assen Georgiev. Dr: Grisha Ostrovski. Ph: Boris Yanakiev. Set: Lyuben Trupkov. Mu: Lyubomir Denev. Cast: Stefan Denev, Dimiter Marin, Rumen Dimitrov, Vanya Tsvetkova, Boyko Iliev, Yordan Gadiev, Nencho Hristov. 82 mins. Prem: July 2.

Story of five boys and a girl during their last free summer after graduation—the period is the early 1950s with all its ramifications.

KUSHTATA / The House. Sc: Vassil Akyov, based on motifs in Grigor Stoykov's memoirs, *Double Life.* Dr: Stefan Dimit-

rov. Ph: Krassimir Kostov. Set: Nikolai Surchadjiev. Mu: Yana Pipkova. Cast: Stanimir Stoylov, Ivan Grigorov, Yossif Surchadjiev, Nikolai Binev, Ivan Yanchev, Anani Yavashev, Ivan Dervishev, Georgi Kaloyanchev, Nevena Andonova. 90 mins. Prem: September 3.

A thriller set in Sofia of the 1940s—the Communists fight the Germans and fascist leaders from the attic of a villa, where a printing press is hidden.

BARIERATA / Barrier. Sc: Pavel Vezhinov, based on his novella with the same title. Dr: Hristo Hrisov. Ph: Atanas Tassev. Set: Stefan Savov. Mu: Kiril Tsibulka. Cast: Innokenti Smoktunovsky, Vanya Tsvetkova, Maria Dimcheva. 111 mins. Prem: November 12.

A film of fantasy and daring. A composer faces a crisis in midlife, but meets a mysterious ethereal creature who persuades him that she can fly and is willing to teach him her secret. Soviet actor Innokenti Smoktunovsky plays the lead.

VOYNATA NA TARALEZHITE / The Porcupines' War. Sc: Mormarev Brothers. Dr: Ivanka Grubcheva. Ph: Yatsek Todorov. Set: Maria Ivanova. Mu: Kiril Tsibulka. Cast: Dimiter Ganev, Maurice Assa, Boris Petrov, Dimiter Dimitrov, Tsvetana Maneva, Vulcho Kamarashev, Angel Lambrev, Vassil Dimitrov. 97 mins. Prem: November 26.

Children's film about grade-school children fighting to get their own basketball court in a residential area.

Rumen Surdjiyski's *Snapshots as Souvenirs* **(1979).**

Hristo Hristov's *Barrier* (1979).

VSICHKO E LYUBOV / All Is Love. Sc: Boyan Papazov. Dr: Borislav Sharaliev. Ph: Stefan Trifonov. Set: Georgi Ivanov. Mu: Vesselin Nikolov. Cast: Ivan Ivanov, Yanina Kasheva, Maria Stefanova, Vulcho Kamarashev, Yordan Spirov. 104 mins. Prem: December 10.

A film on juvenile delinquents. The sweet melodramatic side is balanced by moving realistic scenes. A girl with social standing is in love with a hoodlum.

1980

IGRA NA LYUBOV / Love Game. Sc: Yordan Hadjiev, Vladimir Ganev. Dr: Yanush Vazov. Ph: Tsvetan Chobanski. Set: Anastas Yanakiev. Mu: Georgi Minchev. Cast: Lyuben Chatalov, Yordanka Lyubenova, Rashko Mladenov, Bistra Marchova, Madeleine Cholakova, Rumyana Gaytandjieva. 95 mins. Prem: January 7.

A social comedy about blind dates by telephone.

YOUMROUTSI V PRUSTA / Fists in the Soil. Sc: Ivan Slavkov, Nikola Statkov. Dr: Milen Getov. Ph: Ivailo Trenchev. Set: Vladimir Lekarski. Mu: Toncho Russev. Cast: Ivan Ivanov, Violetta Gindeva, Anton Gorchev, Nikolai Binev, Pepa Nikolova. 85 mins. Prem: January 21.

Patriotic film for the thirty-fifth anniversary of the 1944 revolution. The story centers on a peasant lad who has joined the fascists and lives to regret it.

POCHTI LYUBOVNA ISTORIA / Almost a Love Story. Sc: Eduard Zahariev, Georgi Danailov, Georgi Mishev. Dr: Eduard Zahariev. Ph: Georgi Nikolov. Set: Peter Goranov. Mu: Mitko Shterev. Cast: Marianna Dimitrova, Yavor Spassov, Grigor Vachkov. 85 mins. Prem: February 4.

Eduard Zahariev's *Almost a Love Story* (1980).

A well-to-do and influential man in the provinces is against his son's engagement to a working girl in the factory—because the university should come first. The young couple grapple against odds for their love, but lose in the end.

KRUVTA OSTAVA / The Blood Remains. Sc: Kostadin Kyulyumov. Dr: Borislav Punchev. Ph: Georgi Mateyev. Set: Yuliana Bozhkova. Mu: Alexander Bruzitsov. Cast: Stefan Danailov, Maria Statulova, Radko Dishliyev, Russi Chanev. 140 mins. Prem: February 18.

Set in the resistance days of 1942–44. A loner and anarchist fights to avenge his father's death by the fascists in the September 1923 Uprising, leaving a trail of unsolved killings. Not even joining a partisan band resolves his need to avenge family blood, for his wife and child are killed by his enemies.

SPODELENA LYUBOV / With Shared Love. Sc: Rustam Ibrahimbekov, Katya Gumnerova, Sergei Mikaelian. Dr: Sergei Mikaelian. Ph: Leonid Kalashnikov. Set: Yuri Fomenko. Mu: Kiril Tsibulka. Cast: Velko Kunev, Simeon Morozov, Rosizza Petrova, Veronica Isotova, Georgi Russev, Bogomil Simeonov. (Coproduction with the Soviet Union.) 85 mins. Prem: March 3.

The story of the building of the Drouzhba gas pipeline in the Soviet Union, as experienced by two friends, a Bulgarian and a Russian lad.

DVOYNIKUT / The Double. Sc: Mormarev Brothers. Dr: Nikolai Volev. Ph: Venko Kableshkov. Set: Nikolai Surchadjiev. Mu: Johann Sebastian Bach. Cast: Todor Kolev, Yordanka Kuzmanova, Lyuben Kalinov, Radosveta Vassileva, Pavel Poppandov. 100 mins. Prem: March 17.

Comedy about a scientist who finds a perfect double to represent him abroad and in the public eye—only the double is exactly the opposite in temperament, and this causes merry confusion all the way down the line.

KONTSERT ZA FLEITA I MOMICHE / A Flute Concerto and a Girl. Sc: Angel Wagenstein. Dr: Atanas Kiryakov. Ph: Georgi Nedjalkov. Set: Mony Aledjemov. Mu: Peter Stupel. Cast: Elena Dimitrova, Ilian Simeonov, Marin Yanev, Victor Stoyanov, Dimiter Ivanov, Ivan Gaytandjier. 84 mins. Prem: April 7.

An antifascist theme with a human touch. The scene is a provincial town just as the Germans and Bulgarian fascists are retreating.

TRITE SMURTNI GRIAHA / Three Deadly Sins. Sc: Dimiter Vulev, Lyubomir Sharlandjiev. Dr: Lyubomir Sharlandjiev. Ph: Tsancho Tsanchev. Set: Maria Denichina. Mu: Dimiter Vulchev. Cast: Vassil Popiliev, Georgi Georgiev-Gets, Nevena Kokanova, Sotir Maynolovski, Grigor Vachkov, Irinei Konstantinov, Zinka Drumeva. 69 mins. Prem: April 21.

The setting is a collective farm: two former partisans don't see eye-to-eye on current problems, which in turn sparks a review of past deeds and misdeeds in the resistance struggle.

MOZHE BI . . . FREGATA / Maybe . . . a Frigate. Sc: Atanas Tsenev. Dr: Peter Kaishev. Ph: Svetlana Ganeva. Set: Alexander Djakov. Mu: Angel Mihailov. Cast: Vassil Popov, Dossyo Dossev, Angel Enchev, Neven Enchev, Alexander Lilov. 81 mins. Prem: May 5.

A children's film. During a summer vacation at the seashore, the entire Pioneer Camp is engaged in searching for sunken treasure.

VUZDUSHNIYAT CHOVEK / The Airman. Sc & Dr: Kiran Kolarov. Ph: Radoslav Spassov. Set: Vladislav Schmidt. Mu: Kiril Donchev. Cast: Dimiter Buynozov, Peter Despotov, Boris Lukanov, Annetta Sotirova, Maria Kavardjikova, Grigor Vachkov, Itzhak Fintsi, Nikola Todev. 88 mins. Prem: June 2.

Set in the period of the Personality Cult shortly after the Second World War. A former aviator who sided with the Bulgarian uprising at the end of the war and was decorated for bravery now puts his military plane at the service of fishermen along the coast. A political intrigue follows.

KOLKOTO SINAPENO ZURNO / No Bigger than a Mustard Seed. Sc: Vassil Popov. Dr: Sergei Gyaurov. Ph: Milen Temnyalov. Set: Nikolai Surchadjiev. Cast: Velyo Goranov, Kina Mutafova, Ivan Yanchev. 70 mins. Prem: July 4.

A country doctor, who could have furthered his career with a post in the city, sacrifices his life for the good of the people.

PUTESHESTVIYETO / The Journey. Sc: Vesselin Panayotov. Dr: Iskra Yossifova, Malina Petrova. Ph: Georgi Nikolov. Set: Borislav Neshev. Mu: Bozhidar Petkov. Cast: Stefan Mavrodiev, Plamena Getova, Borislav Tsankov, Ivailo Stoyanov, Edmond Hugassian, Yanaki Ivanov, Ivan Borissov, Lyubcho Vassilev, Ivan Shakirov. 72 mins. Prem: September 22.

Two women directors debut with an unusual children's film. Set in a district of Sofia in 1944, a year of turmoil at the dawn of a new Socialist state, it's about preteenagers roam-

Kiran Kolarov's *The Airman* (1980).

ing the streets to raise money for a fantastic journey to the South Seas—only to experience other adventures of a puzzling nature as the funds mysteriously disappear.

PROZORETSAT / The Window. Sc: Konstantin Iliev, Georgi Stoyanov, based on Iliev's play with the same title. Dr: Georgi Stoyanov. Ph: Hristo Totev. Set: Peter Goranov. Mu: Simeon Pironkov. Cast: Leda Tasseva, Dobrinka Stankova, Plamena Getova, Antoni Genov, Velko Kunev. 89 mins. Prem: October 6.

A psychological drama hemmed in by the confinements of the set and action. The love triangle of man, wife, and mistress is augmented by the birth and adoption of a child. With "a child in common" the trio now face new obligations, while the introduction of two more people adds up to a long night of dialogue in an attic apartment.

UONI / Wonny. Sc: Assen Georgiev, based on Vassil Popov's novel *The Lowlands.* Dr: Vladislav Ikonomov. Ph: Krum Krumov. Set: Vladimir Lekarski. Mu: Kiril Tsibulka. Cast: Georgi Georgiev-Gets, Stoycho Mazgalov, Krystyna Janda. 85 mins. Prem: October 20.

Contemporary theme, about a man with domestic problems who leaves to work on a construction site to sort himself out.

ILYUZIYA / Illusion. Sc: Konstantin Pavlov. Dr: Lyudmil Staikov. Ph: Boris Yanakiev. Set: Zahari Ivanov. Mu: Georgi Genkov. Cast: Russi Chanev, Lyuben Chatalov, Suzanna Kocurikova, Peter Slabakov. 110 mins. Prem: November 3.

A philosophical and historical tract featuring a Poet, an Artist, an Actress, and assorted other characters with metaphoric meaning—during the 1923 uprising.

Lyudmil Staikov's *Illusion* (1980).

KAMIONAT / The Truck. Sc, Dr & Set: Hristo Hristov. Ph: Atanas Tassev. Mu: Kiril Tsibulka. Cast: Djoko Rossich, Stefan Dimitrov, Vesselin Vulkov, Lilyana Kovacheva, Grigor Vachkov, Zhivka Peneva. 107 mins. Prem: November 17.

An exceptional film in a psychological vein. The story parallels Clouzot's *Wages of Fear* (1953) in that a rugged journey by truck over mountain passes in the dead of winter challenges the passengers to the limits of mental and physical endurance. The occasion is the transportation of a dead worker's body in a coffin back to his native village for burial.

GOLYAMOTO NOSHTNO KUPANE / The Big Night Bathe. Sc: Hristo Ganev. Dr: Binka Zhelyazkova. Ph: Plamen Wagenstein. Set: Marie-Thérèse Gospodinova. Mu: Simeon Pironkov. Cast: Malgorzata Braunek, Yuazas Budraitis, Ventsislav Bozhinov, Yanina Kasheva, Nikolai Sotirov, Tanya Shahova, Ilya Karaivanov, Lyuben Chatalov, Ivan Kondov. 152 mins. Prem: December 1.

A fascinating modern parable on Bulgarian traditions. The occasion is the custom of "night bathing" in a resort location on the Black Sea. A group of artists and bored vacationers begin a deadly ritual based on a Thracian game—it leads to tragedy and a reassessment of values.

DAMI KANYAT / Ladies' Choice. Sc: Georgi Mishev. Dr & Set: Ivan Andonov. Ph: Plamen Wagenstein. Mu: Georgi Genkov. Cast: Stefan Danailov, Nevena Kokanova, Tsvetana Maneva, Nadya Todorova, Marianna Dimitrova, Dorothea Toncheva, Maria Statulova, Yordanka Kuzmanova. 94 mins. Prem: December 15.

Comedy about a driving instructor in a provincial town—the girls line up to take lessons from him, and our hero is exhausted.

1981

POHISHTENIE V ZHALTO / Crime in Yellow. Sc: Georgi Danailov, based on Pavel Vezhinov's novella "Incident on a Quiet Street." Dr: Marianna Evstatieva. Ph: Atanas Tassev. Set: Anastas Yanakiev. Mu: Alexander Bruzitsov. Cast: Ivailo Vakavliyev, Simeon Mihailov, Mario Philipov, Martin Stoyanov, Ahmed Aliyev, Konstantin Kotsev, Pavel Poppandov. 74 mins. Prem: January 12.

A remake of Bulgaria's first successful children's film, *The Traces Remain* (1956). Pavel Vezhinov's story was a whodunit with kids in a district of Sofia playing detective when one of their group is mysteriously picked up in a yellow car and is believed to be kidnapped.

TURNOVSKATA TSARITSA / The Queen of Turnovo. Sc & Dr: Yanko Yankov, based on Emilian Stanev's novella with the same title. Ph: Georgi Georgiev. Set: Atanas Velyanov. Mu: Georgi Genkov. Cast: Stefan Danailov, Kamelia Todorova, Elly Skorcheva, Nevena Kokanova, Boris Lukanov. 97 mins. Prem: February 2.

Another of the Turnovo writer's stories set in the past: the period is the Balkan War of 1912 and the principal characters a doctor from the upper classes and his maidservant from the lower. This literary adaptation (the novella was written in 1973) offers a panoramic view of the old city of Turnovo.

DOM ZA NEZHNI DOUSHI / Home for Lonely Souls. Sc: Boyan Papazov. Dr: Evgeni Mihailov. Ph: Elly Mihailova.

Set: Vyacheslav Parapanov. Mu: Bozhidar Petkov. Cast: Plamena Getova, Tsvetana Denkova, Kiryakos Argiropoulos, Nikolai Velichkov, Dora Markova, Marin Mladenov. 78 mins. Prem: February 23.

Fine debut film by the husband-wife team of director Evgeni and camerawoman Elly. A lonely woman engaged as an actress in a theater in the provinces can't come to grips with herself even when an opportunity comes along to play a lead role (a saint who walks on coals). Throughout much of the film a play on satirist Aleko Konstantinov is performed in the background, thus broadening the scope of the story and adding depth to the performance of Plamena Getova in the lead role.

BOYANSKIYAT MAISTOR / Master of Boyana. Sc: Evgeni Konstantinov, Zahari Zhandov, based on motifs in Stoyan Zagorchinov's novel *Festival in Boyana*. Dr: Zahari Zhandov. Ph: Emil Wagenstein. Set: Valentina Yotova. Mu: Vassil Kazandjiev. Cast: Peter Despotov, Emil Markov, Atanas Bozhinov, Yordan Spirov, Boyka Velkova, Lyubomir Dimitrov. 106 mins. Prem: March 9.

The first of the important historical films prepared for the 1,300th anniversary of the founding of Bulgaria in 681. The frescoes in the church of Boyana near Sofia, painted in 1259 by an unknown artist, are world-famous as examples of the then flourishing Turnovo School—the murals preceded Italian art of the Renaissance by two generations, and may have indirectly influenced the Italian masters. Zhandov's story is fiction, but he is faithful to the period.

MILOST ZA ZHIVITE / Mercy for the living. Sc: Nikolai Nikiforov. Dr & Ph: Todor Stoyanov. Set: Violetta Yovcheva. Mu: Rumen Balyozov. Cast: Georgi Georgiev-Gets, Kosta Tsonev, Tsvetana Maneva, Boris Lukanov. 104 mins. Prem: March 30.

An aging partisan fighter and now a trusted leader in his village is dying of cancer, but instead of caring about an operation after a medical checkup, he stubbornly continues on his way of helping others in need.

PRYATELI ZA VECHERYA / Friends to Dinner. Sc: Lyubomir Yanov. Dr: Yakim Yakimov. Ph: Ivan Velchev. Set: Mony Aladjemov. Mu: Alexander Bruzitsov. Cast: Svetoslav Peyev, Maria Kavardjikova, Ivan Grigorov, Annetta Sotirova, Violetta Doneva, Banko Bankov, Peter Petrov, Vesselin Vulkov, Nikolai Kalchev. 80 mins. Prem: April 13.

A social comedy constructed around a gag: What happens when an old sport like Pepi telephones five of his boyhood friends just before midnight to invite them to dinner at his home? They come, together with their wives.

PRISHESTVIE / Advent. Sc: Dimiter Delyan, based on his novel with the same title. Dr: Ivanka Grubcheva. Ph: Yatsek Todorov. Set: Yordanka Peycheva. Mu: Kiril Tsibulka. Cast: Vassil Mihailov, Nikolai Tomov, Maria Statulova, Georgi Georgiev-Gets, Stoycho Mazgalov. 107 mins. Prem: April 27.

A film on ethics: in a provincial town a scientist is researching the phenomenon of flying saucers—his findings are inadvertently published, and an uproar follows.

MERA SPORED MERA / Measure for Measure. Sc: Russi Chanev, Georgi Djulgerov, based on Svoboda Buchvarova's book *Liturgy for St. Elijah's Day*. Dr: Georgi Djulgerov. Ph: Radoslav Spassov. Set: Georgi Todorov. Mu: Bozhidar Petkov. Cast: Russi Chanev, Stefan Mavrodiev, Grigor Vachkov, Katya Ivanova, Tsvetana Maneva, Rumena Trifonova.

Three-part version: 288 mins. Part One: 100 mins. Prem: May 4. Part Two: 84 mins. Prem: May 11. Part Three: 104 mins. Prem: May 18.

Although a shortened "festival version" of this magnificent epic is available, the longer version is highly recommended. This is a film on the Macedonian Question prepared in three parts for the 1,300th anniversary celebrations in 1981. Part One deals with Macedonia under the Turks, 1878–1903, Part Two with the 1903 Ilinden Uprising (on Saint Elijah's Day, August 2) and the short-lived Krushevo Republic, and Part Three with the final years of the revolution, 1906–12.

DISHAI, CHOVECHE! / Breathe, Little Man! Sc: Svetoslav Michev. Dr: Vesselina Gerinska. Ph: Georgi Angelov. Set: Tsveta Marinova. Mu: Kiril Tsibulka. Cast: Ivan Yanchev, Mimosa Bazova, Maxim Kolev, Ivan Djambazov, Svetozar Kokalanov, Hristo Shopov, Momhil Indjov. 72 mins. Prem: July 6.

A youth film. A boy of fourteen enters a school and clinic for children with tuberculosis and has to find his way on his own.

LETALOTO / The Flying Machine. Sc: Boyan Papazov. Dr: Ognyan Gelinov: Ph: Krassimir Kostov. Set: Nikolai Surchadjiev. Mu: Yuri Stupel. Cast: Hristo Gurbov, Krassimir Dokov, Yulia Kozhinkova, Rashko Mladenov, Yordan Spirov. 75 mins. Prem: July 27.

A tragicomedy set during the Balkan Wars of 1912–13. A shepherd is enthusiastic about flying and, together with a Turkish friend, constructs a homemade flying machine. Just when it gets off the ground, the war comes to his mountain village with tragic results.

MASSOVO CHOUDO / Mass Miracle. Sc: Konstantin Pavlov. Dr: Ivan Pavlov. Ph: Plamen Hinkov. Set: Borislav Neshev. Mu: Georgi Genkov. Cast: Dimiter Ganev, Georgi Stefanov, Konstantin Dimchev, Ruth Spassova, Minko Minkov. 74 mins. Prem: August 10.

Impressive debut film by director Ivan Pavlov and cameraman Plamen Hinkov, both graduates of the Sofia Film Academy. It is a film-within-a-film: a second-time candidate for the film academy attempts to make a documentary about a factory as it is being constructed. The idea backfires.

NEPALONOLETIE / Under Age. Sc: Vera Mutafchieva. Dr: Alexander Obreshkov. Ph: Georgi Nikolov. Mu: Simeon Shterev. Cast: Vesselin Rankov, Emil Djurov, Svetlana Atannasova. 92 mins. Prem: September 21.

A youth theme about a lad maturing to manhood on a construction site.

YO-HO-HO. Sc: Valeri Petrov. Dr: Zako Heskia. Ph: Stefan Trifonov. Set: Isidora Seidner. Mu: Kiril Donchev. Cast: Victor Chuchkov, Kiril Varjiyski, Ilya Penev, Anani Anev. 98 mins. Prem: October 5.

A children's film for adults as well as young people. This is Valeri Petrov's best screenplay in the genre since *Knight without Armor* (1966). A boy spending time in a hospital ward makes friends with a young worker with an injured back, who transports the boy and the film to the Caribbean with a fantastic story of pirates on the open sea. The twist comes when daydreams and reality mix.

KHAN ASPARUKH. Sc: Vera Mutafchieva. Dr: Lyudmil Staikov. Ph: Boris Yanakiev. Set: Bogoya Sapundjiev. Mu:

Zako Heskia's *Yo-Ho-Ho* **(1981).**

Simeon Pironkov. Cast: Stoyko Peyev, Antoni Genov, Vanya Tsvetkova, Marie Syur, Yossif Surchadjiev, Peter Slabakov. An epic in three parts. Part One: *Phanagoria*, 112 mins. Prem: October 19. Part Two: *Migration*, 113 mins. Prem: October 26. Part Three: *Land Forever*, 113 mins. Prem: November 3. Total length: 338 mins.

Lyudmil Staikov's *Khan Asparukh* **(1981).**

193

A national epic produced for the 1,300th anniversary of the founding of Bulgaria, celebrated on 20 October 1981 with the general release of the three-part production across the country. *Phanagoria* is set on the steppes of Middle Asia, the land of Great Bulgaria, from where these Turkic people set out under Khan Asparukh in search of a new home. *Migration* is the story of the trek westward to the Danube River over the years and the encounter with the Slavs in the area. *Land Forever* features the decisive battle with the Byzantine emperor Constantine IV Pogonatus. Shot in Eastmancolor, the epic took over a year to make, features a cast of thousands, and compares extremely well with Western spectaculars.

POD EDNO NEBE / Under the Same Sky. Sc: Vladimir Kumin, Iskander Khamrayev. Dr: Iskander Khamrayev. Ph: Georgi Georgiev. Set: Rima Narinian, Eva Yordanova. Mu: Alexander Yossifov. Cast: Naum Shopov, Vladimir Menshov, Tsvetana Maneva, Natalia Fateyeva. (Coproduction with Lenfilm in the Soviet Union.) 75 mins. Prem: unknown.

This is the story of Bulgarian workers leaving their sunny homeland to work on a lumber project in the rugged taiga region of Siberia in the Soviet Union. The Soviet side of a friendship between two men is interpreted by Vladimir Menshov, who as a director won the 1980 Academy Award for Best Foreign Film: *Moscow Doesn't Believe in Tears*.

1982

ORKESTUR BEZ IME / A Nameless Band. Sc: Stanislav Stratiev. Dr: Lyudmil Kirkov. Ph: Victor Chichov. Set: Assya Popova. Mu: Boris Karadimchev. Cast: Velko Kunev, Pavel Popandov, Georgi Mamalev, Filip Trifonov, Maria Kavardjikova, Katerina Evro. 115 mins. Prem: January 4.

Second collaboration between director Kirkov and scriptwriter Stratiev after their successful *Short Sun* (1979). A social satire, in the Black Sea resort area where an amateur band dreams of making it big at a plush hotel, but they resort to too many tricks and lose out in the end.

NASHIYAT SHOSHKANINI / Our Shoshkanini. Sc: Georgi Stoev, Ivailo Manev. Dr: Georgi Stoev. Ph: Milan Ognyanov, Nikolai Tod. Set: Ivailo Manev. Mu: Simeon Shterev, Raycho Lyubenov, Itzhak Fintsi. Cast: Itzhak Fintsi, Mimosa Bazova, Simeon Shterev, Nikolai Nikov, Alexander Kerkov, Kosta Mihailov. 76 mins. Prem: January 18.

A comedy about a mechanic with the soul of a poet and a love for the violin. His playground is at the moment a beergarden, but he dreams of one day performing in a concert hall. Itzhak Fintsi is the "Shoshkanini," a role the popular comedian plays to the hilt.

SRESHTA NA SILITE / A Meeting of the Great Powers. Sc: Vladislav Ikonomov, Nikola Tiholov, based on a novel by Stefan Dichev. Dr: Vladislav Ikonomov. Ph: Krum Krumov. Set: Konstantin Russakov. Mu: Kiril Tsibulka. Cast: Stefan Marvodiev, Vulcho Kamarashev, Vladimir Smirnov, Irsi Krisak, Vassil Buchvarov, Sigmund Fock. 98 mins. Prem: February 1.

Literary adaptation of a historical novel. It deals with the Constantinople Conference of December 1876, at which the Great Powers of Britain, France, Germany, Austria-Hungary, and Russia discussed granting autonomy to two Bulgarian provinces centering around Sofia and Turnovo.

Irina Aktasheva and Hristo Piskov's *Avalanche* (1982).

Turkey was the afflicted member nation during the conference.

LAVINA / Avalanche. Sc & Dr: Irina Aktasheva, Hristo Piskov, based on Blaga Dimitrova's novel with the same title. Ph: Tsvetan Chobanski. Set: Anastas Yanakiev. Mu: Georgi Minchev. Cast: Ivan Ivanov, Vanya Tsvetkova, Lyuben Chatalov, Filip Trifonov, Pavel Poppandov. 153 mins. Prem: February 15.

Faithful adaptation of a much discussed contemporary novel. The theme is mountain climbing, but this sport and the ensuing avalanche are metaphorically applied to life's values and social problems. The message is clear: the individual must triumph over self-interest.

OUDARUT / The Thrust. Sc: Nikolai Nikiforov. Dr: Borislav Sharaliev. Ph: Venets Dimitrov. Set: Maria Ivanova. Cast: Lyubomir Mladenov, Konstantin Dimchev, Mihail Mihailov, Plamen Charov, Stefan Dimitrov, Kosta Tsonev, Ilya Raev, Boris Lukanov, Dimiter Hadjiyanev, Stoyan Stoev, Lyubomir Dimitrov, Georgi Djubrilov. 141 mins. Prem: March 22.

A historical chronicle encompassing the events in Sofia from 26 August to 9 September 1944, the moment of the Communist revolution and the arrival of Soviet troops in the city. The two-part patriotic film was produced for the 1,300th anniversary celebrations of Bulgaria's founding.

EDNA ZHENA NA TRIDESET I TRI / A Woman at Thirty-three. Sc: Boyan Popazov. Dr: Hristo Hristov. Ph: Atanas Tassev. Set: Yordanka Peycheva. Mu: Kiril Tsibulka. Cast: Liliana Kovacheva, Bogdan Glishev, Vesselin Vulkov, Gergana Burdarova, Pavel Spassov. 102 mins. Prem: April 12.

Borislav Sharaliev's *The Thrust* (1982).

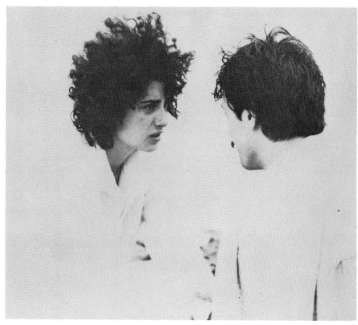

Rumyana Petkova's *Reflections* (1982).

A psychological study of a woman approaching middle age with few prospects for the future: she is divorced, has a small daughter to take care of, holds a job as a secretary, and continues her studies on the side. She is also the object of gossip, backbiting letters, and threatening phone calls—the accusations are false but she cannot prove her innocence, owning to having placed herself in too many compromising situations. Finely acted and splendidly photographed in natural light on locations by Atanas Tassev.

KOMBINA /The Racket. Sc: Vladimir Ganev. Dr: Nikola Rudarov. Ph: Yatsek Todorov. Set: Assya Popova, Vladimir Hikov. Mu: Mitko Shterev. Cast: Ivan Ivanov, Vanya Tsvetkova, Nikolai Sotirov, Vulcho Kamarashev, Mario Stanchev, Ivan Yanchev, Svetoslav Nedelchev. 119 mins. Prem: May 10.

A whodunit about a gang of smugglers. The thriller is set in bars and dives, where young drifters live on the edge of society.

KOUCHE V CHEKMEDZHE / A Dog in the Drawer. Sc: Rada Moskova. Dr: Dimiter Petrov. Ph: Atanas Tassev. Set: Yordanka Peycheva. Cast: Zhivok Garvonov, Maria Statulova, Ruzha Delcheva, Pavel Poppandov, Annetta Sotirova, Ivan Yanchev, Vesselin Prahov, Emil Dimitrov, Martin Stoyanov. 95 mins. Prem: May 24.

Three youngs boys purchase a dog in common, deciding that "Roshko" will spend a day with each in turn. After several mishaps, the five-year-old (and youngest) owner manages to get the dog to his grandparents for a better home out in the country than a cramped city apartment.

OTRAZHENIA / Reflections. Sc: Nevelina Popova. Dr: Rumyana Petkova. Ph: Svetlana Ganeva. Set: Yuliana Bozhkova. Cast: Zhanna Karaivanova, Filip Trifonov, Lyuben Chatalov, Lydia Vulkova, Boris Lukanov. 105 mins. Prem: June 26.

Feminist theme made by a production team of women: scriptwriter, director, camerawoman, art director, and lead actress. It's about three days of reflection in the life of a twenty-year-old student at the university.

TSARSKA PIESSA / Royal Play. Sc: Vlado Daverov. Dr: Ivan Nichev. Ph: Tsvetan Chobanski. Music: Bozhidar Petkov. Set: Elka Todorova. Cast: Todor Kolev, Kosta Tsonev, Dorothea Toncheva, Evstati Stratiev, Lazar Ganev. 72 mins. Prem: July 12.

A play-within-a-play plot: a provincial theater stages a historical drama about a King, Queen, and Counsellor, but it so happens in real life that the King's queen is the lover of the star of the play, the counsellor. Suddenly, in the midst of a performance, the King decides to take command of the embarrassing situation, even though he's considered to be the poorest actor in the company.

SMURTA NA ZAYEKA / Death of the Hare. Sc: Boris Hristov. Dr: Anri Kulev. Ph: Svetlana Ganeva. Set: Yuliana Bozhkova. Mu: Raycho Lyubenov. Cast: Rumena Trifonova, Anton Radichev, Lyubomir Mladenov, Lyuben Chatalov, Maria Kavardjikova. 87 mins. Prem: August 2.

Animation filmmaker Henri Koulev's first feature film. He collaborated with poet Boris Hristov on this experimental attempt to recapture images of a village childhood. An opportunity to film a flooded village was offered by the creation of a man-made lake.

ELEGIYA / Elegy. Sc: Alexander Tomov, based on his novella with the same title. Dr. Eduard Zahariev. Ph: Georgi Nikolov. Set: Georgi Todorov. Cast: Itzhak Fintsi, Anton Radichev, Marianna Dimitrova. 111 mins. Prem: September 27.

Story of a retired railwayman living in a suburb, who is shocked by his son's unfaithfulness to wife and family. He confronts the situation in his own stubborn way: the tragic result is the accidental drowning of a gypsy girl in a swamp.

NAY TEZHKIYAT GRYAH / The Worst Sin. Sc: Dragomir Assenov, based on his novel with the same title. Dr: Ivanka

Grubcheva. Ph: Emil Wagenstein. Set: Valentina Mladenova. Mu: Kiril Tsibulka. Cast: Georgi Cherkalov, Katya Paskaleva, Nikolai Binev, Dossyo Dossev, Boris Lukanov, Vassil Dimitrov, Bela Tsoneva, Georgi Georgiev-Gets. 94 mins. Prem: September 13.

The "worst sin" of a writer is to be untrue to himself: in this case, the aging protagonist suffers when a friend, an artist, dies—he feels himself guilty of the death, and begins to review his past.

PREDOUPREZHDENIYETO / The Warning. Sc: Lyuben Stanev, Juan Antonio Bardem. Dr: Juan Antonio Bardem. Ph: Plamen Wagenstein. Set: Konstantin Russakov. Costumes: Maria Sotirova. Cast: Peter Gyurov, Nevena Kokanova, Boris Lukanov, Assen Dimitrov, Gavril Tsonkov, Dobromir Manev, Alexander Lilov. 180 mins. Prem: October 11.

Spanish director Bardem and several German actors of the GDR collaborated on this historical epic produced on the occasion of the one-hundredth anniversary of Georgi Dimitrov's birth in 1982. The scene is Berlin 1932, the last summer before Hitlers rise to power, followed by the famous Leipzig Trial at which Dimitrov was accused of planning the Reichstag fire. Documentary footage is mixed with the reenactment of the historical events. This was the third major film made on Dimitrov, the two others being Lev Arnstam's *History Lesson* (1957) and Hristo Hristov's *Hammer or Anvil* (1972).

TAINOTO ORUZHIYE / The Secret Weapon. Sc: Boyan Byolchev, based on Boyan Bolgar's novels *The Blue-Eyed with the Short Sword* and *The Victories of the Blue-Eyed.* Dr. Marianna Evstatieva. Ph: Atanas Tassev. Set: Anastas Yanakiev. Mu: Simeon Pironkov. Cast: Lyuben Chatalov, Elvira Inanova, Pavel Poppandov, Yossif Surchadjiev. 99 mins. Prem: November 1.

Youth film: an adventure story set in fourteen-century Bulgaria, the secret weapon being gunpowder.

BYALA MAGIYA / White Magic. Sc: Konstantin Pavlov. Dr: Ivan Andonov. Ph: Victor Chichov. Set: Peter Goranov. Mu: Georgi Genkov. Cast: Peter Slabakov, Georgi Kaloyanchev, Kunka Baeva, Ilka Zafirova, Plamena Getova, Velko Kunev, Ivan Grigorov. 97 mins. Prem: November 22.

A poetic film drawing upon the country's folk heritage. The period is yesteryear, sometime in the 1920s, and the setting is a village in the Rhodope Mountains.

24 CHASSA DUZHD / 24 Hours of Rain. Sc: Vladislav Ikonomov, Nikola Tiholov, based on Yordan Yavkov's story "The Private Teacher." Dr: Vladislav Ikonomov. Ph: Krum Krumov. Set: Konstantin Russakov. Mu: Kiril Tsibulka. Cast: Stefan Mavrodiev, Stefan Danailov, Eva Czikulska, Kiril Varjiyski, Velyo Goranov. 86 mins. Prem: December 6.

Based on a Yordan Yavkov story, "The Private Teacher" (from the collection of his stories in *Evenings at Antimovo*

Juan Antonio Bardem's *The Warning* (1982).

Ivan Andonov's *White Magic* (1982).

Inn, published in 1928), the original was set at the turn-of-the-century and against the background of a moonlit night. The director has moved the action forward to 1931 and introduced the motif of rain for dramatic effect.

SINUT NA MARIA / Maria's Son. Sc: Svetoslav Michev. Dr: Malina Petrova. Ph: Plamen Hinkov. Set: Boris Neshev. Mu: Bozhidar Petkov. Cast: Kiril Varjiyski, Peter Slabakov, Konstantin Dimchev, Vassil Popiliev, Polina Dorostolska. 98 mins. Prem: December 20.

A young journalist decides to look for the father of a ten-year-old boy, the illegitimate son of a young woman who has died and left him an orphan.

1983

MARGI / Margie. Sc: Zheni Radeva. Dr: Lilyana Pencheva. Ph: Georgi Georgiev. Set: Marie-Thérèse Gospodinova, Sonya Despoda. Mu: Bozhidar Petkov. Cast: Lily Mitova, Lyubomir Tsvetkov, Lily Ouzunova, Rossen Bochev, Vladimir Radkov, Tsvetana Maneva, Annetta Sotirova, Velko Kunev. 74 mins. Prem: January 10.

A children's film. A group of youngsters, ages eight to twelve, are planning a school play along the lines of Hans Christian Andersen. The play includes an astronaut, in order to please the science-teacher.

CHOVEK NE SAM UBIVAL / I Never Killed a Man. Sc: Rossen Bossev. Dr: Rashko Ouzunov. Ph: Georgi Mateyev.

Vladislav Ikonomov's *24 Hours of Rain* (1982).

Set: Mony Aladjemov. Mu: Raycho Lyubenov. Cast: Georgi Novakov, Nikola Stefanov, Anani Yavashev, Vulcho Karamashev, Inna Semeonova, Krassimira Petrova, Ivan Yanchev. 89 mins. Prem: January 24.

Part thriller, part psychological drama, the protagonist is a trickster who comes to a provincial town and bites off more than he can chew.

AKO TE IMA / If You Do Exist. Sc & Dr: Ilya Velchev. Ph: Mihail Venkov. Set: Zahari Savov. Mu: Mitko Shterev. Cast: Irène Vladimirova. Peter Terziev, Violetta Buchvarova, Peter Donchev, Boris Lukanov. 116 mins. Prem: February 7.

Youth film about a young couple and first love: he's from an orphanage with a mind of his own, while she's from a well-to-do family with social responsibilities.

MYARKA ZA NEOTKLONENIE / Preventive Detention. Sc: Stefan Kospartov. Dr: Maya Vaptsarova. Ph: Stefan Trifonov. Set: Vladimir Lekarski. Mu: Vesselin Nikolov. Cast: Ivan Ivanov, Stefka Ilieva, Plamen Sirakov, Ibish Orhanov, Yordanka Kuzmanova, Velyo Goranov. 89 mins. Prem: March 4.

A psychological thriller about a young man seeking revenge on his own, outside the law. He has witnessed the rape of the girl he loves.

HOTEL TSENTRAL / Hotel Central. Sc & Dr: Vesselin Branev, based on two short stories by Konstantin Konstantinov. Ph: Yatsek Todorov. Set: Anastas Yanakiev. Mu: Bozhidar Petkov. Cast: Irène Krivoshieva, Reneta Dralcheva, Boryana Puncheva, Zhivko Garvanov, Anton Radichev, Valentin Gadjokov, Boris Lukanov. 105 mins. Prem: March 7.

An entry at the 1983 Venice festival, this quite extraordinary film was made by a scriptwriter who came to directing via a TV serial on Bulgarian uprisings in times of oppression. In *Hotel Central* the historical moment is the 1934 *coup d'etat*, after which parliament was dissolved and a totalitarian rule was established. The central character is a hotel chambermaid in a provincial town, an innocent girl compelled to become a prostitute to serve the interests of the village benefactors. Her behavior, however, unmasks the corruption about her. Both writer-director Vesselin Branev and actress Irène Krivoshieva made names for themselves at home and abroad with this production.

ZAVRASHTANE / The Return Journey. Sc: Raina Tomova. Dr: Stefan Dimitrov. Ph: Atanas Tassev. Set: Petko Bonchev. Mu: Simeon Pironkov. Cast: Rumena Trifonova, Stefan Dimitrov, Erna Zhinova, Ivan Atanassov, Ivan Nestorov. 100 mins. Prem: March 21.

A performing artist returns home to Bulgaria after a long tour, only to discover that the gap is widening between herself and her closest friends and acquaintances—including her daughter.

BON SHANS. INSPEKTORE! / Bonne Chance, Inspector! Sc & Dr: Peter Donev. Ph: Hristo Totev. Set: Georgi Gutsev. Mu: Boris Karadimchev. Cast: Velko Kunev, Georgi Kaloyanchev, Kamelia Todorova, Tatyana Lolova, Yossif Surchadjiev, Stoyan Stoyev, Anton Radichev, Kiril Gospodinov, Dimiter Georgiev. 88 mins. Prem: May 2.

Vesselin Branev's *Hotel Central* **(1983).**

Peter Donev's *Bonne Chance, Inspector!* **(1983).**

An Inspector Clouseau caper, Bulgarian style. The comedy is set in the 1930s, thus allowing for appropriate costumes and decorations from the period. The setting is a provincial town, where the bank is robbed.

GOSPODIN ZA EDIN DEN / King for a Day. Sc: Nikola Statkov, based on two stories in his book *The Lie of Having Lived*. Dr: Nikolai Volev. Ph: Krassimir Kostov. Set: Konstantin Russakov. Mu: Ivan Staikov. Cast: Todor Kolev, Yordanka Stefanova, Itzhak Fintsi, Ivan Grigorov. 87 mins. Prem: May 16.

Set in a mountain village in the 1930s. The antihero is a gullible bumpkin, who one day turns the tables on his fellow villagers by pretending to have struck it rich. In truth he is scratching for funds to sail to America.

POSLEDNI ZHELANIA / Last Wishes. Sc: Marianna Basheva, Rangel Vulchanov. Dr: Rangel Vulchanov. Ph: Radoslav Spassov. Set: Borislav Neshev. Mu: Kiril Donchev. Cast: Stefan Mavrodiev, Antonia Zhekova, Diana Sofronieva, Georgi Mamalev, Lyubomir Ouzunov, Emile Djurov, Aleko Minchev. 102 mins. Prem: August 22.

Presented at the Munich and Montreal festivals in 1983, *Last Wishes* won critical acclaim as a satire on the world powers in Europe just before the First World War reached its explosive climax. The royal families congregate on a battlefield during a truce to continue their family spats in an absurd setting. A photographer contrasts royal amusements with the harsh realities of war and killing.

Nikolai Volev's *King for a Day* **(1983).**

ZAVURTETE USICHKI SFERI / Spin the Spheres. Sc: Nikola Petrov. Dr: Ilko Dundakov. Ph: Boyko Kalev. Set: Evgeni Apostolov. Mu: Angel Mihailov. Cast: Mihail Elenov, Chavdar Monov, Georgi Kishkilov, Maya Zhurkova. 75 mins. Prem: September 5.

A film for youth. During the Second World War, the boys in an orphanage rebel against mistreatment at the institution. The leader of the group dies fighting for justice.

PRILIV NA NEZHNOST / A Surge of Tenderness. Sc: Rudenko Yordanov, based on his novella with the same title. Dr: Kosta Bikov. Ph: Dimiter Lissicharov. Set: Ivan Andreyev. Mu: Kiril Donchev. Cast: Lyuben Chatalov, Kamelia Todorova, Pavel Poppandov, Peter Slabakov, Nikolai Volev. 95 mins. Prem: September 9.

At the end of the Second World War, a new society is being built in Bulgaria. These difficult years are reviewed in the figure of a young man returning home to do his part in bringing about historical change.

ZLATNATA REKA / The Golden River. Sc: Georgi Bogdanov. Dr: Ivanka Grubcheva. Ph: Emil Wagenstein. Set: Valentina Mladenova. Mu: Mitko Shterev. Cast: Mihail Mihailov, Peter Slabakov, Nikola Chiprianov, Stoine Pavlin, Pepa Nikolova, Nikola Todev, Igor Markovski, Katya Filipova, Maria Statulova. 112 mins. Prem: October 31.

Set in a village that has now become a factory town owing to the construction of a cement plant. The protagonists are all "lost souls" who search for a new meaning in life—now that they are thrown together in a house with a mortgage on it.

TRETOTO LITSE / The Third Side of the Coin. Sc: Yordan Kostov, Yanush Vazov. Dr: Yanush Vazov. Ph: Tsvetan Chobanski. Set: Anastas Yanakiev. Cast: Yossif Surchadiev, Georgi Stoyanov, Anton Radichev, Oyler Stoyanov, Ernestina Zhineva, Nikolai Binev, Assen Milanov, Ivan Chervenkov. 87 mins. Prem: October 17.

A crime thriller. A stash of ancient coins, some of which are being sold for high profits on the art market, induces an amateur detective to begin his own investigation.

ORISSIA / Destiny. Sc & Dr: Nikola Korabov, based on Nikolai Haitov's short story "Dervish Seed." Ph: Plamen Somov. Set: Tsvetana Yankova, Elyana Stoyanova. Cast: Maria Hristova, Eleftery Elefterov, Hristo Gurbov, Lyuben Chatalov, Yordan Spirov, Leda Tasseva. 86 mins. Prem: October 31.

A Romeo and Juliet tale set in the distant past in the Rhodope Mountains, the favorite setting for Nikolai Haitov stories. Because of a twist of fate, the two young lovers are denied marriage and spend forty years of their lives with other mates—but time has not diminished the longing for each other.

RAVNOVESSIE / Balance. Sc: Stanislav Stratiev, based on his novella "Wild Bees." Dr: Lyudmil Kirkov. Ph: Dimko Minov. Set: Georgi Todorov. Mu: Boris Karadimchev. Cast: Pavel Poppandov, Plamena Getova, Georgi Georgiev-Gets, Katerina Evro, Konstantin Kotsev, Luchezar Stoyanov,

Ivanka Grubcheva's *The Golden River* (1983).

Nikola Korabov's *Destiny* (1983).

Lyudmil Kirkov's *Balance* (1983).

Vanya Tsvetkova, Stefan Danailov, Ivan Djambazov, Lyuben Chatalov. 140 mins. Prem: November 14.

The third and best collaborative effort between director Lyudmil Kirkov and scriptwriter Stanislav Stratiev (following *Short Sun* and *A Nameless Band*). The twist in this social drama has to do with filmmaking itself: the fates of three minor figures in a production unit on location—Milko, Elena, and Maria—are contrasted with the bloodless romanticism in the film scenario. One of the year's best productions and a film with remarkable psychological depth, it features the talented Plamena Getova as Elena, Milko's wife, in a finely sketched performance. *Balance* won a Silver Prize at the 1983 Moscow festival.

KONSTANTIN FILOSOF / Constantine the Philosopher.
Sc: Nikola Russev. Dr: Georgi Stoyanov. Ph: Hristo Totev. Set: Angel Ahryanov, Boyanka Ahryanova, Georgi Gutsev. Mu: Simeon Pironkov. Cast: Russi Chanev, Konstantin Tsanev, Naum Shopov, Itzhak Fintsi, Dobrinka Stankova, Elly Skorcheva, Velko Kunev, Rashko Mladenov, Nevena Kokanova, Vitomir Saruivanov. Two parts: 240 mins. Prem: restricted release until completion of Part Three.

The story of Cyril (Constantine) and Methodius, the brother-saints who were missionaries to the Slav peoples in Moravia and trained their zealous disciples for the later conversion of the Bulgarians in 864–65. The central figure is Cyril-Constantine (827–69), whose brief life of forty-two years was marked for greatness from the very beginning. He was a monk from Salonica whose first official post was that of librarian at the Church of Saint Sofia in Constan-

tinople, thereafter succeeding the patriarch Photius as teacher of philosophy at the city's university while still in his twenties—thus the title *Constantine the Philosopher*. This section covers those years in Constantinople before the brothers embark on their mission. Part Three, now in preparation, follows Cyril-Constantine on his journeys until his death at forty-two in the year 869.

1984

DELO NO. 205/1913 / Case No. 205/1913. Sc: Kiran Kolarov, Ivan Dechev, based on Nikola Gayderov's book *The Drama of Yavorov's Life*. Dr: Kiran Kolarov. Ph: Radoslav Spassov. Set: Peter Goranov. Mu: Kiril Donchev. Cast: Yavor Milushev, Katya Ivanova, Bogdan Glishev. Stoyan Stoev, Plamen Sirakov, Boris Lukanov, Martin Penchev, Vulcho Kamarashev. Two parts: 158 mins. Prem: January 23.

This is a portrait of one of the great figures in Bulgarian literature, Peyo Yavorov (1878–1914). The poet committed suicide, this act following the suicide of his wife, Lora Karavelova. The team of Kiran Kolarov and Ivan Dechev attempt to retrace this troubled relationship through letters written by Lora to Yavorov, as well as through other documented evidence and interviews with contemporaries. The film captures the atmosphere of the turn-of-the-century, a fruitful period in the ripening of Bulgarian literature.

681 A.D. / THE GLORY OF KHAN. This edited version of the three-part *Khan Asparukh*, produced in 1981, was made for a Warner Brothers release abroad under the supervi-

Georgi Stoyanov's *Constantine the Philosopher* **(1983).**

Georgi Stoyanov's *Constantine the Philosopher* **(1983).**

Georgi Stoyanov's *Constantine the Philosopher* (1983).

Georgi Stoyanov's *Constantine the Philosopher* (1983).

Kiran Kolarov's *Case No. 205/1913* **(1984).**

sion of Steven Bickel and Thomas Marshall. The synchronized English-language version was presented in Bulgarian theaters with Bulgarian subtitles. 95 mins. Prem: February 13.

VIBRATSIA / Vibration. Sc: Vikenti Marinov. Dr: Todor Stoyanov. Ph: Tsvetan Chobanski. Set: Ivan Andreev. Mu: Angel Mikhailov. Cast: Nikolai Sotirov, Boris Arabov, Daniel Mishev, Maya Baburska, Kiril Zlatkov, Nelly Monegjikova. 87 mins. Prem: March 15.

A contemporary theme. The vibration in the title refers to a faulty turbine in a nuclear power station. The potential disaster triggers, in turn, psychological conflicts.

VKOUS NA BISSER / A Taste of Pearl. Sc: Assen Georgiev. Dr: Villy Tsankov. Ph: Krassimir Kostov. Set: Nikolai Surchadjiev. Mu: Boris Karadimchev. Cast: Ventsislav Kissyov, Ingeborg Rotte, Andrea Chernitski, Georgi Cherkelov, Anani Yavashev, Yossif Surchadjiev. 83 mins. Prem: March 19.

A romance between a young East German Ballerina and a Bulgarian composer. She has come to a Black Sea resort town to participate in a World Ballet Competition.

GORE NA CHERESHATA / Up in the Cherry Tree. Sc: Rada Moskova. Dr: Marianna Evstatieva. Ph: Atanas Tassev. Set: Vladimir Lekarski. Cast: Vesselin Prahov, Konstantin Kotsev, Lyuben Chatalov, Anton Gorchev, Dobrinka Stankova, Lyuba Alexieva. 90 mins. Prem: April 2.

Children's film, about kids in a big city and a convenient cherry tree in the neighbor's backyard.

NA GOSPOZHITSATA I NEINATA MUZHKA KOMPANIA / To the Miss and Her Male Company. Sc: Margarit Minkov. Dr: Ivan Dobchev. Ph: Dimko Minov. Set: Georgi Gutsev. Cast: Naum Shopov, Plamena Getova, Ivan Ivanov, Nikola Todev, Marin Mladenov, Stefan Iliev. 84 mins. Prem: April 22.

Sofia during the Second World War. The resistance works its way into the environs of the Titanic Nightclub. The entertainers at the club awaken in various ways to the revolution at their doorstep.

POETUT I DYAVOLUT / The Poet and the Devil. Sc: Stefan Prodev, Ivan Rossenov. Dr: Ivan Rossenov. Ph: Svetlana Ganeva. Set: Anastas Yanakiev. Mu: Bozhidar Petkov. Cast: Vladimir Penev, Elefteri Elefterov, Zhanna Karaivanova, Vulcho Kamarashev, Krustan Djankov, Lyuben Chatalov, Katya Paskaleva. 82 mins. Prem: April 30.

A biography of poet Hristo Smyrnenski (1896–1923). Smyrnenski died at twenty-seven, and the film encompasses the events of the tragic 1920s.

ZELENITE POLYA / Green Fields. Sc: Alexander Tomov, based on his short story, "Mitri and the Little Horse." Dr: Plamen Maslarov. Ph: Plamen Somov. Set: Georgi Todorov. Mu: Stefan Dimitrov. Cast: Stefan Mavrodiev, Marianna Dimitrova, Velko Kunev, Velcho Kamarashev, Lyuben Chatalov. 81 mins. Prem: May 21.

Situation comedy about a rustic type living a lonely existence in an urban community—so he goes out and buys a horse to keep himself company. This is a moral parable with some fresh new twists on the migration from the land to the city.

SPASSENIETO / The Rescue: Sc: Serafim Severnyak, Peter Peichev, based on Severnyak's novel, *Ohrid Ballad.* Dr: Borislav Punchev. Ph: Borislav Punchev, Petko Bonchev, Ivan Gekov. Set: Petko Bonchev. Mu: Simeon Pironkov. Cast: Kosta Tsonev, Jan Novitski, Mihal Bajor, Nevena Kokanova, Stoycho Mazgalov, Sotir Maynolovski, Anton Radichev, Alicia Jachiewicz. Two parts. 141 mins. Prem: May 28.

War story. The setting is a small Bulgarian town, and the rescue mission involves twenty-five Bulgarian POWs in the hands of the Nazis during the German retreat.

TAINATA NA APOLONIA /Apollonia's Secret. Sc: Atanas Tsenev, Jan Fleischer, Ivo Toman, based on Robert Louis Stevenson's novel, *The Wrecker.* Dr: Ivo Toman. Ph: Viktor Ružicka. Set: Bogoya Sapundjiev, Miloš Chervinka. Mu: Ivan Kurz. Cast: David Vejražka, Jan Pichocinski, Olga Shoberova, Stoycho Mazgalov, Yavor Miloshev, Peter

Ivan Dobchev's *To the Miss and Her Male Company* (1984).

Slabakov. (Coproduction with Czechoslovakia.) 95 mins.

Based on a minor Robert Louis Stevenson novel penned in 1892, the original was titled *The Wrecker* while the Czech release preferred *The Derelict* over *Apollonia's Secret*. The action has been transferred to a Bulgarian port on the Black Sea at the turn of the century, and the adventure concerns a shipwrecked Greek merchant ship called the *Apollonia* whose treasure of costly pelts is her secret.

PROLETNO TAINSTVO—ZHENA ZA MONASSI / The Rite of Spring—A Wife for Monassi. A feature film in two parts. 80 mins.

1. PROLETNO TAINSTVO / The Rite of Spring. Sc: Donvena Pandurska, based on the libretto by Igor Stravinsky and Nikolai Reorich. Dr: Mihail Pandurski. Ph: Atanas Tassev. Set: Maria Trendafilova. Mu: Igor Stravinsky. Cast: Performers of the Arabesque Ballet Company. 40 mins.

A ballet-film, this performance of Igor Stravinsky's classic also features Herbert von Karajan conducting the Berlin Philharmonic Orchestra during a visit to Sofia. The occasion was the national celebration of the 1,300 anniversary of the founding of Bulgaria, due to a cancellation two years earlier when Karajan fell ill.

2. ZHENA ZA MONASSI /A Wife for Monassi. Sc: Slave

Makedonski. Dr: Krassimer Atanassov. Ph: Zheko Manev. Set: Krassimir Atanassov. Cast: Ivan Grigorov, Ilya Palagachev, Blagoy Pilarski, Yulia Djivdjorska. 40 mins.

Set in the 1930s, the film deals with customs in a small mountain village: a younger son wishes to marry, but has to wait for the older unmarried brother to marry before seeking his own happiness. The situation is resolved by the younger brother, Monassi, through his own resourcefulness in the end.

OTKOGA TE CHAKAM / It's Nice to See You. Sc: Lilyana Mihailova, based on her novella with the same title. Dr: Anna Petkova. Ph: Stefan Trifonov. Set: Tsvetana Yankova. Cast: Tsvetana Maneva, Georgi Georgiev-Gets, Assen Milanov, Peter Slabakov, Georgi Kaloyanchev, Elena Stefanova, Leda Tasseva. 106 mins.

Screenplay writer Lilyana Mihailova came to cinema from television, but she also has written several books of prose and poetry. She collaborated with a young graduate of the Sofia Film School, Anna Petkova, who quickly established a reputation for herself in the field of the documentary. This is a complex psychological story of a young social worker dealing with the elderly and the lonely.

STENATA / The Dam. Sc: Vladimir Ganev. Dr: Emil Tsanev. Ph: Dimiter Lisicharov. Set: Borislav Neshev. Mu:

Kiril Donchev. Cast: Georgi Georgiev-Gets, Aneta Sotirova, Peter Slabakov, Pavel Poppandov, Velko Kunev, Ivan Ivanov. 98 mins.

After an important dam has been built that effectively serves the community with needed water and electricity, the civil engineer who brought it to completion is investigated for irregularities in getting the job done rather than sticking to the rules and risking failure.

NE SE SARDI CHOVECHE / Ludo. Sc: Kiril Topalov. Dr: Ivailo Trenchev. Ph: Svetoslav Mechkuyevski. Set: Evgeni Apostolov. Mu: Mitko Shterev. Cast: Tsvetana Maneva, Irène Krivoshieva, Yavor Milushev, Ivan Dervishev, Rumena Trifonova, Dimiter Djumaliev, Stefan Vladimirov, Iva Dimitrova. 91 mins.

Cameraman-turned-director Ivailo Trenchev makes a children's film: it's about a lad abandoned by his mother. Ludo's extra twist of fate is that he was born out of wedlock.

SUBESSEDNIK PO ZHELANIE / Question Time. Sc: Vladimir Ganev, Hristo Hristov. Dr: Hristo Hristov. Ph: Atanas Tassev. Set: Yordanka Peycheva. Mu: Victor Chuchkov. Cast: Vassil Mihailov, Lilyana Kovacheva, Ivan Kondov, Vassil Popiliev, Zhana Karayordanova, Vulcho Karmarashev. 97 mins.

Based on a true story (the fate of Hristov's actor-friend Tsviatko Nikolov): a popular TV actor is told by an examining doctor that he is suffering from leukemia and has only a few months more to live. Instead of seeking treatment to help prolong his life, the actor decides to tidy up his personal affairs and complete his other obligations as best he can with the time that is left to him.

CHERNITE LEBEDI / The Black Swans. Sc & Dr: Ivan Nichev, based on a novel with the same title by Bogomil Rainov. Ph: Richard Lenchevski. Set: Ani Markova. Mu: Bozhidar Petkov. Cast: Diana Rainova, Dorothea Toncheva, Zornitsa Popova, Todor Kolev, Donka Shishmanova. 106 mins.

The story of a ballerina at the critical age of thirty-three. The heroine retraces the events in her life over the past twenty years, a period in which she saw her dreams crumble to ashes. She realizes now that her goals are beyond reach.

PUTIAT NA MOUSIKANTITE / Traveling Musicians. Sc: Dimiter Shumnaliev. Dr: Igor Kyulyumov. Ph: Victor Chichov. Set: Georgi Todorov. Mu: Stefan Dimitrov, Alexander Brazitsov. Cast: Anya Pencheva, Itzhak Fintsi, Nikola Sotirov, Velko Kunev, Georgi Novakov, Rashko Mladenov, Vesselin Borizov, Pavel Poppandov. 96 mins.

Set during the immediate postwar years, this is a tale of a band of musicians moving from town to town to play for anyone on any occasion. The group now must take a political stance, and each musician decides differently.

YAN BIBIYAN. Sc: Atanas Tsenev, Vassil Apostolov. Dr: Vassil Apostolov. Ph: Krassimir Kostov. Set: Boris Neshev. Mu: Villi Kazassyan. Cast: Michael Donchev, Georgi Kaloyanchev, Nikola Todev, Tsvetana Maneva. 84 mins.

A children's film, blending real life with animated puppets. This experimental feature stars the puppet ragamuffin Yan Bibiyan (created by Lyubomir Tsakev) in his own mythical kingdom open only to those who are gifted with imagination and fantasy.

POSLEDNOTO PRIKLYUCHENIE / The Last Adventure. Sc: Pavel Vezhinov. Dr: Yakim Yakimov. Ph: Tsvetan Chobanski. Set: Sonya Kalcheva. Mu: Kiril Tsibulka. Cast: Ekaterina Evro, Marius Donkin, Jürgen Zartmann, Anton Gorchev. 100 mins.

The last screen play written by the prolific Pavel Vezhinov. A love triangle in which a once married and divorced woman with child has to choose between two new men in her life.

BORIS PURVI / Boris the First. Sc: Angel Wagenstein. Dr: Borislav Sharaliev. Ph: Venets Dimitrov. Set: Maria Ivanova. Mu: Vesselin Nikolov. Cast: Stefan Danailov, Antoni Genov, Ventsislav Kissyov, Kosta Tsonev, Aneta Petrovska, Boris

Borislav Sharaliev's *Boris the First* **(1984).**

Borislav Sharaliev's *Boris the First* **(1984).**

Borislav Sharaliev's *Boris the First* **(1984).**

Lukanov, Stoyan Stoev, Plamen Donchev, Peter Petrov, Ivan Ivanov. An epic in two parts. Part One: *The Conversion to Christianity*, 120 mins. Part Two: *Discourse on Letters*, 120 mins. Total length: 240 mins.

The last of the grand historical epics produced to celebrate the 1,300th anniversary of the founding of Bulgaria in 681. Khan Boris ascended to the throne in 852, was converted to Christianity in 864 (possibly 865), and reigned for thirty-seven years until 889, when he retired to a monastery—only to return four years later to depose a wayward son on the throne (Vladimir), and appoint his brother, Simeon, in his place. It was Simeon who heralded the beginning of the "Golden Age" during the First Bulgarian Empire, but the way was prepared by his father (who took the name of Michael at his baptism to testify to his conversion). Boris the First realized that the introduction of Christianity would open new vistas, for traditional Bulgarian paganism had already fallen into spiritual bankruptcy. But should he as a converted pagan king, or khan, embrace Rome or Constantinople? And what of his people, and those Bulgarian chieftans who preferred the ancient ways? To achieve his ends, Boris had to execute fifty-four rebels and, later, return from retirement to depose his own son. Nevertheless, by choosing Constantinople and ultimately favoring his son Simeon, Boris the First laid the foundations for a long-lasting Slavonic, and Bulgarian, culture. [Golden Rose winner at 1984 Varna Festival of Bulgarian Feature Films.]

ZABRAVETE TOZI SLOUCHAI / Just Forget That Case. Sc: Georgi Danailov, Krassimir Spassov, based on Danailov's play *The Autumn of an Investigating Magistrate*. Dr: Krassimir Spassov. Ph: Radoslav Spassov. Set: Georgi Todorov. Mu: Kiril Donchev. Cast: Filip Trifonov, Boris Lukanov, Ljubomir Kabakchiev, Tsvetana Maneva, Ruth Spassova, Tanya Shanova, Dorotea Toncheva, Stefan Iliev. 97 mins.

A new young magistrate is assigned to replace an older colleague in a small provincial town. He stumbles across a network of longstanding corruption that can be linked to the office of the mayor.

TAZI KRUV TRYABVASHE DA SE PROLEE / Blood That Had to Be Shed. Sc: Dragomir Assenov, Leon Daniel, based on Assenov's novel with the same title. Ph: Dimiter Lisicharov. Set: Violeta Yovcheva. Mu: Vassil Kazandjiev. Cast: Vesselin Rankov, Ognyan Ouzunov, Todor Atanassov, Maya Dimitrova, Anani Yavashev, Nikolai Sotirov, Peter Despotov, Katya Ivanova, Stefan Danailov, Marin Yanev, Adriana Adreeva, Lilyana Kovacheva. 95 mins.

A patriotic film produced to celebrate the fortieth anniversary of the founding of a Communist youth organization known as the People's Militia in September 1944.

1985

DENYAT NA VLADETELITE / The Day of the Rulers. Sc: Nikola Tiholov, Vadislav Ikonomov. Dr: Vladislav Ikonomov. Ph: Krum Krumov. Set: Maria Ivanova. Mu: Kiril Tsibulka. Cast: Vassil Mihailov, Lyuben Chatalov, Georgi Georgiev-Gets, Velyo Foranov, Stefan Mavrodiev, Vulcho Kamarashev, Pavel Pappandov, Stoycho Mazgalov.

Made with the sets and trappings left over from the major epics produced for the 1,300th anniversary celebrations in 1981, this is a film in two parts telling the story of Khan Krum during the crucial years of his reign, A.D. 803–14. Khan Krum—known in Bulgarian history as "The Conqueror"—expanded the kingdom handed down to him a century earlier by Khan Asparukh (died 701). From his capital at Pliska he first captured the Byzantine fortress at Serdica (Sofia) in 809, and this action in turn prompted the sacking of Pliska that same year, and again in 811, by the Greek Emperor Nicephorus I. This led to a showdown between the two leaders at Vurbishki Pass in July 811 (where the epic was partially filmed): Nicephorus perished in that battle, the first time since 378 that a Greek emperor had fallen in battle against the barbarians. Krum died three years later, as a result of a burst blood vessel, at the height of his power.

MUZH ZA MAMA / A Husband for Mom. Sc: Kalina Kovacheva. Dr: Marianna Evstatieva. Ph: Hristo Totev. Set: Assya Popova. Mu: Angel Mihailov. Cast: Vesselin Prahov, Tsvetana Maneva, Pavel Pappandov, Bogdan Glishev, Emil Markov.

The young son of a divorced mother decides it's high time for him to seek a mate for his mother, who will also be a father to his own liking. He assembles a task-force of friends at school to help him in the search.

ROMANTICHNA ISTORIA / A Romantic Story. Sc: Alexander Tomov. Dr: Milen Nikolov. Ph: Georgi Georgiev. Set: Vladimir Lekarski. Mu: Alexander Burzitsov. Cast: Ivan Ivanov, Irène Krivoshieva.

A love story set in the 1970s. A young man with little money and a menial job as a bartender in a Black Sea resort hotel pretends he's a playboy with newly found wealth, in order to impress a girlfriend, who is also aching for the finer things of life.

TAZI HOUBAVA ZRYALA / This Fine Age of Maturity. Sc: Lyuben Stanev, based on his novella with the same title. Dr: Hacho Boyadjiev. Ph: Boris Yanakiev. Set: Yordanka Peycheva. Mu: Willy Kayassyan. Cast: Kosta Tsonev, Ruzha Delcheva, Assen Milanov, Velko Kunev, Nevena Kokanova, Vanya Tsvetkova, Katya Paskaleva, Dosyo Dossev, Boris Lukanov, Nikolai Sotirov.

A drama critic approaching fifty reluctantly comes to the realization that he has been making too many compromises of late in his private and professional life. Up to now, he has believed himself to be holding to the ideals of his youth.

SMURTTA MOZHE DA POCHAKA / Death Can Wait Awhile. Sc: Alexander Tomov, based on a story in his collection titled *Elegies of Birds—The Hypothesis*. Dr: Evgeni Mihailov. Ph: Elly Mihailova. Set: Boris Neshev. Mu: Bozhidar Petkov. Cast: Todor Kolev, Momchil Karamitev, Dilyana Hadjiyankova, Ilya Karaivanov, Ginda Stanchev, Nikolai Nachkov.

A psychological thriller set in 1930. A detective with a yen for Nietzsche and Dostoevski traces the actions of a young loner who has a liking for Karl Marx. In the course of this complex plot the hunter becomes the hunted.

SKUPI MOI, SKUPA MOYA / My Darling, My Darling.
Sc: Plamen Maslarov, Eduard Zahariev, based on a story in Alexander Tomov's collection titled *The Saintly Ana*. Dr: Eduard Zahariev. Ph: Stefan Trifonov. Set: Georgi Gutsev. Cast: Marianna Dimitrova, Plamen Sirakov, Ivan Donve, Anton Radichev, Itzak Fintsi, Stoyan Stoev, Ana Guncheva.

A young couple with two small children moves from the provinces to Sofia, whereupon their lives go through a series of changes. A portrait of a contemporary working-class family in Bulgaria.

DA SE LYUBIM NA INAT / Let's Love Each Other Out of Spite. Sc & Dr: Nikolai Volev, based on Chavdar Shinov's novel with the same title. Ph: Krassimir Kostov. Set: Konstantin Russakov. Mu: Ivan Staikov. Cast: Velko Kunev, Maria Statulova, Ivan Velko, Leda Tasseva, Marieta Popova, Yordan Spirov, Yulia Kozhinkova, Atanassi Iliev, Prodan Prodanov.

A comedy focusing on a father-son relationship. Both are going through a crisis, but still love each other "out of spite."

ZLA PAMET / Bitter Memories. Sc: Konstantin Pavlov. Dr: Docho Bodjakov. Ph: Alexander Ivanov. Set: Ivan Andreev. Mu: Kiril Tsibulka. Cast: Katya Paskaleva, Stefan Mavrodiev, Dora Todorova, Daniela Nikova, Dimiter Tanev, Tsocho Kerkelezov.

Poet Konstantin Pavlov pens another moral and philosophical debate on fascism and its aftermath. The central character is a mother who has lost her husband in the September Uprising of 1923 and her son on the eve of the Socialist Revolution in 1944.

MANEVRI NA PETIA ETAZH / Maneuvers on the Fifth Floor. Sc: Chavdar Shinov. Dr: Peter Vassilev. Ph: Pavel Milkov. Set: Violeta Yovcheva. Mu: Peter Stupel. Cast: Stefan Danielov, Velko Kunev, Anton Radichev, Maria Stefanova, Ventsislav Vulchev, Aneta Sotirova, Maria Statulova, Iskra Radeva, Ivan Grigorov.

Veteran comic director Peter Vassilev's latest film is about three friends pitted against each other in a make-believe contest.

VIK ZA POMOSHT / A Cry for Help. Sc: Boyan Byolchev, based on his novel *Saturn's Ring*. Dr: Nikola Rudarov. Set: Maria Deenichina. Mu: Mitko Shterev. Cast: Ivailo Geraskov, Vesselin Nedyalkov, Elzhana Popova, Pavel Poppandov, Elena Rainova, Violeta Bachevanova.

A crime thriller. The central character is a loser: having committed an absurd and pointless crime, he finds himself the object of a manhunt.

NAREKOHME GI MONTEKI I KAPULETI / We Called Them Montagues and Capulets. Sc: Donyo Donev, Dimo Bolyarov. Dr & Design: Donyo Donev. Ph: Vera Doneva. Mu: Emil Pavlov.

A full-length feature cartoon loosely based on Shakespeare's *Romeo and Juliet*. The war between the two competing families in this case is capped by a typical Bulgarian peasant wedding feast.

HERAKTERISTIKA / Reference. Sc: Alexander Tomov, based on a short story in his collection titled *The Saintly Ana*. Dr: Hristo Hristov. Ph: Atanas Tassev. Set: Yordanka Peycheva. Mu: Victor Chuchkov. Cast: Ivailo Geraskov, Georgeta Nikolova, Atanas Atanassov, Liliana Kovacheva, Vassil Mihailov, Itzak Fintsi, Georgi Kaloyanchev.

A tale about honesty amid corruption in the working class. The setting is the taxi-driving milieu, the title referring to a letter of recommendation a foreman is asked to write for an undisciplined driver who is involved in shady affairs on the side.

INDEX OF FILM TITLES